RAILWAYS AND THE HOLC

Editor:
Robin Jones
Editorial consultant:
Rabbi Dr Walter Rothschild
Design:
Michael Baumber
Group production editor:
Tim Hartley

Production manager:
Craig Lamb
Marketing manager:
Charlotte Park
Publishing director:
Dan Savage
Commercial director:
Nigel Hole
Managing director:
Brian Hill

Published by:
Mortons Media Group Ltd, Media
Centre, Morton Way,
Horncastle, Lincs LN9 6JR.
Tel: 01507 523456

Printed by
William Gibbons & Sons,
Wolverhampton

A HERITAGE RAILWAY PUBLICATION
Special thanks to Dr Alfred Gottwaldt, of
Deutsches Technikmuseum, Berlin, and Beth
Shalom, Nottinghamshire.

*Pictures marked thus are published under a
Creative Commons licence, the full details of
which can be found at
www.creativecommons.org

HERITAGE RAILWAY

MORTONS
MEDIA GROUP LTD

Nazi re-enactors at an East Lancashire Railway wartime weekend in spring 2012, shortly before officials of the line ordered them off the premises. MANCHESTER EVENING NEWS

FOREWORD

'Wartime Weekends' at heritage railways across Britain are hugely popular with the general public, attendances frequently exceeding those of ordinary steam galas or other crowd-pulling events on the lines.

Thousands of re-enactors in period uniforms and civilian clothing turn out, along with vintage and restored military vehicles, to entertain a family audience with lashings of 'Forties nostalgia'.

Several years ago, in response to complaints and observations from members of the Jewish community, the Heritage Railway Association, the umbrella body for preserved railways, asked its members to desist from allowing re-enactors to turn out in SS uniforms or to display swastikas, in order to avoid causing offence.

"What was all the fuss about?" some people asked. "It is only a bit of fun, and it is educating people about life in the Second World War, and the fact that Britain stood alone against the tyranny of Nazi Europe."

That may be so, but when did SS guards ever force people onto British trains, at stations in England, Scotland or Wales? Thankfully, at huge cost to our nation and our allies, they never did.

On the continent, the fact is that in millions of cases, railway platforms were among the last things people ever saw. The image of deportees waiting to board trains – not just cattle trucks but also ordinary passenger carriages – is understandably as deeply offensive to many Jews (or Poles or Ukrainians or Belgians or Dutch or French or Italians or Serbs or Greeks or Russians...) as, for instance, a carnival float depicting IRA bombers in the middle of Birmingham city centre or Warrington, or turning out in a fancy dress parade in Manchester dressed as Myra Hindley or Ian Brady.

No, it is not just a case of playing the bogey man 'for a bit of fun', just like donning silly masks at Halloween. Nor should it ever be considered as an exclusive Jewish sensitivity.

For while the Holocaust indeed began as the persecution of an accomplished race of people who for centuries had been illogically persecuted for reasons which few could remember, and who had become an ideal scapegoat in the rantings of an accomplished rabble-rouser and his henchmen on the continent, it soon snowballed into an all-out war on humanity.

After the Jews, it was the Poles who took a sizeable hit in terms of population numbers, and then anyone whom the Nazis simply did not like, or who was considered 'different', even ordinary German people joined the victims. Had history taken an alternative course at so many points, millions of British subjects would likely have met a similar fate.

One might ask: "Yet it is so long ago, and surely wartime re-enactments with SS officers are no different to medieval jousting events or mock battles between Roundheads and Cavaliers?"

Well, let's put this "long ago" into context. In 2012, music fans were paying £1000 and more for a ticket to see Mick Jagger and the Rolling Stones. Paul McCartney is of a similar vintage. In September, I saw the Beach Boys' 50th anniversary concert at Wembley Arena. The lead singer, Mike Love, is – in his early 70s – infinitely fitter than I have ever been in my life.

Love was born in March 1941, and during his infant years, halfway around the world from the safety of California, Operation Reinhard would have been in full swing and millions of people, many of them harmless women, children and the elderly, were being transported by train to their deaths in the Nazi death camps. I don't know if he ever saw newsreels in the cinemas of the day: I can recall at the age of four, when I was otherwise immersed in fairy tales, stories on the TV news about a wall being built through a big city called Berlin by some bad guys. I knew not why, or even where this place was, but I simply remembered being fascinated by the idea of a big city being cut in half.

The point here is not the durability of Sixties music or the accuracy of early boyhood memories, but the fact that the Holocaust took place within the lifetime of people who are living and working today.

It cannot be dismissed as a few pages of old blurred archive pictures in school history books, as filler material on low-budget TV channels or the stuff of boxed video sets available for a few pounds from car boot sales.

Its horrors are still very much on our doorstep, if not in our midst, and by dismissing, sanitising or making light of them, we have not learned the many enormous lessons it has to give.

A re-enactment for bona fide education purposes, such as the making of a film highlighting the evils of the Third Reich – no problem; but family entertainment with a general helping of historically inaccurate artistic licence thrown in – never.

In the spring of 2012, several individuals dressed in SS uniforms 'invaded' without invitations a 'Wartime Weekend' event at the East Lancashire Railway, whose officials rightly asked them to leave as soon as they were brought to their attention. The escapade made headlines in both the regional and national press and, again, Jewish people expressed outrage.

It may well be that those SS re-enactors who were thrust into the media spotlight have no political axe to grind against anyone, and were merely following what they regard as a hobby. Yet the same view might not be taken by those who lost their entire extended families, who were seen for the last time either boarding deportation trains or being selected for the gas chambers after they disembarked on arrival – that is, if they had survived the horrendous journeys in appalling conditions at the hands of railwaymen who were either "only obeying orders" or simply did not care that starving people were transported for days in conditions in which they were packed like sardines, conditions that might just about cause their deaths before the journey's end.

Later in 2012, loud anti-Semitic chants were heard at a Tottenham Hotspur football match, again generating public disdain.

In recent years, there has been a subtle rise of the far right in many countries across Europe, with the danger that old scapegoats will potentially again be much sought after as a recession darkens Europe, just as it did in the late Twenties and Thirties.

A 'far right' party is not necessarily a fascist one holding Nazi views or sympathies: Indeed, it's often the case that large sections of their manifestos by and large seem eminently reasonable to 'ordinary members of the public' – who often vote for them as a means of protesting against the mainstream parties, rather than professing genuine support. However, can the same be said for those supporters holding far more extremist views, who so often find in such organisations a friendly bolthole?

Hitler was the Great Unraveller. He took the extremely democratic Weimar Republic – a state struggling to overcome the constraints placed upon Germany after the First World War – and unwound the

nation's society century by century, back to the times when there was no universal vote, no elected leader, no protection for even sizeable minorities, when states were run by despots and there was no freedom for individual expression; back before the dawn of human rights, back into the Neanderthal age, when one primitive tribe would show no mercy or take no prisoners in their petty squabbles with everyone else.

Yet the big difference, and the danger presented to all of the world, was that between 1939 and 1945, such a mentality was combined with cutting-edge technology.

The juxtaposition of SS uniforms with railways in any setting is even more offensive for one primary reason: It was only the railways that made the Holocaust possible.

As outlined in the pages to come, the Holocaust was an infernal mixture of three separate concepts coming together in the wrong place at the wrong time: ancestral and irrational hatred of the Jews at a time when ordinary Germans were, with some justification, smarting at the outcome of the First World War, a conflict which they had not themselves started, and the desire for a scapegoat; the theory of eugenics and the idea of a master race, which began not in Buchenwald but in a Birmingham suburb; and arguably the greatest fruit of the Industrial Revolution, mass rapid transport in the form of the steam railway.

Without the railways, the Nazi regime would not have been able to deport millions of victims to the concentration camps of the conquered eastern territories, out of sight of the German population whose opinion had, surprisingly, managed to curb Hitler's

previous extermination of the handicapped and disabled.

Britain gave the world the railways and the power to change the globe forever. Yet Germany under Hitler created a railroad network to hell, plumbing new depths of depravity with the concept, for the sake of the twisted cause of racial 'purity'.

In Britain, engine drivers and their crews were hailed as heroes for breaking technological barriers and setting new world speed records and they were the boyhood stars of their day, long before pop idols or millionaire footballers.

Yet on the other side of the North Sea, their counterparts were either turning a blind eye to what was going on... or else they simply went along with their orders out of duty. However, it seems some even relished and profited from the death trains, Nazi ideology, propaganda and laws shielding them from personal liability and moral responsibility under the cover of the excuse of legality.

Even in France, railwaymen carried out their deportation train duties with zeal, even submitting bills for running them after the country had been liberated.

The railways made the modern world. As outlined stage by stage in this book, they also allowed the worst of humanity to shame it.

Even after nearly seven decades, there must never be the slightest acceptance of the evil of the Nazi regime, even if it manifests itself only as 'harmless' dressing up in costumes at fun events.

When we say 'Never Again!' we must all show that we mean it.

Robin Jones

Der Fuhrer Adolf Hitler once said: "The personification of the devil as the symbol of all evil assumes the living shape of the Jew." It is therefore ironic that history now regards Hitler as a defining personification of evil, but he was also a serial bungler whose illogical military strategies helped Germany lose the Second World War.

Introduction

By Rabbi Dr Walter Rothschild

The history of what is known as the Second World War (normally dated 1939-45, though it started earlier and in some respects has not ended even yet) is much more complicated than most people think, and the end result was also much closer than most people realise.

My father always used to say: "We ought to be grateful to Hitler, because without him we would never have won the war"... and he was essentially right, however gruesome that might seem.

Hitler was a charismatic madman who convinced professionals – even the military – to obey him. But he was a terrible strategist.

Here are some examples. Firstly, he called off the daytime Luftwaffe air attacks on Britain just as many believe the RAF was about to lose the 'Battle of Britain' – its supply of planes running out, its pilots exhausted, its bases damaged – and turned to the night blitz instead, giving the RAF an opportunity to recover.

Secondly, he opened a Second Front with the Soviet Union before he had quite settled Great Britain on the western flank of his 'empire'. He refused to follow advice to pull the entire 6th Army out of Stalingrad in the winter of 1942/43 before it was encircled and lost.

Thirdly, if he had not demanded that the Luftwaffe have a jet bomber rather than jet fighter, the Messerschmitt Me 262 would have been ready earlier (prototypes flew in 1941 – but in November 1943 Hitler demanded that production be restricted only to a bomber version which took longer to develop) and would have been able to wipe out those formations of RAF and USAF Lancasters, Halifaxes, B17s and Liberators – which would have been thoroughly outclassed.

Then he refused to let the Wehrmacht withdraw and regroup until it was too late and he kept up the belief in a non-existent secret weapon and a reserve army right up until Berlin was already occupied...

There are many other examples. Had the V2 rockets come on stream even a few months earlier they could have brought Britain to its knees, for there was no defence against them possible – only a desperate lunge forward to capture possible firing sites.

What might have happened had Japan not treacherously entered the war with its attacks in the Pacific and brought the USA into the conflict? Without the Americans, Britain and its Imperial forces would never have been able to conquer Europe in 1944-45, landing in Italy and in France. Without the American atom bomb, the Pacific War could have lasted another few dreadful years.

As a schoolboy in England one grew up with the patriotic myths of Dunkirk, the Battle of Britain, the Blitz, D-Day – somehow, in hindsight, it all seemed so obvious.

This is not the place for an extensive history of the conflict, but anyone who is interested will find a lot of information which will reveal to the thinking reader how close in reality it all was.

There are the famous 'what if?' questions – what if the Nazis had got through the Ukraine and Caucasus to Turkey in 1941? What if Rommel had beaten Montgomery at El Alamein in October 1942 and got through to Egypt and blocked the Suez Canal? What if Malta had fallen? What if the Germans had not had their heavy water experiments in Norway sabotaged in 1943 and had developed the nuclear fission bomb?

One could even add another hypothetical factor. What if Hitler had not been a fanatical and obsessive racist?

Would not Jewish citizens have been just as prepared to fight for their motherland in the Second as they had in the First World War?

Instead of which, those who could flee or escape brought their knowledge to the use of the Allies...

One should also not forget that the original Nazi plans for the war in 1938 (Anschluss with Austria in March, annexation of Sudetenland in September) and 1939 (Blitzkrieg into Poland, France, Belgium, the Netherlands, Denmark) and 1940 (Yugoslavia, Greece, Crete, etc.) 1941 (the invasion of Russia) involved – in contrast to the use of railways in the First World War – mainly use of aeroplanes for preliminary bombing and then armour and road transport for the invasion. Railways were to be used only for the transport of supplies and reinforcements.

With regard to the German railways, the Reichsbahn had been starved of funds in the 1920s and 1930s and the number of new locomotives in 1939 was actually very small. Transport in the occupied countries was dependent on the local motive power and stock which was captured.

Only in Russia did this tactic not work, and for two reasons – firstly, the Russians were able to withdraw or disable most of their railway stock before the Wehrmacht could capture it, and secondly, the different

> "They refer to me as an uneducated barbarian. Yes, we are barbarians. We want to be barbarians, it is an honoured title to us. We shall rejuvenate the world. This world is near its end."
> Adolf Hitler

Ty42-148, a Polish-built Kriegslok built in 1946, photographed on a freight working at Tloki in Poland in 1998. This type of locomotive was turned out by the Third Reich in vast numbers during the later stages of the Second World War and was among those used on deportation trains. TREVOR JONES

gauge held up the quick use of German locomotivess and wagons.

This was another example of Hitler's bad planning. Long and complex operations involving the regauging of lines and stations, reconstruction of bridges and depots and workshops were the consequence.

Then Prussian locomotive types proved incapable of dealing with the very low winter temperatures. Quickly – but too late – plans were laid for construction of simplified Kriegslok or 'war loco' types and

simplified wagons. Some of the locomotives would even have condensing tenders to make them less dependent on the erratic water supplies. Thousands of these engines were built, but too late to change the course of the war and many of those in use later had actually been built from parts left lying in locomotive factories when the war ended.

So when you read this book, beware of falling into the 'hindsight' trap.

No one in 1940 could have predicted how the world would look two, three or five years

later. When Britain was fighting for its existence in 1940, Russia was adhering to the August 1939 Molotov-Ribbentrop Non-Aggression Pact with Germany and Franklin Delano Roosevelt's America was isolationist and doing its best to keep out of the conflict.

Although the Nazis had been racist and anti-Semitic, it was not really until the Wannsee Conference of bureaucrats in Berlin in January 1942 that the real plans were laid for an industrial-style mass killing of Jews throughout Europe and North Africa.

"Providence has ordained that I should be the greatest liberator of humanity. I am freeing man from the restraints of an intelligence that has taken charge, from the dirty and degrading self-mortification of a false vision called conscience and morality, and from the demands of a freedom and independence which only a very few can bear."
Adolf Hitler

German troops standing at Munich station in 1937. DR ALFRED GOTTWALD COLLECTION

Throughout many parts of the world, the railways worked to serve the different sides. Along the east coast of the USA the railroads had suddenly to move vast amounts of oil because German U-boats were threatening the coastal tanker fleet. Across the USA, transcontinental trains moved troops and materials. Railways in Africa and Asia were extended or re-equipped and railwaymen worked longer hours or were drafted to serve in military transport units. New lines were built or projected in North Africa, the Middle East, the Far East. Factories turned out new locomotives, wagons and rails and everything that was needed down to nuts and bolts. Locomotives were carried in convoys across the Atlantic and Pacific, to serve in Iran, Egypt or Turkey.

Each side sought to destroy the railways of the other, knowing just how valuable and important they were. The use of railways to deport civilians was just one dreadful element in what Josef Goebbels had proclaimed to be a 'Total War', i.e. a war without any geographical or moral boundaries, without distinction between combatants and noncombatants, a war where the status of neutrality was not respected, nor the rights of prisoners, nor the most basic of human rights.

Those of us who were fortunate enough to have been born after it was formally ended should stand in respect and awe before those who were forced to participate in it and who survived it. And we should never treat it as 'a game'.

THE NIGHTMARE

One of those what if? questions of course just has to be: what if the eagle really had landed in 1940?

What if the Wehrmacht had successfully landed in England in their gliders and landing barges during the planned Operation Sealion? What would have been the consequences?

Well, based on what happened in, say, Belgium or the Netherlands, the answer is fairly obvious. A new government would have been established, probably under Oswald Mosley.

(Compare with Seyss-Inquart in Holland or Quisling in Norway, or the Vichy regime under Pétain in France.) Whether or not the abdicated former King Edward VIII would have been brought back can remain a matter for speculation – there would certainly have been an attempt to 'legitimate' the system, as there had been in Yugoslavia (where the pro-Nazi Regent Prince Paul deposed King Peter II in April 1941) or Romania (where King Carol II had wanted to remain neutral but was deposed by the fascist Ion Antonescu in September 1940).

The German officials would have gone to the town halls and taken over the administration of cities, towns and villages, appointing their own 'Gauleiters' and other staff but keeping the local civilians to do the work. All anti-Mosley MPs and civil servants, trades unionists, any protesting Church of England and free church clergy, anti-Nazi

A gallery of a handful of around 100,000 Nazi victims of the Ravensbrück concentration camp for women and children 56 miles to the north of Berlin. While inmates included Jews and gypsies, the biggest nationality represented there was Polish, and the prisoners even included German women who had been sent there for refusing to marry. ROBIN JONES

WARSAW

The 'master race' soldiers overcome a group of 'dangerously subversive' Jewish women and small children during the Nazi's subjugation of the Warsaw Ghetto uprising in May 1943.

The image was part of a report to Heinrich Himmler, the original caption in German translating as 'forcibly pulled out of dug-outs'.

Only the little boy in the centre survived the subsequent deportation to the death camps.

The SS soldier facing him with an MP18 sub-machine gun is Josef Blösche, a former farmhand and waiter, who Jews had nicknamed 'Frankenstein' following his raping and then killing of women from the ghetto.

Following what was clearly his finest hour, he received the German War Merit Cross for his actions during the uprising.

Blösche evaded prosecution for many years after the war because his face was scarred in an accident at work in 1946.

However, East German police arrested him in January 1967. At

his trial in April 1969, he was found guilty of having been involved in the deportation of 300,000 Jews, and of murdering of up to 2000 including newborn infants, pregnant women, handicapped persons, and the elderly.

He was executed in Leipzig on July 29, 1969, by a shot through the neck.

---

intellectuals, jazz music players (yes, they were a victim of Nazi persecution too – ever think the Holocaust is defined merely by race or ideology), modern artists, homosexuals, Communists, Social Democrats, refugees from mainland Europe and other 'undesirables' would have been rounded up and placed initially in concentration camps.

Where? Well, Dachau is a town just north of Munich, Sachsenhausen a village near the town of Oranienburg on the electrified S-Bahn just north of Berlin – so one could position, say, a camp outside Luton for London and Rawtenstall north of Manchester for the north west.

Probably another in the south west – maybe near Exeter – and one in South Wales (a lot of trades unionists and devout Methodists there!) – let us say, up in the valleys near Newport, so it could also scoop up people from the Cotswolds. Perhaps one at Stourbridge for the West Midlands; one in the Lowlands of Scotland – maybe near Castlecary.

And of course, there would be plenty of POW camps for the demobilised and defeated soldiers, held as prisoners of war until they could be released as ideologically

sound and perhaps called up to join the Wehrmacht. Those who refused to toe the line could be disposed of with a bullet in the back of the neck. Maybe a special camp for Women (like Ravensbrück) would be established. And we are not talking yet about labour camps or subsidiary camps near industries.

Then the prisoners would be rounded up by lorry or even bus and driven to the goods depots – say, at West Hampstead or Accrington. Trains of maybe 40 12T goods vans, with guards' brake vans marshalled at front and rear and maybe an old Midland coach in the middle for the escort troops, headed perhaps by an LMS Fowler 7F 0-8-0, would then depart every evening for the north – in each van 30 to 40 men and women, standing, no seats, no toilet, no food.

On arrival they would be shouted out of the wagons and put into barbed-wire compounds. If they were lucky they would be put to hard labour, if not – or too old, too weak, too ill – they would simply be allowed to die. Senior officers would be shot.

And then the sequence of administrative orders would appear, on posters, on the BBC radio, in the newspapers. The Jews would have to wear a distinctive yellow star. Able-

bodied men would have to report for work in the 'Reich'. All the munitions factories would be working three shifts, with slave labour too – Hitler would want every tank, every shell, every aeroplane for his planned attack on the Soviet Union.

There would have been plenty of people who would have gone along with the new system the way they went along with any system. If some of their neighbours or colleagues began to disappear, well, that was just one of those things. That LNER J27s were hauling trains of vans up into the Kielder Forest where the 'passengers' would be forced to get out, dig their own mass pits and then be shot into them, would not be something one would really believe, even if a neighbour's son's cousin's school friend told him this. Who would want to believe this?

This is the nightmare that was avoided – but only just – by a combination of heroism, determination, luck (think of the weather on certain days and weeks that held up the German invasion fleet) and Nazi bad planning.

But please think like this, and the story becomes much closer, much more intense.

So what happened?

No one can say that the period from 1918

OSWALD MOSLEY

The British 'would-be' Hitler: Oswald Mosley, the Labour MP who founded the British Union of Fascists, pictured at his wedding to his first wife, Lady Cythnia Curzon, second daughter of Foreign Secretary George Curzon, Lord Curzon of Kedleston, who gave his name to the Curzon Line, a proposed armistice demarcation line between Poland and Russia in the First World War.

In October 1936 Mosley and the BUF attempted to march through an area of London with a high proportion of Jewish residents, and violence resulted as protesters tried to block the march with police trying to force it through. The incident came to be known as the Battle of Cable Street.

Mosley was interned during the Second World War. His followers included Tarka the Otter novelist Henry Williamson and the future Lord Haw Haw, William Joyce.

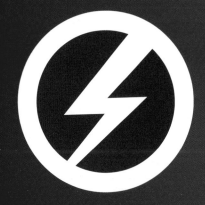

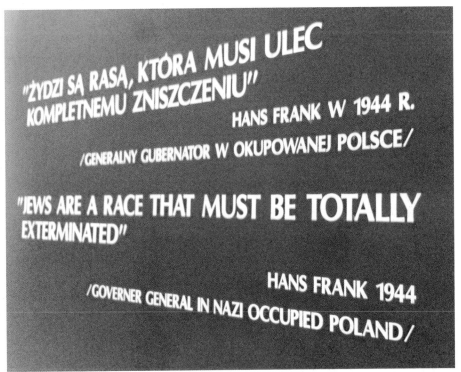

Sign in Auschwitz recalling a definite statement by the Nazi ruler of Poland. AHP

to 1939 was peaceful, calm and happy, even though one often speaks of the 'inter-war period'. The effects of the 1914-1918 war were everywhere – missing men, crippled men, the new borders (often artificial) imposed in Europe and elsewhere, the economic collapse and depression.

The period saw the rise of Fascism under Mussolini in Italy from 1922; of Austro-Fascism in Austria under Dollfuss from 1933 (he was assassinated by Nazis in July 1934 during an attempted coup, and was later succeeded by Schuschnigg); the Fascist takeover of Spain under Franco in 1936 which succeeded despite the desperate civil war fought by Republicans he had ousted and their idealistic helpers from all over Europe.

All these illustrate that this was no golden age. But for most people who were simply struggling to get by, most of this was not directly relevant. They lived their daily lives, tried to earn a living, to bring up their children, they went to school or to work, or they were enjoying a quiet retirement – they read the papers and worried but they did not necessarily all get involved in simplistic blame-everyone-else nationalistic politics.

And then consider yourself as one of these people. Minding your own business. But then suddenly one day, while you drink your breakfast coffee in Brussels or Amsterdam or Paris or Copenhagen or Warsaw or Riga, foreign aeroplanes appear overhead, tanks roll through the streets, soldiers in grey uniforms march through the town, soldiers in black uniforms come after them...

And then for no apparent reason you are told you may no longer go to school, or buy a cinema ticket, you must surrender your driving licence and your radio, you must wear a distinctive symbol on your clothing, you are sacked from your job,

you may no longer use public transport – one crazy rule after another, all designed to make your life difficult...

Your bank account is closed, your savings confiscated, pension no longer paid, your business and then your flat is confiscated, you are told to move and to live in a poor part of town in cramped quarters, maybe the whole family in one room...

And then you are ordered to appear at the city goods yard early one morning, and there is a list of what you may take, because you are to be 'Resettled in the East' – or maybe the soldiers just come running into the house and grab you before you can even get properly dressed, and drag you down the stairs to waiting lories... no neighbour would dream of interfering, it would be too dangerous for them as well...

It is too easy to write about 'deportation trains' and just think of the trains that shamed the world.

The trains themselves were only a part of the experience. The people were not just transported, they were uprooted, traumatised, humiliated and tortured on the way. Before you were even pushed into the closed, windowless goods wagons (not cattle vans – cattle were treated much better, as it was accepted that they needed air and light and straw and regular stops for feeding and cleaning) you had already been dragged from your social roots.

You had no idea of where you were being sent. You had no idea why – for you had – normally – not done anything wrong. (And even prisoners of war or captured resistance fighters, who knew that they had fought and resisted the invader, could still find no good explanation for why another country had invaded and oppressed their own, for why it had even been necessary to fight in defence or to fight in resistance.)

You had no idea how long the journey

would take. There were certainly differences between some of the journeys – from Saloniki in Greece or Skopje in Macedonia all the way to Poland, from Drancy near Paris or Westerbork in northeast Holland, from Zagreb to the killing fields at Jasenovac – there were differences depending on whether it was summer or winter, whether you thirsted or froze – but some things were probably universal.

In the train you had no privacy. You had to stand for days, crammed up against family or strangers. No food and no water. No view. Little indication of time passing.

There was nowhere to go to the toilet. Read that sentence again. There was nowhere to go to the toilet.

Maybe there was a bucket in the van, but no privacy, no toilet paper, no way of washing.

In front of your colleagues or customers or neighbours or congregants or pupils or your own family, in front of men and women, you had to squat there – presumably having held back as long as possible beforehand.

All social restrictions and taboos were broken. Imagine being with small children, who cried with hunger and thirst, who wanted to be held, to be put down, let out, who soiled themselves – and there was nothing you could do. People, many people, died on the way. Their corpses stayed in the wagon with you.

The Nazis were clever. At the death camp of Treblinka there was a platform with a fake station building and a fake clock (made of wood) so that those getting out might think they had come to a real place and not just a fenced-off clearing in the wood.

In Auschwitz-Birkenau and other places the poor passengers were told they could go to get a shower. Who would not run there, in such circumstances? Who would possibly think that a government in the throes of a war would have wasted valuable railway resources, engines and drivers and wagons and guards and coal, just to take you several hundred kilometres to be killed?

What we know now – they did not know then.

The above describes deportation of people to their extermination camps. But the railways were used for many flows of human cargoes. There were the Zwangsarbeiter – forced labourers, actually slaves, people simply dragged off the streets or from a cafe in a police raid in Brussels or Paris or called up in the Ukraine – and transported to work in the mines, in the fields, in the factories – even to Peenemünde to work on the V1 or the dreadful underground concentration camps in tunnels at Nordhausen where V2 rockets were built.

Many French and Belgian civilians were burned to death here hours or days before the Americans liberated the area – just as in Leipzig, the American troops found piles of warm ash that had been living people only minutes earlier... murdered before they could be freed.

The entire male population of Putten in the Netherlands was dragged off in October

Nightmare scenario: a platoon of 'German soldiers' lines up at Leicester North station. Reprisals against the civilian population would have been catastrophic had the Nazis managed to invade, and Britain's railways would have played a key role in their subjugation of the country, all but certainly with the help of collaborators as was the case in every other occupied country. Thankfully it never happened, and so such scenes never became reality on these shores. The picture on the Great Central railway was taken several years before Heritage Railway Association members outlawed the wearing of Nazi uniforms at heritage railway wartime weekends, because of the increasing awareness of the offence that such inaccurate depictions caused.
ROBIN JONES

What if? 'German officers' demand the production of passports and identity cards. This scene, taken at Leicester North station on the Great Central Railway during a 1940s event in 2004, could have been commonplace throughout Britain had the V2 rocket campaign led to Hitler winning the war. In fairness, this picture was taken several years before Heritage Railway Association members outlawed the wearing of Nazi uniforms at heritage railway wartime weekends, one reason, offence apart, was that it was historically inaccurate as the Nazis had never invaded mainland Britain.
ROBIN JONES

The infamous Arbeit Macht Frei slogan (labour makes (you) free) which appeared above the entrances to both extermination and concentration camps (in this case Dachau), one of many aspects to a complicated deception aimed at luring incoming prisoners into the misbelief that if they worked hard, they would be rewarded. Many of them died in the gas chambers at the extermination camps within the hour.

1944 to Neuengamme near Hamburg and then in goods wagons to Ladelund, on the German-Danish border, and worked to death building a totally useless anti-tank ditch.

Russian POWs were treated worse than Western ones – in Buchenwald some were put into a barbed-wire compound and allowed to starve to death in front of the other inmates... even looked at the thousands who died building the Trans-Sahara Railway in 1941-43 or in the Far East on the Burma Railway and other lines – one, built mostly by Dutch and Australian prisoners of the Japanese to Pakan Baroe on Sumatra, was finally opened the day before the Hiroshima bomb and all had died in vain. It was never used...

It is important therefore to have a broad perspective and to read as much history as one can stomach. The railways were used not just for Jews or Sinti, but for almost everyone. Later on in 1944 and 1945 they were used to transport Germans fleeing the Russian advance, and then after the total collapse of Germany there were former prisoners and slaves and displaced persons travelling all over Europe in open goods wagons or any vehicle imaginable, desperate just to keep moving and head home – wherever home was and whoever was now in charge there.

Hungry civilians took the trains out into the country to trade their remaining possessions with farmers and come home with potatoes or eggs or fruit – there were no supermarkets then, you haggled or you starved. It was called 'Hamstering'.

A girl stands amid the ruins of houses following a V2 rocket strike on Battersea on January 27, 1945, in which 17 people were killed and 20 houses destroyed.

"The struggle for world domination will be fought entirely between us, between Germans and Jews. All else is facade and illusion. Behind England stands Israel, and behind France, and behind the United States. Even when we have driven the Jew out of Germany, he remains our world enemy."
Adolf Hitler

If ever there was on earth an embodiment of the mythical gates of hell, it is the entrance to the Auschwitz-Birkenau camp, the terminus for thousands of deportation trains. The ultimate monument to Nazi ideology, it was not, however, built by Satan, but by man.

During the Second World War Two, so many people travelled not for fun but because they had to or they were forced to. Many went in one direction only and never came back – they ended up in mass graves or military cemeteries or as piles of ash in the wind.

People travelled without luxury, without comfort, without even the basics.

People became freight, not passengers.

Local railwaymen were coerced into service, military railwaymen undertook specific tasks nearer the Fronts. Troops, supplies, wounded, prisoners, displaced civilians, booty (including wagon-loads of human hair from Auschwitz that were sent to a cable factory near Roth, south of Nuremberg) – all went by rail. There was no petrol for engines and little rubber for tyres, so steam locomotives and – not to be forgotten – the E44 and E94 'Wartime Electric Locomotives' where these could be used – did the haulage.

This book can only scratch the surface of the story. There are books in German and other languages, but in the nature of things there are few original documents that survived and almost no pictures. Normally any photography was forbidden.

Orders were given to destroy all timetables and operational documents after the trains had run – only rarely does a working timetable, a guard's report, or anything similar, survive.

Experts who have spent decades researching all report the same thing – there is anecdotal evidence, sometimes memoirs of survivors, but rarely any contemporary reports.

But that does not mean it did not happen...

Rabbi Dr Walter Rothschild
Berlin

The scene moments after disgusted American soldiers shot SS troops in the coalyard at Dachau, after viewing what had been going on inside the camp.

THE V2 ROCKET

After Allied troops began sweeping across Europe in the wake of the D-Day landings, Hitler responded by launching an all-out V2 rocket attack on London. An estimated 2754 civilians were killed in London by V2 attacks, with another 6523 injured, making it two people killed per V2 rocket.

A total of 160 were killed and 108 seriously injured in one mid-afternoon explosion on November 25, 1944, when a Woolworths department store in New Cross, south east London, was hit. Had Hitler started the V2 rocket programme several months earlier, would the outcome of the war have changed?

Despite such carnage, history records that more people were killed building the V2s than in the raids themselves. The Nazis used slave labour at the construction sites, bringing into sharp focus the role of the rocket designer, Wernher von Braun, who surrendered to the Americans and became a pivotal figure in the space race.

At the Mittelbau-Dora concentration camp, 20,000 inmates, died from illness, beatings, hangings and intolerable working conditions. Von Braun himself described conditions at the Mittelwerk construction plant as "repulsive", but denied seeing any deaths or beatings. However, he admitted in a letter dated August 15, 1944 that he had personally picked slaves from the Buchenald concentration camp, and at least one witness later said that von Braun stood by and watched as prisoners were hung by chains from hoists.

Above:
Two VIP guests on board the
German train which set a world speed
record in 1936 were Heinrich Himmler and
Reinhard Heydrich, who were to pencil in railways as the key
element in their plans for the 'Final Solution'.

H IJACKED BY HELL
Railway history

B ACK in 1771, a vehicle which
resembled a huge road cart with a
massive kettle fixed to its front,
emitted huge clouds of steam, ran out of
control and crashed into a wall in Paris.

What some regarded as the world's first
car crash ended its inventor's bid for fame
and fortune, and while it may have gone
down in history's 'good try' category, it also
brought scorn and ridicule to its inventor.

Nicolas-Joseph Cugnot was a trained
military engineer from Void-Vacon in
Lorraine, who experimented with working
models of steam engine-powered vehicles
for the French Army, intended for
transporting cannons.

His work began in 1765, and two years
later, had progressed to the point where
he produced two full-sized working
steam vehicles.

Seeking to invent the first self-propelled
vehicle – the transport equivalent of the
philosopher's stone, the goal of medieval
alchemists who desired to find the means of

turning base metals into gold – Cugnot had
become one of the first people to
successfully employ a device for
converting the reciprocating motion of a
steam piston into rotary motion by means
of a ratchet arrangement.

However, his three-wheeled steam dray
(or 'fardier à vapeur') which boasted a speed
of 2.25mph (the fire needed to be lit every
quarter of a mile) and could carry four
passengers, proved highly unstable due to
its poor weight distribution, hence the
accident when it smashed into the wall of
the Arsenal.

His experiments were abandoned after
trials between Paris and Vincennes and at
Meudon, but while the French army lost
interest in the fanciful idea of self-propelled
vehicles, King Louis XV nonetheless
granted Cugnot a pension and ordered his
fardier to be preserved; it can be seen in
the Conservatoire National des Arts et
Métiers today.

It would not be France, but Cornwall that

would change the world.

It would be in the duchy at the
westernmost tip of England that the crucial
bridge link of transport technology between
the Industrial Revolution and the modern age
would be forged.

CORNWALL'S EUREKA MOMENT
Today, Cornwall with its stunning romantic
coastal landscapes, wild untamed moors and
quaint fishing harbours is regarded as one of
Britain's top destinations for holidays at home.

Two centuries ago, however, you would
not want to go there on holiday. Much of the
landscape in the 18th and 19th centuries
was about as enticing as that of the South
Wales valleys in the 20th century, or that of
the Black Country in the West Midlands.

Huge engine houses pumped water out of
tin and copper mines and belched out
clouds of black smoke above the mining
villages with their tiny cottages, in which
miners' families lived on the meagre wages

Germany's fastest steam locomotive: Class 05 No. 05 001 set a world record in 1936 when Deutsche Reichsbahn-Gesellschaft was desperately trying to impress its Nazi overloads, in particular Himmler and Heydrich who were on board. In 1935, No. 001 was presented at the 100 Years of German Railways propaganda exhibition in Nuremberg. It is now a static exhibit inside the Deutsche Bahn Museum in Nuremberg.
ROBIN JONES

up production and boosting profits?

Also, was there a better way of transporting the huge components that made up those giant beam engines across land from the harbours to the mines? Would it not be absolutely wonderful if they could get there under their own steam?

Scottish inventor William Murdoch was taken on by Boulton & Watt to oversee the firm's stationary steam engine business in Cornwall.

While there, he began making his own plans for a steam carriage or road locomotive, which would greatly improve on Cugnot's design.

Watt was less than impressed when he was told of Murdoch's intentions. He said that there was no future in the concept and tried to persuade Murdoch to discontinue his experiments.

Murdoch built a model which visitors to his house in 1784 witnessed running around his living room in Redruth. It is the first recorded example in Britain of a man-made machine moving around completely under its own power, and is now displayed at the Thinktank science museum at Millennium Point in Birmingham.

In 1795, Murdoch gave a demonstration of his steam carriage in the Rivers Great Room at the Kings Head Hotel in Truro. It was the first public demonstration given in Britain of steam locomotion in action.

An often-told story is that one night Murdoch tested his carriage outside on the open road only to find that it ran away, leaving him to chase after it. On his way he encountered a local churchman who had believed he had seen the devil pass by, never having seen a steam carriage before, with its burning fire and billowing smoke.

Taking up the baton after Murdoch was another Cornishman, the great mining engineer Richard Trevithick.

He believed that the way forward was using high-pressure or 'strong' steam to power a self-propelled vehicle. Watt was horrified, and went as far as saying that Trevithick should be hanged for his experiments with it.

The problem was that nobody before had managed to contain high-pressure steam – previous attempts had led to fatal accidents. Safe containment of the pressure was essential: this was the one hurdle which had to be overcome before anything else.

It was Trevithick who came up with the answer: the cylindrical boiler, which would allow pistons to be driven by high-pressure steam. Eureka!

The cylindrical boiler was the key ingredient in the formula which could turn the mass of steam engineering knowledge used to build the giant pumping engines to produce a revolutionary and efficient form of transport. High-pressure steam on wheels was the end result.

This key ingredient was used on every steam engine that followed Trevithick, where it was to be found on a railway locomotive, traction engine, electric power station or nuclear submarine.

derived from some very inhospitable and precarious working conditions. Muscular woman known as bal maidens ('bal' being Cornish for mine) would hammer the extracted ore prior to its refining. The average life expectancy for those who toiled underground was not great.

Mining in Cornwall began around 2150 BC, the early Bronze Age. The peninsula's fame as a source of metals spread far and wide, and there was a vibrant trade with the Mediterranean for tin and copper. Britain was one of the places identified as the Cassiterides – the Tin Islands – marked on ancient seafarers' maps, and St Michael's Mount, near Penzance, has often been suggested as one of the great tin ports for the Mediterranean traders.

However, it was the work of steam pioneers like James Watt and Matthew Boulton, architects of the Industrial Revolution, who made it possible for the rich mineral veins beneath the Cornish landscape to be exploited on a massive

scale. The key to expanding Cornish mining to an industrial scale lay in keeping the mine shafts dry, and so their beam engines would pump out water night and day while the miners toiled below.

The finished ore would be taken to the nearest port by horse-drawn cart for distribution to other parts of Britain and export abroad. Road communications between Cornwall and the rest of Britain were, despite the duchy's renowned mineral wealth and huge industrial output, very poor. Indeed, as late as the 1890s, when the London & South Western Railway was still completing its expansion to Padstow, it despatched three tank engines by sea to run on the Bodmin & Wadebridge Railway, which it had owned since 1846.

Yet, despite such poor land links, Cornwall was the most valuable nonferrous mining area in the world. What if a more efficient means could be found by which ore could be taken to those ports from the mining regions several miles inland, thereby greatly stepping

Trevithick set about designing a road locomotive, and produced one which lacked the inadequacies of Cugnot's cumbersome machines. However, backward technology for 1500 years had seen Britain all but lose the art of road building that the Romans had imported with them, so Trevithick's first vehicle, designed to run on the public highway, immediately sank into mud and potholes.

He then looked at the railway concept, which for centuries had been a tried and tested method of carrying bulk loads in horse-drawn wagons from a mine, quarry or place of manufacture to a transhipment point, and placed his vehicle on rails.

An early Trevithick railway locomotive ran at Ironbridge in 1802, and the first public demonstration of one was given by Trevithick on the Penydarren Tramroad at Merthyr Tydfil two years later, to settle a bet.

His locomotive cracked the cast-iron rails because of its weight, but succeeded in hauling loaded wagons from a mine to a canal wharf far more efficiently than horse power could achieve.

Trevithick not only won his bet, but he had lit the blue touchpaper, sparking off a series of events that changed the face of the world by providing a transport system that would see human society take a huge evolutionary leap forward within a relatively short space of time. The ability to quickly and efficiently move bulk loads without man or animal power in harness held out the promise of an enormous liberating principle. The world would never be the same again.

Trevithick experimented with more steam railway locomotives, including *Catch-me-who-Can*, which ran on a trainset-like circle of track on a site near the future Euston station in 1808, hauling a carriage, and thereby forming the world's first passenger train.

Yet, despite the fact he proved that a railway locomotive could be a reality, nobody came forward to order a batch of his locomotives. Faced with indifference, Trevithick turned his attention elsewhere, but his invention had, however, by no means gone unnoticed.

As the Napoleonic Wars raged, the British Army had the need for a seemingly endless supply of horses and hay. Accordingly, horses became in short supply while the cost of feed rocketed. Mine owners in the north of England turned again to Trevithick's ideas. As with trying to conquer the difficult Cornish terrain, raw necessity became the mother of invention.

Engineer John Blenkinsop saw steam locomotives as the future and persuaded Matthew Murray to build several for Middleton Colliery, near Leeds – the first, *Salamanca*, made its debut in 1812. It was

the world's first commercially successful steam locomotive, and the first to have two cylinders. It was named after Sir Arthur Wellesley's (late the Duke of Wellington's) victory at the Battle of Salamanca which took place the same year.

Other mine owners followed suit, and from the many steam engine designers and builders who appeared to satisfy demand, two names acquired early pre-eminence: George Stephenson and his son Robert.

In 1814, Stephenson designed his first locomotive for Killingworth Colliery in County Durham, which became known as the 'cradle of the railways', and in 1820 began work on the Hetton Railway from Hetton Colliery in Durham to Sunderland. It was the world's first purpose-built steam-operated railway.

Afterwards, the Stephensons surveyed the route for the Stockton & Darlington Railway, which when opened in 1825 was the world's first public steam railway.

George Stephenson acquired even greater fame with the opening on September 15, 1830 of the Liverpool & Manchester Railway, the world's first inter-city line, for which he and his son had designed the locomotive *Rocket*.

In the wake of its resounding success, Stephenson was offered the position of chief engineer for many other railways. He partially designed the Grand Junction Railway linking the Liverpool & Manchester to Birmingham, and which, when opened on July 4, 1837, was the first trunk railway to be completed in England, and probably the world's first long-distance railway using steam traction.

A SLOW START

It took 26 years from that first public demonstration at Penydarren (and six decades from Cugnot's car crash) to the opening of the Liverpool & Manchester Railway for the steam railway concept to catch on big time. The railway revolution may be said to have started with a whimper, but after the Liverpool & Manchester, it quickly became a big bang.

The Railway mania of the 1840s saw speculative schemes for lines mushroom across Britain. Not all were successful, but by the end of that decade, we saw the basis of what became the country's national network forming into place.

At the same time, British steam railway technology was in increasing demand all over the world. In 1828, Pioneer locomotive builder Foster, Rastrick & Company constructed and exported the *Stourbridge Lion*, which became the first steam locomotive to be operated in the USA, and indeed one of the first to operate outside Britain.

Robert Stephenson set up a locomotive building works in Newcastle, and in 1835 designed and built a 2-2-2 tender locomotive

for the Bavarian Ludwig Railway (Bayerische Ludwigsbahn) for service between Nuremberg and Fürth.

Named *Der Adler* (The Eagle), it was the first steam locomotive used successfully for the commercial transport of freight and passengers in Germany.

It is impossible to overstate the dramatic impact which railways made, firstly in Britain, and then around the globe, in Victorian times. They effectively shrunk the continents: far-flung countries and isolated towns and cities which would take many days to reach on horseback or foot could be accessed from ports and harbours within a few hours. Thanks to the 'iron horse', human achievement was suddenly spiralling ahead at an alarming pace.

In the Stephensons' day, Britain was still a predominantly rural country, although the Industrial Revolution had been steadily changing that for decades, with poor farm labourers drawn to rapidly-expanding towns where the promise of regular jobs in factories, using modern equipment to mass produce goods, was too good to miss.

TIME FOR A CHANGE

The railways were a physical 'internet', bringing cities and countryside closer together than their inhabitants had ever dreamed possible. They facilitated the movement of the workforce gravitating from the shires to the towns and cities, and for a sizeable proportion of the population, allowed them to travel more than a few miles from their birthplace for the first time. Before the advent of the railways, many people in Britain had never seen the sea.

One of the earliest by-products of steam railways was the standardisation of time. Before the railways, localities tended to have their own time zones, which could differ from that of the capital by half an hour or more. With the arrival of the railway, the train guard would have his pocket watch set to the time of Big Ben, and the places on the route would fall in line.

Railways not only promoted massive industrial expansion, with the provision of bulk supplies of coal from the mining areas such as South Wales and Yorkshire, and mineral ores to blast furnaces, but also opened up new markets for fresh country produce, providing outlets for milk and perishables to a mass market, cutting the cost of food and improving living conditions. That great British tradition of fish and chips has its origin in the railway coming to Grimsby, the once-great North Sea trawler port. >>

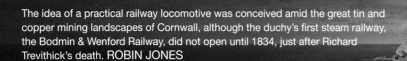

The idea of a practical railway locomotive was conceived amid the great tin and copper mining landscapes of Cornwall, although the duchy's first steam railway, the Bodmin & Wenford Railway, did not open until 1834, just after Richard Trevithick's death. ROBIN JONES

>> Eventually, with the rise in working conditions and holidays, railways would create a tourist economy, offering the prospect of a week at the seaside.

The benefits which railways brought to human society are encyclopaedic. The ready availability of cheap food in bulk help raise living standards, and every house had access to coal for a fire.

They also paved the way for the development of road and eventually air transport, which created our world in which anywhere can be reached inside a day.

CENTURY OF CHANGE

At the start of the 19th century, steam railways were unknown. By the end of the century, the entire fabric of the country was based around them, or in association with them. The impact that they made on the human race was seismic, akin to a reinvention of the wheel, which they literally were.

However, like every human innovation from the dawn of time, railways were also a double-edged sword.

While railways were a force with immense power to do good, in human hands, they could, history was to prove, became a tool for acts of unthinkable evil.

Trevithick, Stephenson et al had given the world one of the greatest inventions in the history of the human race.

Unwittingly, they had also provided humanity the means by which, under certain circumstances, mass murder and destruction on a continent-wide scale could be facilitated, if such a great gift found itself in the wrong hands, and if nobody willing to lift a finger to stop it happening.

Railways were not just a gift created from the ingenuity and technological progress which followed in the wake of the Industrial Revolution.

Like every empowering invention or school of thought, they would also be a challenge for the human race. One day, the use of railways would test mankind's core values beyond any extremity that had gone before, and in the process would find the world sadly wanting.

The crew that drove *Flying Scotsman* at 100mph were feted as national heroes when they arrived back at King's Cross on November 30, 1934, and were idolised by youngsters everywhere. NRM

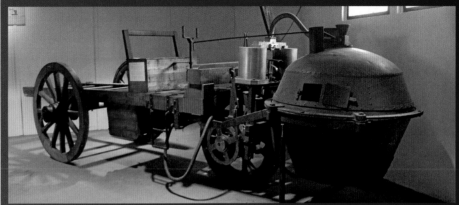

A modern-day replica of Nicolas-Joseph Cugnot's 18th century attempt at building the world's first self-propelled vehicle using extremely basic steam technology can be seen inside the DB Museum in Nuremberg. ROBIN JONES

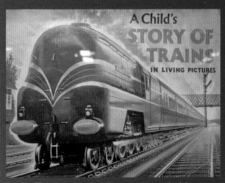

In the Thirties the public, young and old, were enchanted by railways, which cashed in on the adulation with a range of souvenirs to suit all pockets, like this book featuring a streamlined LMS Princess Coronation Pacific on its cover. ROBIN JONES

A child's block puzzle of one of Nazi Germany's new autobahns, which provided an alternative to rail transport. ROBIN JONES

DAWN OF THE DARKER SIDE

Railways inevitably became part of the field of human conflict. One of the first uses of military railways came in the severe winter of 1855 to establish a more reliable supply of British Army soldiers in the Balaklava positions during the Crimean War.

A decade later, the United States Military Railroad, known as the City Point Railroad, was extended to Petersburg during the Siege of Petersburg in the American Civil War.

After that conflict, in which, incidentally, slavery and racial suppression was a primary factor, railways became more frequently used for military operations. They played a part in the Austro-Prussian War of 1866 and the Franco-Prussian War of 1870/71, after which Germany laid many new lines for strategic reasons.

The German army had a special Railway Brigade and by the time of the outbreak of World War One, had drawn up precise railway timetables for troop movements.

The Great War was unlike anything that had gone before, with the products of technological progress over the previous century bringing death and destruction on an industrial scale.

That conflict has also been described as the world's first great railway war. On both sides, railways brought troops, armaments and equipment to the front lines, and brought back the wounded and the dead, as well as soldiers going home on leave and then returning to the battlefields.

In many places on the Western Front, extensive narrow gauge networks were laid in the trenches, with the British company Motor-Rail of Bedfordshire supplying engines that did not run on steam. The company's

Simplex petrol-engined locomotives did not emit clouds smoke and therefore give away their positions to the enemy.

Fast forward – literally – to the zenith of the steam age, the Thirties, where speed was of the essence.

By this time much of the patterns of British society had long since been shaped by the railway. A sizeable proportion of the population was employed by the 'Big Four' companies, the Southern, London, Midland & Scottish, London & North Eastern and Great Western railways.

The railway community was a society within a society, with its own rules and its own hierarchy, extending from station porters and engine cleaners at the bottom of the ladders to chief mechanical engineers and directors at the top.

In many towns and cities, the

Two replicas of Germany's first commercial steam locomotive, the British-built *Der Adler*, exist. The first was built in 1935 and is still operational, while the second, pictured here on display in the DB Museum at Nuremberg, was built by Deutsche Bundesbahn apprentices in 1952 and used as an exhibit at trade fairs. The beer barrels featured on both replicas were never carried by the original, and were added to the first in 1935 as an advertisement for the Lederer Brewery. ROBIN JONES

The replica maker's plate highlights the Newcastle origin of *Der Adler*. ROBIN JONES

Not *Rocket* on the Liverpool & Manchester Railway, but a slightly later Stephenson locomotive, *Der Adler*, depicted hauling its first train in Germany. The painting is in the DB Museum in Nuremberg.

stationmaster was regarded as equal if not higher than the local mayor, and there are reports of many of them attired in top hats and tails. Ordinary railway staff were trusted as a veritable backbone of society.

The continual process of locomotive development seemed unstoppable; every new express passenger type won more fans and admirers.

Engine drivers were the idols of, and role models for, many a schoolboy, in those days when pop stars and millionaire footballers did not exist. Their dream was to board the footplate of a glamorous locomotive, and maybe take a short ride to the engine shed if nobody in authority was watching.

Such adulation did not go unnoticed by the railway companies' marketing departments, which turned out volumes of merchandise ranging from boys' books of trains to jigsaws and puzzles.

THE RIVALS

What captured the public imagination at large in the period following the great depression were the races from London to Scotland by the LNER and its great rival, the LMS. Such rivalry produced the fastest and some of the most powerful express steam locomotives that the world had ever known.

LNER chief mechanical engineer Nigel Gresley's powerful A1 Pacifics came to the fore with the launch of the daily 'Flying Scotsman' named train from King's Cross to Edinburgh Waverley in 1928. *Flying Scotsman* the locomotive, A1 No. 4472, became the first in the world to officially reach 100mph, on Stoke Bank on the East Coast Main Line on November 30, 1934, with 61-year-old driver William Sparshatt becoming a hero overnight.

When GWR 4-4-0 No. 3440 *City of Truro* allegedly reached 102.3mph on Wellington Bank in Somerset in 1904, the GWR hid the fact for several years for fear that speed would scare passengers off trains. By the Thirties, there was no holding the LNER back: it wanted to show the world it could beat allcomers.

However, it was only rivalry between Britain's east and west coast routes that was foremost in the minds of the LNER directors at the time. It was competition from abroad, and a new threat to steam traction, then still the undisputed norm in Britain.

In Germany, streamlined two-car diesel

electric railcar set named Flying Hamburger quickly became the fastest train in the world. State railway Deutsche Reichsbahn-Gesellschaft ordered the 98-seater Class SVT 877 set in 1932 from manufacturer Waggon und Maschinenbau AG Gorlitz and introduced it on the Berlin–Hamburg line the following year, when, coincidentally, Hitler came to power.

Wind tunnel experiments were used to design the streamlining, following on from the development of the high-speed inter-urban railcar Bullet two years previously. Each of the two vehicles had a 12-cylinder Maybach diesel engine with a direct current generator directly coupled to it, which drove a Tatzlager traction motor. The Flying Hamburger recorded a then-amazing average speed of 77.4mph over the 178-mile journey, decades ahead of its time, and indicated that the future of mass transport lay in diesel power, not steam.German locomotive builder Henschel-Werke responded by building a streamlined express steam train that could compete with the Flying Hamburger. The Henschel-Wegmann Train ran non-stop express services between Berlin and Dresden from June 1936 to August 1939. Gresley took a trip on this train and was so impressed that the LNER seriously considered buying one.

The manufacturers were asked to design a Flying Hamburger for the LNER, but could not guarantee the speeds the original one had displayed in Germany. The chief general manager of the LNER, Sir Ralph Wedgwood, suggested that with an ordinary Pacific engine, faster overall speeds could be maintained with a train of much greater weight, capacity, and comfort, and so Gresley followed the steam route.

In March 1935, A3 No. 2750 *Papyrus* reached 108mph going down Stoke Bank while hauling 217 tons, maintaining a speed above 100mph for 12½ consecutive miles, the world record for a non-streamlined locomotive, shared with a French Chapelon Pacific.

Streamlining, however, was by then viewed as the way forward, not only to produce aerodynamic designs, but to produce a stylish 'futuristic' locomotive outline for publicity purposes. Gresley was given the green light to produce his 'Silver Jubilee' streamlined trains, with his

distinctive A4 Pacifics at their head.

A trial run on September 27, 1935 saw No. 2509 *Silver Link*, twice reach 112mph and sustain an average speed of 100mph for 43 consecutive miles.

The LMS responded to this and other feats involving the A4s. Its Chief Mechanical Engineer William Stanier had already built a class of 13 new express passenger Pacifics, the Princess Royal class, to haul the 'Royal Scot' from Euston to Glasgow Central, and planned a six-hour non-stop service from London to Glasgow.

On a test run, Crewe North senior driver Tom Clark, chosen to drive No. 6201 *Princess Elizabeth* from Euston to Glasgow Central, along with fireman Charles Fleet and passed fireman Albert Shaw, and on November 16 1936, they managed it in five hours 53 minutes 38 seconds. The following day, the return journey took five hours 44 minutes 14 seconds.

The footplate crew were instantly feted as national heroes, and daily newspapers ran front page headlines proclaiming "London-Glasgow Under 6 Hours", "401 Miles Non Stop", "Railway Ambition Achieved". Everyone loved them, and few schoolboys did not want to be anything but an engine driver.

A SMASHING TIME

Stanier's response to the A4s, the streamlined and somewhat bulbous Princess Coronation class Pacifics, went one better. On June 29, 1937, Tom Clark reached Euston from Crewe in two hours 9 minutes 45 seconds, with the press trip preceding the launch of the 'Coronation Scot' on July 5. He covered the 158 miles back to Crewe in one hour 59 minutes and reclaimed the record with a top speed of 114 mph, just south of the town, when the train travelled so fast over a series of points that the crockery in the dining car came crashing down. Wonderful stuff to grip the public imagination!

While the crockery incident caused the LMS and LNER to agree an end to further potentially hazardous record-breaking attempts, the Germans had other ideas.

They also wanted to see if steam traction could better their Flying Hamburger, and Borsig locomotive works built three Class 05 streamlined 4-6-4s.The second of these, No. 05002, seized the world steam locomotive speed record on May 11, 1936, when it reached 124.5mph while hauling a 197 ton train on the Berlin-Hamburg line.

The Germans had reclaimed the crown, but despite outward experiences, the record run was not intentional.

The German state railways had become increasingly agitated about Hitler's apparent switch of support from rail to road.

While work on the first autobahns had been started under the Weimar Republic, just days after the Nazi takeover in 1933, Hitler announced his support for an ambitious autobahn construction project and appointed Fritz Todt, the Inspector General of German Road Construction, to head it.

ROAD TO CONQUEST

By 1936, 130,000 workers were directly employed in its construction, as well as an additional 270,000 in the supply chain for construction equipment, steel, concrete, signage and maintenance equipment. In rural areas, new camps to house the workers were built near construction sites.

The Nazi propaganda ministry turned the building of the autobahns into a significant publicity exercise that attracted international attention. They were the first limited-access, high-speed road network in the world, with the first section from Frankfurt-am-Main to Darmstadt opening in 1935.

Despite the fact that the German Army still saw the railways as the preferred means of travel because of lower fuel costs, the railway authorities became worried. What if the situation changed?

A special three-leg train was laid on for Nazi top brass to showcase the advantages that the rail network could offer.

All went well until the final leg, when a series of red signals hampered the train's progress. Fearing that the guests on board would lose patience, the jittery organisers of the trip told the locomotive crew in no uncertain terms to put their foot down all the way to Hamburg. They did, and a new record was somewhat inadvertently set.

The special train covered the 70.1 miles from Wittenberge to a signal stop before Berlin-Spandau in 48 min 32 sec, at an average start-stop speed of 86.66mph.

A little over two years later, on July 3, 1938, Gresley seized back the crown, when four-month-old A4 No. 4468 *Mallard*, the first of the class to be fitted with the Kylchap double-blastpipe to improve its performance, was taken by Doncaster driver Joe Duddington who had a reputation for running trains hard when needed, and fireman Tommy Bray and inspector Sam Jenkins, down Stoke Bank with the needle in the dynamometer car behind the engine registering 126mph, at milepost 90¼, between Little Bytham and Essendine. The record has never been beaten.

The Nazi propaganda machine was silent.

However, a less well-known fact is that among the VIP guests on that trip to Hamburg in 1936 were two men who were to have very different intentions for their nation's railway system other than trying to break a speed record.

Their names were Heinrich Himmler and Reinhard Heydrich.

Between them, a few years later, they were to orchestrate a plan by which millions of innocent people from all over Europe were to be transported by rail in horrific circumstances to special camps in which they were to be murdered, most within hours of their arrival.

It was the railways that made mass killings on such an industrial scale possible. Without the railways, it would have been impossible for the Nazis to move trainloads of people from the corners of occupied Europe to their many killing fields, which had Auschwitz at the hub of their demonic network.

The Germany of the Thirties was similar to Britain in so many ways. The Holocaust was not the result of age-old tribal warfare in some backward third-world country when the law of the jungle reigned supreme, but the actions of a highly-cultured nation which had produced the likes of Goethe, Bach, Beethoven and Mendelsson (who, incidentally, was born a Jew).

HEROES AND VILLAINS

German railwaymen would have been little different to those in Britain. Basically decent people, their camaraderie, their pride in conscientiously carrying out their duties to the letter, their roles in their communities, would have been very much the same. Perhaps their youngsters idolised engine drivers in much the same way.

So why, why, why, how could it ever have happened? What turned pillars of the community and schoolboy heroes into accessories to mass murder on an unprecedented scale within a few years?

What's more, if Operation Sealion had been successful and the Nazis had conquered Britain, what part would our railways and their staff have played in furthering their unthinkable crimes? Should we delude ourselves that faced with occupation by tyranny, we would have behaved in a markedly different way?

By 1942, a path had somehow led from the genius of Trevithick to the trains that shamed the world. A great gift had been given to mankind, a challenge to use it for the greater good implicitly lay within, and humanity failed in the worst possible way.

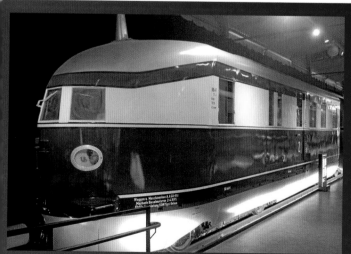

The Flying Hamburger and similar trains introduced from 1933 considerably reduced journey times between major German cities, proving extremely popular and creating an express train network capable of competing with both private cars and air transport. The Flying Hamburger carriage on display in the DB Museum in Nuremberg was built in 1931 and was the first high-speed multiple units manufactured by Maschinenbau AG Görlitz for the Reichsbahn. Taken out of service in 1957, it was restored to its original condition in the Nuremberg repair shop. ROBIN JONES

Mallard pictured on Sunday, July 3, 1938 at Barkston on the East Coast Main Line just prior to its record-breaking run. The streamline A4 Pacific reached a speed of 126mph on a straight stretch of track between Grantham and Peterborough, achieving a new world record for steam locomotives. NRM

Racial cleansing
GERMANY WAS NOT ALONE

John Harvey Kellogg, co-founder of the Kellogg Company, was an early American eugenics pioneer.

US eugenics pioneer Charles Benedict Davenport maintained connections with Nazi institutions and publications before and during the Second World War. It was only when the excesses of Nazi Germany became apparent to the world that eugenics became discredited, but even in some parts of the globe, the principle is still practised. In 1994, for example, China introduced restrictions on marriages involving citizens with certain disabilities and diseases.

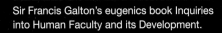

Sir Francis Galton's eugenics book Inquiries into Human Faculty and its Development.

Sir Francis Galton who, inspired by his half-cousin Charles Darwin, came up with the theory of eugenics.

Wildlife conservationist and eugenicist Madison Grant. Not only did he list Hitler among his following, but his work was mentioned in a document compiled by Norwegian mass murderer Anders Behring Breivik, who killed 77 people in a bombing attack and shooting in 2011.

Master of the extreme jingoistic rant as he was, Hitler did not devise the concept of racial cleansing as a means of creating a nation of supermen: in fact, a quick analysis shows that he and his associates had very few, if any, truly original ideas of their own.

Just as the British invented the concentration camp during the Boer Wars in South Africa, it was an Englishman who came up with the 'scientific' idea of eugenics, a word which he coined in 1883.

Sir Francis Galton (1822-1911) was a half-cousin of Charles Darwin, whose ground-breaking but highly-controversial 1859 work On The Origin Of Species written using evidence from his 1830s voyages aboard HMS Beagle postulated the theory that natural selection, not creation, was the reason for the diversity of life.

Taking mankind out of the dark ages in which many in his day still held to the belief that the world was only a few thousand years old, after having been created in six days, Darwin laid the foundation stone of evolutionary biology, doing for science what Richard Trevithick had done for transport.

His half-cousin was highly influenced by Darwin's work. Sir Francis undertook research in the field of selective breeding and in 1869 published a book called Hereditary Genius.

In it, he outlined the lives of several accomplished men from 'good' families. These good families, he said, were more likely to produce intelligent and talented children.

Such observations led him to the conclusion that it was possible to produce a highly gifted race of men through arranged marriages, a process which he termed 'positive' eugenics.

There again, it would be possible to attain a similar goal by 'discouraging' inferior people to breed at all – a form of 'negative' eugenics. His term eugenics derived from the Greek word eu (good or well) and the suffix -genĒs (born).

The question therefore arises – how far is the leap from positive eugenics to the deliberate promotion of a 'master race', and from negative eugenics to wiping out anyone and everyone that you don't like at a particular time?

It would be wrong to suggest that Galton's ideas were directly responsible for mass murder, any more than blaming the philosopher Karl Marx who came up with the idea of communism for the estimated deaths of up to 20 million Soviet citizens through purges and famine under Josef Stalin before Hitler had even come to power. As an aside, it might be considered that once Hitler reneged on the Nazi-Soviet pact and launched Operation Barbarossa in 1941, Britain and the USA joined forces with the bigger monster far away in order to defeat the slightly less big monster on the doorstep.

Sir Francis was born in Sparkbrook, Birmingham and was a descendant of Samuel John Galton, who was a founding member of the city's Lunar Society, which also included Matthew Boulton and James Watt among its members. A child prodigy, Galton could read at the age of two, and by six had moved on to the works of Shakespeare. He went on to study mathematics at Cambridge. In 1850 he joined the Royal Geographical Society, and made an exhibition to the little-explored South West Africa, now known as Namibia.

A prolific writer, among his many contributions to the world of science was the popular weather map, first published in The Times on April 1, 1875.

In the later 1880s, he wrote a controversial letter to this newspaper, headlined 'Africa for the Chinese'. In it, he argued that the Chinese, as a race capable of high civilisation, should be encouraged to emigrate to Africa and displace the supposedly 'inferior' indigenous black population.

He spent much of his later life exploring variation in human populations and its implications. He set up a research programme which looked at why people across the world were different. The study looked at not only their mental characteristics but their height, facial images and event fingerprint patterns. He looked in depth at twins, in a bid to ascertain whether intelligence was inherited or acquired. His method envisaged testing to see if twins who were similar at birth ended up becoming very different people if brought up in totally different circumstances.

More than any other area, Galton studied the upper classes of Britain, and came to the conclusion that their social positions were due to a superior genetic makeup.

In 1909, the first edition of the Eugenics Review, the journal of the Eugenics Education Society, was published, with Sir Francis, the organisation's president, writing the foreword to the first volume.

He died just two weeks before the First International Congress of Eugenics was held in July 1912. Amongst those in attendance was Winston Churchill.

RACIAL PURITY IN THE USA

It was not in Britain or Germany, but in the United States, the 'land of the free', where Galton's theories made the most immediate and resounding impact.

Founded in 1894 by three recent Harvard University graduates, the Immigration Restriction League was the first US organisation associated officially with eugenics. It wanted to stop 'inferior races' from entering the US.

Eugenics was greeted Stateside with fervour in the early 20th century. Proponents considered Nordic, Germanic and Anglo-Saxon peoples to be genetically superior. Indeed, their campaign led to sterilisation laws which were passed in more than half the states many years before the swastika first appeared as a Nazi symbol.

In 1907, Indiana became the first state to enact sterilisation legislation, followed closely by Washington and California in 1909. Sterilisation rates in the US remained low until the 1927 Supreme Court case Buck v Bell approved the forced sterilisation of patients at a Virginia home for 'the mentally retarded'.

It is estimated that around 60,000 compulsory sterilisations were performed in the US from 1909 right up to the Sixties, with about a third of them in California. In North Carolina, sterilisation was considered appropriate for anyone with an IQ of 70 or lower, and social workers had the power to designate people for such operations. It was seen as a cheap and effective way of preventing unwanted pregnancies.

By 1917, 15 US states had introduced eugenics laws to sterilise epileptics, people with mental illness and regular criminals. Broadly speaking, the US policy saw men sterilised to treat their aggression and to eliminate their criminal behaviour, while women were sterilised to control the results of their sexuality.

In the two decades that followed, the policy of sterilising certain mental health patients was adopted in Belgium, Brazil, Canada and Sweden.

In 1906, John Harvey Kellogg, best known for the invention of corn flakes as a breakfast cereal, helped found the Race Betterment Foundation, which became a focal point of the American eugenics movements. Although Kellogg had personally adopted several black children, he favoured racial segregation as he believed that inter-marriage would damage the gene pool.

The eugenics movement also received substantial funding from the estate of railroad magnate Edward 'Ned' Harriman, who by the time he died in 1909 controlled the Union Pacific, Southern Pacific, Illinios Central, Saint Joseph and Grand Island and Central of Georgia railroads. He left a fortune estimated at $100 million.

The Carnegie Institution for Science, which had been established to support scientific research, and the Rockefeller Foundation, founded in 1913 by the multi-millionaire Rockefeller family "to promote the well-being of mankind throughout the world" also gave significant financial support. Indeed, the latter funded German eugenics programs, including one that employed a certain Josef Mengele prior to the Second World War.

The Harriman railroad fortune funded local charities, such as the New York Bureau of Industries and Immigration, to seek out Jewish, Italian and other immigrants in New York and other crowded cities and subject them to deportation, confinement or forced sterilisation.

In 1911, the Eugenics Records Office was founded in Cold Spring Harbor, New York by >>

>> biologist and leading eugenicist Charles B Davenport, using Harriman and Carnegie Institution money. Five years earlier, Davenport had set up the American Breeder's Association which was the first official organisation in the US wholly dedicated to eugenics. He and others began to call for solutions to the problem of 'unfit' members of society. Davenport himself favoured restrictions on immigration while others called for segregation.

A third, Madison Grant – a lawyer, wildlife conservationist, and historian as well as a eugenicist – went much further. In 1916, his book The Passing of the Great Race was published. In it, he argued the case for the "Nordic race" being the prime mover in human development, and argued against immigrants from other races diluting its gene pool. He argued the case for the separation, quarantine, and eventual collapse of "undesirable" traits and "worthless race types" from the pool and the promotion, spread, and eventual restoration of desirable traits and "worthwhile race types" which would boost Nordic society, and called for the segregating of "unfavourable" races in ghettos.

He wrote: "A rigid system of selection through the elimination of those who are weak or unfit – in other words social failures – would solve the whole question in 100 years, as well as enable us to get rid of the undesirables who crowd our jails, hospitals, and insane asylums. The individual himself can be nourished, educated and protected by the community during his lifetime, but the state through sterilisation must see to it that his line stops with him, or else future generations will be cursed with an ever increasing load of misguided sentimentalism. This is a practical, merciful, and inevitable solution of the whole problem, and can be applied to an ever widening circle of social discards, beginning always with the criminal, the

diseased, and the insane, and extending gradually to types which may be called weaklings rather than defectives, and perhaps ultimately to worthless race types."

The Nordics were, for Grant, the height of civilisation, a master race, "characterised by certain unique specialisations, namely, wavy brown or blond hair and blue, gray or light brown eyes, fair skin, high, narrow and straight nose, which are associated with great stature, and a long skull, as well as with abundant head and body hair".

Although the book was never a best seller, Grant served as the vice president of the Immigration Restriction League from 1922 until his death in 1937. He also contributed statistics for the US's Immigration Act of 1924 to set limitations on immigration from certain European countries. He was a close friend of several US presidents, including Theodore Roosevelt and Herbert Hoover.

Grant's biggest fan, however, appeared to be none other than Adolf Hitler. In the early Thirties, he wrote to Grant praising Passing of the Great Race as "his Bible".

The American Eugenics Society was founded in 1926. Two years later there were 376 separate university courses in some of the United States' leading schools, enrolling more than 20,000 students, which included eugenics in the curriculum.

Supporters of eugenics in the USA backed a restriction on immigration from nations with 'inferior' stock, and called for the sterilisation of what they termed "insane, retarded, and epileptic" people. They held that through selective breeding, the human species should direct its own evolution.

The Third International Congress in 1932 discussed the 'problem' of African-Americans. Delegates said that sterilisation should be used to 'cut off bad stock'. Among several Nazi attendees were Dr Ernst Rudin, who had been given passage by the

Hamburg-Amerika Shipping Line, partially owned by the Harriman family. When he went back to Germany, Rudin oversaw the policy of sterilising "the retarded, deaf, blind and alcoholic".

A report on the results of sterilisation in California was published as a book by the biologist Paul Popenoe. The Nazi government held it up as proof that sterilisation programmes could be feasible, humane and successful.

However, it is only a small leap in thought from sterilising someone whose lineage you wish to end, to eradicating them outright. In 1911, a report from the Carnegie Institute recommended euthanasia as a recommended solution for cleaning society of unfit genetic attributes.

There were those who suggested setting up local gas chambers for this very purpose.

Yet even some of the more extreme eugenicists held back, fearing that the American public would quickly turn against a large-scale euthanasia policy.

That did not stop killings by the back door, as doctors found other ways around the problem. A mental institution in Lincoln, Illinois, fed its incoming patients milk infected with tuberculosis, on the basis that genetically-fit individuals would resist the virus. They achieved annual mortality rates of up to 40%.

The Illinois Homeopathic Medicine Association in 1931 called for the right to practise euthanasia on "imbeciles", and the Euthanasia Society of America was founded in 1938.

THE NUREMBERG LAWS
Like a disease in its own right, the implementation of policies of sterilisation on eugenic grounds spread like wildfire from California to Germany, where there seemed to be a very receptive audience, at least in some quarters.

Compulsory sterilisation laws were included in the 1935 Nuremberg racial hygiene laws, one of the first pieces of major legislation enacted by the Nazis after they came to power. Differing from the eugenics laws passed in US states, the Nuremberg Laws – introduced at the annual Nuremberg Rally of the Nazi Party – included anti-semitism.

Harry H Laughlin, director of the Eugenics Record Office, often boasted that his Model Eugenic Sterilization laws had been implemented in the Nuremberg Laws.

In 1936, Heidelberg University in Germany awarded Laughlin an honorary doctorate for his work on the "science of racial cleansing".

By 1934, more than 5000 people every month were being sterilised in Germany against their will. California eugenics leader C M Goethe told a colleague: "You will be interested to know that your work has played a powerful part in shaping the opinions of the group of intellectuals who are behind Hitler in this epoch-making program. Everywhere I sensed that their opinions have been tremendously stimulated by American thought.

Hartheim Euthanasia Centre, where more than 18,000 people were murdered under Aktion T4. DRALON*

"I want you, my dear friend, to carry this thought with you for the rest of your life, that you have really jolted into action a great government of 60 million people."

Eugenics already had a foothold in Germany even before Hitler came to power. As early as 1920, psychiatrist Alfred Hoche and law professor Karl Binding recommended killing those judged to be "life unworthy of life". Their book, Die Freigabe der Vernichtung Lebensunwertem Lebens (Allowing the Destruction of Life Unworthy of Living), became a key Nazi reader. Hitler espoused similar ideas. In Mein Kampf he wrote: "He who is bodily and mentally not sound and deserving may not perpetuate this misfortune in the bodies of his children. The völkische state has to perform the most gigantic rearing-task here. One day, however, it will appear as a deed greater than the most victorious wars of our present bourgeois era."

After the passing of the Nuremberg Laws, the German Interior Ministry, under Wilhelm Frick, established special Hereditary Health Courts which had the power to examine those living in nursing homes, asylums, prisons, aged care homes and special schools to choose those to be sterilised.

As many 360,000 people were sterilised under this law between 1933-39. However, the rate of sterilisation diminished after 1937, when during a labour shortage, anyone capable of working was exempted from this law.

MASS MURDER BEGINS

The ante was raised in 1939, when Hitler received a somewhat astonishing letter from the father of a five-month-old boy, Gerhard Kretschmar, who had been born blind and deformed, with a leg and parts of an arm missing.

The baby's father, farmhand Richard Kretschmar, from Pomssen, near Leipzig, asked for Hitler's permission to kill him. Hitler was clearly inspired to the point that he sent his own doctor to see the family, after which the boy was given a lethal drug. He took between three and five days to die.

This was the cataclysmic turning point. It gave the Nazis the excuse they wanted, to create a 'Nordic' master race.

A few days later, 15 top psychiatrists were told to report to Hitler's Chancellery. They were told that a secret euthanasia programme was to be introduced.

In August 1939, a month after the baby's death, the Interior Ministry issued a decree ordering the killing of mentally and physically disabled children.

The euthanasia programme became known as Aktion T4. The name was taken from its Berlin base at a villa in Tiergartenstrasse No. 4. The establishment was known as Gemeinnützige Stiftung für Heil und Anstaltspflege (the Charitable Foundation for Curative and Institutional Care – overtones here of the Committee for Public Safety through which Maximilien Robespierre ordered the massacres of the French Revolution).

In charge of Aktion T4 were Reichsleiter Philipp Bouhler, the head of Hitler's private

chancellery, and Dr Karl Brandt, the Fuhrer's own physician.

In 1935, Hitler had told the Reich Doctors' leader, Dr Gerhard Wagner, that killing those deemed unfit to live "could be more smoothly and easily carried out in war". Indeed, the outbreak of the Second World War provided many excuses for the would-be euthanasia practitioners. Several disabled and mentally handicapped people, even when sterilised, needed special care – the Nazis had been making that point for several years in propaganda leaflets, posters and films – and would take public resources away from the war effort. Medical facilities, doctors and nurses would be needed to treat wounded servicemen

Nazi doctor Dr Hermann Pfannmüller, who was also at the core of T4, said: "The idea is unbearable to me that the best, the flower of our youth must lose its life at the front in order that feebleminded and irresponsible asocial elements can have a secure existence in the asylum."

NO 'MERCY'

In August 1939, the Interior Ministry ordered doctors and midwives to report all cases of newborn babies with severe disabilities. All children under three with malformations, spastic conditions, Down's syndrome or suffering from "idiocy" were to be killed. The final consent to "mercy killing" was given by a panel of medical experts, with the approval of three members needed.

In some areas, parents, especially Catholics, refused to co-operate. They were told that their youngsters were to be sent to 'special sections' for children where they would receive better treatment. After 'assessment' of a few weeks, they were murdered by phenol injection, with their deaths being recorded as pneumonia.

After the war broke out, the age limit was raised, and approvals made more quickly.

Those designated as 'juvenile delinquents' could be killed… as well as Jewish children (purely because of their race) and 'Jewish-Aryan' half breeds.

Often parents were told in no uncertain terms that they could lose custody of all their children if they refused to comply, even though they suspected the truth of what was going on.

At first, the methods of killing ranged from drugging patients or starving them. More than 5000 children had been murdered by 1941, and the last to die was Richard Jenne on May 29, 1945 in the Kaufbeuren-Irsee state hospital in Bavaria… three weeks after US troops occupied the town.

The relatives received fake letters of condolence and told lies about how the victims died. The doctors involved worked under false names. The policy was not meant to be made public. As was the case with the more extreme US eugenicists, the Nazi hierarchy suspected that the general public might not be ready to accept it.

Brandt and Bouhler expanded the programme to adults and in July 1939 they arranged for a national register of all

Dr Karl Brandt, Hitler's personal physician, who headed the administration of Aktion T4.

Viktor Hermann Brack, the organiser of Aktion T4, who 'progressed' to gassing Jews in death camps and authorised medical experiments using X-rays to sterilise prisoners. Sentenced to death in 1947, he was executed in 1948.

Philipp Bouhler, head of the T4 programme. During the official stage of Aktion T4, 70,273 people were murdered, but the Nuremberg Trials heard evidence that German and Austrian physicians continued killing patients after October 1941, soon after Hitler publicly ordered the programme to stop, and that about 275,000 people were killed under T4. Captured and arrested on May 10, 1945 by US troops, he committed suicide nine days later.

Sonnenstein Castle housed the Sonnenstein Euthanasia Centre. DAWEI*

The price of life: this 1938 pro-sterilisation poster reads: "60,000 Reichsmarks is what this person suffering from a hereditary defect costs the people's community during his lifetime. Fellow citizen, that is your money too."

Brandt during the 'Doctors' Trial' at Nuremberg on August 20, 1947. He and six others were found guilty of crimes against humanity and they were hanged at Landsberg Prison on June 2, 1948.

"We do not stand alone". This Nazi poster from 1936 contained flags of other countries which already had enacted compulsory sterilisation legislation or were said to be thinking of doing so. The US and UK flags are there...

institutionalised people with mental illnesses or physical disabilities. In October that year, Hitler signed a 'euthanasia decree' backdated to September 1, 1939 which empowered the pair to carry out the programme of "mercy death after a discerning diagnosis". Hitler bypassed the country's health ministry, fearing that it was insufficiently pro-Nazi and might raise objections.

Following the invasion of Poland, the SS emptied the hospitals and asylums of the westernmost part of the country, in anticipation of the creation of 'Lebensraum' for good Aryan Germans, and killed around 17,000 inmates, mainly by shooting.

With a renewed emphasis placed on freeing-up medical facilities near the Polish border for wounded soldiers, it was then decided to extend the adult T4 programme into Germany.

Around 8000 Germans died in this early initiative, with many of them being transported to Poland (out of sight, out of mind as far as the general German public was

concerned) for the purpose. At the start of 1940, six hospitals had been turned over to the programme with this as their sole purpose.

Eventually, Aktion T4 extended to 296 medical facilities in Germany, Austria, Poland and Czechoslovakia. Buses run by the Community Patients Transports Service and manned by SS officers in white doctor-style coats shipped patients from their institutions to the euthanasia centres, where most were murdered within 24 hours. Many were told to go to what appeared to be a shower block, where they were gassed with carbon monoxide.

Each killing centre included a crematorium where the bodies were taken for disposal. Their families received letters explaining that owing to wartime regulations it would not be possible to visit relatives in these centres. Falsified death certificates and a random urn of ashes were eventually sent to the relatives.

One of those who worked at the

Hartheim killing centre was none other than Franz Stangl, later commandant of both the Treblinka and Sobibor death camps.

In Posen, Heinrich Himmler himself witnessed a trial gassing whereby patients were killed by carbon monoxide gas in an improved gas chamber that had been devised by Dr Albert Widmann, chief chemist of the German Criminal Police.

Often the victims were placed in a van and the exhaust fumes pipes back inside to suffocate them.

Nurses at the euthanasia centres often had to swear an oath of loyalty, pledging never to speak about what went on in the clinic, under pain of death. Former nurse Luise Erdmann said: "I was used to obeying strictly the orders of the physicians. I was brought up and instructed to do so. I was aware of the fact that a person was killed but I didn't see it as a murder but as a release."

A particularly ominous factor during the T4 campaign was the removal of thousands of brains from euthanasia victims, demonstrating the way in which Nazi-era 'medical research' was connected to the killings.

Hitler had told Bouhler that the T4 paper trail must never lead back to him. He was fully aware of what the public reaction in Germany and the newly-annexed Austria would likely to be if knowledge of the mass murder programme became widespread. Stiff opposition from the Roman Catholic church was feared, even though the Vatican had signed a 'peace accord' with Hitler when the Nazis came to power.

The Reichskonkordat, a treaty between the Holy See and the Nazi administration, that guaranteed the rights of the Catholic church in Germany, was signed on July 20, 1933 by Vatican Secretary of State Eugenio Pacelli, who later became Pope Pius XII, and German Vice Chancellor Franz von Papen. Historians have long claimed that this document, signed on behalf of the then Pope Pius XI, effectively gave legitimacy to the actions of the Third Reich and stifled Catholic criticism of its excesses.

Nonetheless, the Catholic church had succeeded in 1935 in halting the passing of a law to allow euthanasia, after sending a private memorandum against the plans.

HITLER BOWS TO PUBLIC OPINION!

Because it was largely conducted on home territory, the Nazis struggled to keep T4 a secret. Many of the bereaved families quickly saw through the ruse of the death certificates, and local residents soon became aware of the one-way traffic.

As rumours of the fate of the patients spread in 1940, many families took their relatives out of institutions and cared for them at home, or switched them to private clinics where T4 did not extend, often with assistance of the medics. In other cases, doctors revised their diagnoses so that patients were taken out of the T4 remit.

That year, even Nazi Party members wrote letters of protest about T4 to the Nazi administration.

Ashes containing human hair rained down on the town of Hadamar, where in the spring of 1941, children shouted in the streets that people were being taken away in buses to be gassed.

Discontent erupted into an open protest, mainly by large crowds of Catholic residents, including party members, at Absberg in Franconia in February 1941, and kick-started others. Such protests were unheard of in wartime Germany where dissenters might fear the worst.

As medical facilities began to fill up with Germany's war wounded, the rumour mill went into overdrive again, suggesting that maimed and disabled German soldiers might soon be sent for 'special treatment'.

Protestant churchmen protested privately against T4, but did not speak out publicly. However, when Reinhold Sautter, the Supreme Church Councillor of Württemberg's State Church, upbraided Nazi Ministerial Councillor Eugen Stähle over the euthanasia carried out in Grafeneck Castle,

he was shocked to be told: "The fifth commandment, Thou shalt not kill, is no commandment of God but a Jewish invention and cannot claim any validity any more."

In July 1941, a pastoral letter from German bishops was read out in all churches, restating that killing, apart from in self-defence, was wrong. Shortly afterwards, the Catholic Bishop of Münster in Westphalia, Clemens August Graf von Galen, not only publicly denounced the T4 in a sermon, but telegrammed his text to Hitler, pleading for his help.

He wrote: "It is a terrible, unjust and catastrophic thing when man opposes his will to the will of God."

The German press toed the line and did not report the sermon, which nonetheless was dropped on Germany army units by RAF pilots.

Galen publicly attacked the Nazis again that August, also condemning the closing of Catholic institutions and religious persecution.

Nazis asked for Galen to be arrested, but in stepped the Shakespeare of the weasel word, Propaganda Minister Joseph Goebbels, who advised Hitler that such an action could lead to a revolt in Westphalia. A unique incident in August saw Hitler jeered by crowds in the Bavarian town of Hof. Hitler was enraged, but fellow leading Nazis advised him not to seek a confrontation with the church at such a crucial moment in the war.

Rather than risk the wrath of the people by imprisoning their bishops, Hitler took what was for him the extremely unusual and never-to-be-repeated step of bowing to public opinion. On August 24, 1941, he cancelled the T4 programme (although as stated above, it continued in a smaller form far more clandestinely until 1945).

He also ordered no further provocation of the churches. That in itself was to beg another question – what would have happened if the Vatican had spoken out against the even greater evil that the Third Reich was to shortly enact?

For Hitler, Himmler and Heydrich, a stern lesson had been learned.

Aktion T4, which is said to have claimed between 275,000 and 300,000 victims, floundered because it had effectively been carried out in next to broad daylight, right in the heart of Germany.

But... what if the intended victims were secretly taken out of Germany, to the occupied territories in the east, which by then were under the iron grip of military control, and where nobody would dare to ask questions about their appalling treatment or fate, let alone protest?

Gassing people in the back of vans would no longer suffice, if only for the colossal numbers that were to be scheduled for extermination.

The key ingredient already criss-crossed Germany, Austria, Poland and all other occupied countries like a labyrinth.

The railways.

A steel-railed highway soon led from the germ of an idea concocted by a Victorian scientist in Birmingham to the physical gates of hell itself.

Commemorative plaque on the wall of bunker No. 17 in artillery wall of Fort VII in Poznań, which was used as an improvised gas chamber in the T4 programme. RADOMIL*

The Berlin villa at No. 4 Tiergartenstraße has long since been demolished. The spot marked by a plaque set in the pavement commemorates the victims of the Nazi euthanasia programme.

The Galton Arms, the village pub in Himbleton, Worcestershire, the name of which reflects the influential family of engineer Sir Douglas Strutt Galton KCB who lived in Himbleton Manor house, and who counted eugenics inventor Sir Francis Galton as a cousin. ROBIN JONES

BLIND HATRED
the ultimate conclusion

The Memorial to the Murdered Jews of Europe, laid
out on a 4.7 acre site between Potsdamer Platz and
the Brandenburg Gate in Berlin city centre, was
designed by the American architect Peter
Eisenmann. The centrepiece of the Holocaust
memorial is the Field of Stelae, covered with more
than 2500 geometrically arranged concrete pillars. It
is possible to walk through the unevenly sloping field
of pillars from all four sides. The strong columns, all
slightly different in size, evoke a disorienting, wave-
like feeling. Eisenmann said: "The enormity and
scale of the horror of the Holocaust is such that any
attempt to represent it by traditional means is
inevitably inadequate." Next door is an underground
museum below the field of pillars, which is an
exhibition on Nazi terror in Europe containing the
names of all known Jewish Holocaust victims.

In 1980, as a trainee reporter on a weekly newspaper in the Black Country, I was despatched to a press conference called by the far-right group the National Front, in advance of a potentially highly-confrontational march through ethnic areas of West Bromwich.

As I entered the room hired for the press conference, I was asked to sign in by a smartly-dressed boy who appeared to be aged about 14. "Who do you work for?" he asked. I told him. "Huh!" he immediately sneered. "Owned by Jews!"

I did not know whether to laugh or cry. The boy seemed like a somewhat quaint replication of a member of the Hitler Youth from 45 years before, whom I had read about in history books, or seen in archive films on TV, complete with exactly the right attitude, mannerism and phraseology.

Indeed I did not even know until then that my employers, light years further up the company hierarchy, were Jewish: in fact, I could not have cared less, then or now, as I was happy with the job. Even less, I could not work out what this lad could possibly have had personally against them – at that age he probably would not have even studied the Second World War in history lessons, let alone met any Jews himself.

Was he merely acknowledging that in order to be a member of a far-right party, you had to fall into line with prescribed views and act the part... doing the literally 'right' thing in their eyes?

Joking apart, the incident was a classic case of how hatred can be passed down the generations, despite the severe lessons of the past. The lad had probably never met a Jewish person in his life, or might have struggled to point out where Israel is on the globe. In turn, he might retort with party mantra by saying I am a 'victim', no, a 'tool', in a great Jewish conspiracy to take over the world and like the public at large, fail to recognise the 'evil' in every last member of this despised nation, 'Hitler was right, the Holocaust never happened', et al.

At around the same time I investigated several tiny far-right groups that appeared to be mushrooming in Britain during the bleak years of the recession that marked the very early years of the Margaret Thatcher government in the late Seventies and early Eighties, skinheads making up a fair proportion of their members. It seemed that several groups as opposed to one big one existed merely because their organisers could not agree who would be leader: every one of them wanted to be, or rather played at being, Hitler.

I always wondered why they wanted to emulate as far as possible, and make palatable to potential recruits, the Nazis, whose bizarre and illogical ideology had in its day failed at every turn. In doing so, they could only perpetuate the mistakes of the past, the biggest of which is the hate mantra against a race of great artists, musicians, writers, scientists, businessmen and in general great achievers, who had contributed far more positivity to the world than anything that came out of the Reich Chancellery over 12 demonic years.

Nevertheless, the fact that there are still people around to chant the ancient party dogma parrot fashion and convince even a few non-thinkers, despite the appalling lessons of the Holocaust, can never be a laughing matter, and in the light of the fact that the National Socialist Party was once also tiny (as the German Workers Party) – Hitler was member number 4 – it is indeed scary.

Second World War re-enactors may have considered it to be harmless fun to dress up in Nazi uniforms for special weekends at heritage railways, thinking that there is a huge natural gulf between historical costume drama and joining a far-right organisation, but both appear to have the same result – the normalising of the abnormal, the acceptance of the utterly unacceptable.

The biggest question both for me, and for historians, scholars and theologians alike, is: Why have the Jews been hated over two millennia?

The question has sometimes been phrased in the more conspiratorial style: Surely all the nations that have expelled or persecuted them in the past can't all be wrong, and they must have done something to deserve it?

Between the years 250 and 1948 there were more than 80 expulsions of Jews from European countries, including England, France, Austria, Germany, Lithuania, Spain and Portugal. Why, despite the multiple benefits that they brought to many countries in the centuries following their dispersal from the native homeland, do they appear to be hated more than any other group?

Nobody appears to have satisfactorily answered that question. Maybe this is because there is no answer. Historical analysis reveals that the hatred is irrational.

Hitler made much of the role played by major Jewish bankers in the world economy in the early 20th century, the First World War and the Wall Street Crash of 1929, blaming the nation for everyone else's plight. The reality was that these bankers accounted for a mere handful of Jews, and the vast majority were ordinary hard-working people, many of who had fought for Germany in the First World War, who had never owned a business of their own, and were struggling on or below the breadline just like everyone else. And in any case, not all the bankers and industrialists were Jews by any means.

Resentment of Jews because they were deemed to possess too much wealth and power does not explain why Jews in Poland and Russia were hated despite being among the poorest members of the community and having no influence.

Then there is the tired old rhetoric that the Jews deserved what they got because they killed Jesus. This idea of the vengeful God quickly collapses when it is pointed out that Jesus himself was Jewish, preached the Old Testament, and had a band of followers who were also Jews. As he was crucified under Roman jurisdiction, then logically we should persecute all Italians?

Among supposed reasons for resentment is that wherever Jews settled, they remain as an isolated or even elite group, refusing to mix with the local society while profiting from it. But is it not true of all immigrant communities, since time began, that they will seek their own? It is said that Southampton is the Polish capital of Britain because immigrants now account for 10% of the population. Similarly, the ITV programme Little England in 2011/2 has homed in on the ex-pat English community that has settled in the Dordogne.

From the late 18th century onwards, many Jews in Europe, including Germany, tried harder to assimilate, so if this is the reason for them being hated, it should have stopped there.

However, some eugenicists openly demanded that Jews should not be allowed to marry 'Nordics', and the Nuremberg Laws incorporated this into legislation.

Then there is the theory that Jews are hated because they are 'inferior'. This argument falls down because Jews are not a 'race'. Anyone can become a Jew if they so wish, regardless of their race, creed or colour.

The 'arrogance' of Jews claiming to be the 'chosen' people has been given as another reason. Yet how many Christian sects have argued on the doorsteps that only their followers will be saved come judgment day?

The writer Rabbi Kalman Packouz said: "Every other hated group is hated for a relatively defined reason. We Jews, however, are hated in paradoxes: Jews are hated for being a lazy and inferior race – but also for dominating the economy and taking over the world. We are hated for stubbornly maintaining our separateness and, when we do assimilate, for posing a threat to racial purity through intermarriages. We are seen as pacifists and as warmongers; as capitalist exploiters and as revolutionary communists; possessed of a chosen-people mentality, as well as of an inferiority complex. It seems that we just can't win."

The British Prime Minister David Lloyd George stated in 1923: "Of all the extreme fanaticism which plays havoc in man's nature, there is not one as irrational as anti-Semitism... If the Jews are rich (these fanatics) are victims of theft. If they are poor, they are victims of ridicule. If they take sides in a war, it is because they wish to take advantage from the spilling of non-Jewish blood. If they espouse peace, it is because they are scared by their natures or traitors. If the Jew dwells in a foreign land he is persecuted and expelled. If he wishes to return to his own land, he is prevented from doing so."

This author's over-simplistic view, for >>

The cover of an early Russian edition of The Protocols of the Elders of Zion.

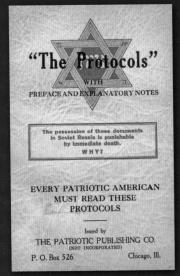

An American edition of The Protocols, published in 1934, 13 years after they have been proven beyond all doubt to be a fake.

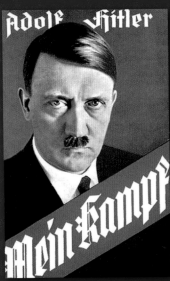

Manual of hate: Hitler's rambling diatribe containing lengthy rants against Jews was published in 1925/26 and had sold 10 million copies by the end of the war.

Clifford's Tower in York, built on the site of a royal castle where in 1190, around 150 Jews were massacred. It is a textbook case of Jewish persecution which so often over the centuries has been purely for the financial gain of the protagonists yet dressed up in a pseudo-religious, political or historical motive. DUNCAN HARRIS*

Der Stürmer was a weekly tabloid published by Julius Streicher from 1923 to 1945. It contained regular anti-Semitic rants and caricatures, and Hitler said it was his favourite paper. It was a key part of Nazi propaganda. This is a cartoon from the Christmas 1929 edition urging Germans to avoid buying from Jewish shops.

The Wannsee villa where Reinhard Heydrick took 90 minutes to order the destruction of Europe's Jews. JEAN-PIERRE DALBÉRA*

>>

what it is worth, is that Jews have been resented mainly because they are great survivors. Driven out of their homeland and dispersed across Europe, they became despised where they settled for no other reason than being 'the outsiders', just as black and Asian immigrants were treated by swathes of the indigenous British population in the Fifties, Sixties and Seventies.

Jewish people have always placed a great emphasis on education. An educated person will usually have a far greater chance of surviving – and thriving – than someone who never seeks to better his or her condition, and then becomes content to resent those that do. 'Why should he have that when I can't?' is a basic negative sentiment that dates back to the dawn of humanity. Sadly, it extends from the petty-minded to the wilfully oppressive, and forms a brilliant basis for scapegoating when times get hard, when any excuse for persecution becomes nailed to the mast.

Also, if you keep repeating a myth that someone or something is unwholesome, then in the human psyche it becomes enshrined as established fact, maybe even centuries after any original cause for complaint had vanished.

WHERE DID IT ALL START?

Historians have traced anti-Semitism back to outbursts against Jews in Alexandria in the third century, in several cases simply because they did not recognise the local gods. In the same way most Jews were not attracted to Christianity as preached by Paul to the pagans because, unlike most of the pagans of the time, they already believed in the concept of a single knowing and loving god, and so these aspects of the new religion were not new for them. On the contrary, they had problems believing that this God would send a son in human form to be crucified merely to make a theological point. But this refusal annoyed those people propagating the new faith – and it still does.

When Christianity, the new 'Jewish sect', became the state religion of the Roman Empire, the general attitude to Jews, who represented the 'old order', deteriorated.

Under Islamic rulers from the ninth century, Jews were initially allowed more freedom to practice their religion than in medieval Christendom, until Muslim pogroms (or violent mob attacks) against them began in countries such as Spain in the 11th century.

Christian persecution of Jews peaked during the Crusades, with several communities in Germany and elsewhere destroyed.

On March 16, 1190, a wave of anti-Semitic riots culminated in the massacre of an estimated 150 Jews, the entire Jewish community of York, who had taken refuge in the town royal castle where Clifford's Tower now stands. The chronicler William of Newburgh described the rioters as York acting "without any scruple of Christian conscientiousness" in wiping out the Jewish community.

At this time, anti-Semitism ran high throughout western Europe, but in this case, the rioters were egged on by powerful locals who had borrowed heavily from Jews, and saw their deaths as an easy and practical way to pay off their debts.

All Jews were expelled from England in 1290, and 100,000 were ordered to leave France in 1396.

Jews were used as scapegoats for the Black Death which decimated Europe in the mid-14th century, with communities destroyed in the wake of rumours that they had deliberately poisoned wells. In 1348, 900 Jews were burned alive in Strasbourg, before the plague had even struck.

The German reformist Martin Luther started out by expressing concern for the plight of Jews in Europe and wanted to convert them to Christianity. However, later in life, when he felt angry that they rejected this, he denounced them and urged for harsh persecution and expulsion.

He successfully campaigned against the Jews in Saxony, Brandenburg and Silesia. In August 1536, Elector of Saxony John Frederick issued a mandate banning Jews from inhabiting, engaging in business in, or passing through his realm.

Historians consider Luther's anti-Semitism contributed significantly to the rise of such attitudes in Germany. Most anti-Jewish books published in the Third Reich referred back to Luther, and Himmler spoke admiringly of his writings.

During the Khmelnytsky Uprising in the 17th century, Cossacks massacred tens of thousands of Jews in Ukraine. In 1744, Frederick II of Prussia restricted the number of Jews allowed to live in Breslau to just 10 'protected' Jewish families and encouraged a similar practice in other Prussian cities. In 1752 the Archduchess of Austria, Maria Theresa, restricted each Jewish family to one son.

WAGNERIAN ACCUSATION

In 1850 the German composer Richard Wagner published, under an assumed name, an attack on Jewish rivals, Jewishness in Music. In it, he accused Jews of being a harmful foreign element in German culture. Grimms' Fairy Tales by brothers Jacob and Wilhelm Grimm contains several anti-Semitic depictions of Jews.

However, flying in the face of those who condemned German Jews for isolationism and other reasons, the second half of the 19th century saw far greater assimilation in the country, after gaining legal equality from 1848 and marriages between Jews and Gentiles became commonplace.

A higher percentage of German Jews fought in the First World War than that of any other ethnic, religious or political group in the country. Not only did around 12,000 die for Germany, but it was a Jewish lieutenant, Hugo Gutmann, who awarded the Iron Cross, First Class, to a 29-year-old corporal, for bravery. hat man's name was Adolf Hitler.

In the post-war Weimar Republic, which

has been described by some historians as the most democratic state ever created, German Jews served in high political positions such as those of foreign minister and vice chancellor.

Indeed, the Weimar constitution itself was written by the Jew Hugo Preuss, who was afterwards made minister of the interior. German Jews also played significant roles in postwar culture such publishing, theatre, graphic art, cinema, music, law and popular entertainment, as well as other fields such as law, medicine and architecture.

Between 1900 and 1924, around 1.75 million Jews migrated to the United States, taking their percentage of the population from 1% to 3.5%. In this period of the 20th century, they experienced worsening discrimination in the US, with restrictions placed on them with regard to jobs, access to residential areas and enrolment at colleges.

Among the leading figures who espoused anti-Semitic views was none other than Henry Ford, the car manufacturer. From 1919 to 1927 he had his own newspaper, *The Dearborn Independent*, also known as The Ford International Weekly, which reached a circulation of 900,000. It became subject to lawsuits regarding the anti-Semitic material that it ran, and this led to its closure.

THE BIGGEST CONSPIRACY

In 1903, The Protocols of the Elders of Zion was published in Russia. It purported to be a copy of a Jewish masterplan to take over the world. It is set out as a document of the minutes of a late 19th century meeting of Jewish leaders discussing the way to achieve their goals by undermining the morals of Gentiles and controlling the press and the world's economies.

For anti-Semitists, it was manna from heaven. The book was a huge success and was translated into several languages and sold all over the world in the early 20th century. The aforementioned Henry Ford funded the printing of half a million copies. In 1921, he held up the book as proof of a Jewish threat: "The only statement I care to make about the Protocols is that they fit in with what is going on. They are 16 years old, and they have fitted the world situation up to this time."

There was, however, one big problem with the Protocols. The book was a fake.

In 1921, it was demonstrated in *The Times* that swathes of text in the Protocols had been lifted from a very different work, Maurice Joly's fiction Dialogue in Hell, an attack on the political ambitions of the French emperor Napoleon III is portrayed by the non-Jewish character Machiavelli and plots to rule the world.

Compare and contrast the texts: in Dialogue in Hell, a section reads: "How are loans made? By the issue of bonds entailing on the Government the obligation to pay interest proportionate to the capital it has been paid. Thus, if a loan is at 5%, the State, after 20 years, has paid out a sum equal to

the borrowed capital. When 40 years have expired it has paid double, after 60 years triple: yet it remains debtor for the entire capital sum."

In The Protocols of the Elders of Zion, this emerges as: "A loan is an issue of Government paper which entails an obligation to pay interest amounting to a percentage of the total sum of the borrowed money. If a loan is at 5%, then in 20 years the Government would have unnecessarily paid out a sum equal to that of the loan in order to cover the percentage. In 40 years it will have paid twice; and in 60 thrice that amount, but the loan will still remain as an unpaid debt."

There are many more 'comparisons' between the two works to be made. What's more, Dialogue in Hell itself 'borrowed' heavily from Les Mystères du Peuple, a mid-19th century novel by Eugene Sue.

That should have been an end to anyone taking the Protocols seriously, but why let facts get in the way of a good rant?

Accordingly, the Protocols were seized by the Nazis for their propaganda campaign against the Jews, and the book was made required reading for German students. Hitler blamed the humiliating Treaty of Versailles which ended the First World War and the soaring inflation of 1923 as efforts by international Jewry to destroy Germany, just as had been predicted in the Protocols.

In Mein Kampf he wrote: "To what extent the whole existence of this people is based on a continuous lie is shown incomparably by the Protocols of the Wise Men of Zion, so infinitely hated by the Jews. They are based on a forgery, The Frankfurter Zeitung moans and screams once every week: the best proof that they are authentic.

"The important thing is that with positively terrifying certainty they reveal the nature and activity of the Jewish people and expose their inner contexts as well as their ultimate final aims."

At first, Weimar citizens paid little heed to Hitler's meandering rants about Jews, especially as the country had recovered from many of its financial woes. His Nazi Party did badly in pre-1929 elections.

However, the Wall Street Crash and the Great Depression changed everything. Hitler perceived that more and more Germans would readily appreciate a scapegoat for soaring unemployment and another round of economic collapse, and he had the perfect one polished, ready and waiting.

THE TERROR BEGINS

In 1920, Hitler outlined to the tiny Nazi Party his Five Points of National Socialism. One ran thus: "None but members of the nation may be citizens of the State. None but those of German blood may be members of the nation. No Jew, therefore, may be a member of the nation."

In a speech in Munich in 1922, he expanded the theme of the Jews: "His is no master people; he is an exploiter: the Jews are a people of robbers.

"Foreign people, foreign workmen build

him his temples, it is foreigners who create and work for him, it is foreigners who shed their blood for him."

Mein Kampf, written while Hitler was serving a prison sentence for his role in the attempted coup in Munich known as the Beer Hall Putsch in 1923, contains numerous references to 'filthy Jews'.

Hitler also capitalised on a backlash against the 'decadence' of the Weimar Republic, criticising its replacement of core 'German' values with those of the western world, and for many, sounded the right note. It was no time to be a scapegoat.

After Hitler came to power on January 30, 1933, Jewish people became the 'Untermenschen' – the sub-humans.

Members of Hitler's private army the Sturm Abteilung (stormtroopers or brownshirts), stopped Germans from patronising Jewish shops, and within a year they were all marked with the yellow Star of David or had the word Juden written on the window. SA men stood outside the shops to deter anyone from entering. It was an amateurish bully-boy attempt to economically bankrupt traders and shopkeepers.

Special seats for Jews were allocated on trains and buses, and well as park benches. They were restricted to them – in much the same way there was still black and white segregation on parts of the US at the time.

Anti-Semitism was added to the school curriculum, while Jewish pupils were ridiculed by teachers and bullied in the playgrounds.

MARRIAGE GUIDELINES

After the Nuremberg Laws were passed in 1935, the Jews lost rights as German citizens. Again, the eugenics movement came into play in the minds of the legislators. Marriage between Jews and non-Jews was banned.

This watershed marked the start of serious violence against German Jews, and many were allowed to leave the country on payment of a fine.

The bulk of the Jewish population could not afford to leave, and increasingly found that shops would not sell them food or medicines.

It was a 'bovver boy' approach by the administration of a country once respected for its high culture, and which tacitly encouraged the yob element among its population to do its dirty work, to soften up the Jews for worse to come.

With the eyes of the world watching, the 'my fist is bigger than yours' approach towards the Jews eased off during the 1936 Berlin Olympics, but restarted once the international press had gone home.

The Zionist leadership in the British Mandate of Palestine claimed in February 1938 that according to "a very reliable private source—one which can be traced back to the highest echelons of the SS leadership" there was "an intention to carry out a genuine and dramatic pogrom in Germany on a large scale in the near future".

It seemed the Nazis were looking for an excuse for a major crackdown on Jews, and it was noted that with arms of the party short of money, Jewish property held out the prospect of rich pickings.

In August 1938 the Nazis announced the cancellation of residence permits for foreigners, including German-born Jews of foreign origin. On October 28, 1938, Hitler ordered the expulsion of more than 12,000 Polish-born Jews overnight, permitting them to take just one suitcase per person. After the Jews left their homes, Nazi officers and neighbours swooped vulture-like to seize their property.

The deportees were taken away by trucks to the nearest railway station. The streets were full of people shouting: "Juden raus! Auf nach Palästina!" ("Jews out, out to Palestine.").

They were placed on trains to the Polish border, but Poland refused to accept them and border guards sent them back into Germany.

An impasse remained for several days over the dispute, leaving the Jews without food or a roof over their heads. Eventually, 4000 were permitted to move into Poland, but the other 8000 were blocked at the border, where makeshift refugee camps sprang up. It was said that some were shot trying to get back into Germany.

At Bentschen, others were incarcerated in a forced labour camp, until they were freed shortly before the outbreak of the Second World War.

However, it had set a precedent for the use of railways to remove Jews and other undesirables from Germany.

Herschel Grynszpan, a 17-year-old German Jew who had fled to Paris, was told of his family's expulsion to Poland in a postcard sent by his sister.

In a rage he bought a revolver and a box of bullets, and asked to see an official at the German embassy.

On November 7 he was shown to the office of German diplomat Ernst Eduard vom Rath, and shot him three times in the abdomen. Vom Rath died of his wounds two days later.

It was a poor choice of revenge victim for young Herschel, for vom Rath was known to have anti-Nazi views because of their treatment of the Jews, and was being investigated by the Gestapo as a result. Yet the shooting was exactly the excuse that the Nazis had been looking for. The next day, Germany responded by banning Jewish children from German state elementary schools.

The publication of all Jewish newspapers and magazines was stopped, and all Jewish cultural activities suspended.

That day, Hitler and Goebbels gave the nod and wink for the public at large to take reprisals against all Jews into their own hands, a sort of official unofficial pogrom.

It became known around the world as Kristallnacht, or 'crystal night', because of the colossal amount of shards of glass from the smashed windows of around 7500 Jewish

shops, houses and synagogues. Early on November 10, Reinhard Heydrich issued secret guidelines to the police and SA. Police were to stand back and not interfere with rioting, except to arrest 'healthy male Jews', who would be sent to concentration camps.

SA and SS units sprang into action, dressed in civilian clothes and armed with sledgehammers and axes. Every item of Jewish property was fair game, but synagogues too close to non-Jewish property were to be smashed rather than set on fire, Jewish businesses or dwellings could be destroyed but not looted, and there should be no attacks on non-Jews.

Nearly 100 Jews were beaten to death while over 30,000 men were taken to concentration camps like Dachau, Buchenwald and Sachsenhausen, later to be freed on condition they left Germany, apart from around 2000 who perished in custody. Official figures released by Heydrich stated that 191 synagogues were destroyed, 100,000 Jews were arrested; 174 people were arrested for looting Jewish shops and 815 Jewish businesses were destroyed.

A separate pogrom took place in Vienna with most of the city's 94 Jewish religious houses destroyed or damaged.

HOLOCAUST 'BEGINNING'

Not content with the wholesale murder and destruction of Kristallnacht, for 'its' part in it, the Jewish community was fined a billion Reichsmarks. In addition, it cost four million marks to repair the windows.

Daily Telegraph correspondent Hugh Greene wrote from Berlin: "Mob law ruled in Berlin throughout the afternoon and evening and hordes of hooligans indulged in an orgy of destruction.

"I have seen several anti-Jewish outbreaks in Germany during the last five years, but never anything as nauseating as this. Racial hatred and hysteria seemed to have taken complete hold of otherwise decent people.

"I saw fashionably dressed women clapping their hands and screaming with glee, while respectable middle-class mothers held up their babies to see the 'fun'."

Goebbels stated that Kristallnacht was the result of the "healthy instincts" of the anti-Semitic German race which "has no desire to have its rights restricted or to be provoked in the future by parasites of the Jewish race".

However, Goebbels called a halt to the rioting on November 11, and immediately afterwards the Nazi hierarchy set about deciding what to do next.

In the transcript of a meeting the following day, Hermann Goering, the founder of the Gestapo and commander-in-chief of the Luftwaffe, said: "I have received a letter written on the Führer's orders requesting that the Jewish question be now, once and for all, coordinated and solved one way or another.

"I should not want to leave any doubt, gentlemen, as to the aim of today's meeting. We have not come together merely to talk again, but to make decisions, and I implore competent agencies to take all measures for the elimination of the Jew from the German economy, and to submit them to me. It is obvious that we will have to manage a final account with the Jews."

Martin Sasse, a leading member of the German Christian movements, immediately published a collection of Luther's writings with an introduction which celebrated the occasion thus: "On November 10, 1938, on Luther's birthday, the synagogues are burning in Germany."

The persecution continued, and over the next 10 months more than 115,000 Jews fled the country, leaving the Nazis to seize the property and businesses they left behind. Regrettably, many foreign countries, including the United States, Canada, Britain, and France, were unwilling to admit very large numbers of refugees.

There was, however, a loathing towards the events of Kristallnacht from a sizeable silent minority or even majority of German people, who were sickened by mob rule and street violence as espoused by the SA in previous years. The British Embassy at Berlin and British consular offices throughout the country received many expressions of disquiet from the German public about the anti-Jewish actions.

Nonetheless, Kristallnacht was the night that discrimination changed to violence and physical damage, and when Jewish property and assets became fair game for a government readying itself for war.

It is seen by many as the first day proper of the Holocaust.

GOERING'S DIKTAT

As if the Third Reich had not anything better to do after the outbreak of war on September 1, 1939, new restrictions were imposed on Jews remaining in Germany.

A strict curfew was imposed on Jews who were also banned from entering designated areas in many cities.

Food rationing was introduced, with Jews allocated, at first, reduced rations, followed by limitations on times when food could be bought by them, and then on which stores they could use. The effect, as intended, was to deprive Jewish households of the most basic essentials.

Jews were also ordered to hand over possessions considered essential to the war effort such as radios, cameras, bicycles, electrical appliances and other valuables.

In September 1941, another decree banned Jews from using public transport. Further emigration was banned.

That same month, the Government ordered Jews over the age of six to wear the yellow Jewish Star (Magen David) on their outermost garment.

New residence regulations forced Jews to live in designated areas of German cities, concentrating them in 'Judenhäuser' (Jewish houses) while those fit to work were ordered to undertake forced labour.

Tens of thousands of Jews from Germany and Austria were deported to the Lublin

The Nazis awarded Henry Ford the Grand Cross of the German Eagle on his 75th birthday, July 30, 1938. It was a diplomatic and honorary award given to prominent foreigners who were considered sympathetic to Nazism.

Car manufacturing giant Henry Ford published several anti-Semitic articles in his own newspaper.

The edition of Henry Ford's *Dearborn Independent* that started a seven-year crusade against Jews.

Ford Model Ts on an assembly line.

district of Poland at the end of 1939. The first deportations of Austrian Jews began in October that year, with around 1500 Jews taken to the Polish town of Nisko. Between February and March 1941, another 5000 were deported to Poland

Goering had asked what was to be done about the Jewish question. The German invasion of the Soviet Union under Operation Barbarossa in 1941 produced answers for him.

The occupation of large parts of the Soviet Union would bring another four million Jews under Third Reich jurisdiction.

Goering, by now the Reichsmarshall and the second most powerful Nazi, and Himmler took Hitler's comments over the total conquest of European Russia as authority to proceed with the 'Final Solution' of the Jewish problem. On July 31, 1941, Goering authorised Heydrich to draw up a blueprint.

Himmler, Heydrich's superior, wanted the Jews exterminated, and set about the task in the occupied territories, using murder squads, known as Einsatzgruppen, for massacres in which the victims were taken to forest clearings or pits and shot – again, out of sight, out of mind of the German

population who had successfully opposed Aktion T4.

On November 29, 1941, 1000 German Jews arrived at the Latvian capital Riga by train. Rudolf Lange, commander of Einsatzkommando 2, shot them almost immediately. Similar actions were taking place throughout parts of the Soviet Union that the Nazis had over-run and the Baltic states of Latvia, Lithuania and Estonia.

Mass murder on a hitherto-unknown industrial scale was now being perpetuated.

However, both Lange and his superiors saw the practical limitations of such actions. Due to the high cost of bullets, and the fact that even hardened SS troops baulked at the idea of shooting German as opposed to Soviet Jews, it would only ever be a small-scale solution in the grand Nazi scheme.

CATASTROPHIC INVASION

So Heydrich worked on a plan to send Jews eastwards, out of the gaze of German people to 'labour camps' in the occupied territories. Rather than stage mass shootings, inmates would be killed if they could not work once inside the perimeter fences, while the rest would be worked or starved to death.

Hitler's bungling over Operation Barbarossa had led to a delayed start to the campaign, while his army was busy with mopping up operations in the Balkans. The lost few weeks proved catastrophic, for when the German armies reached Russia, they were bogged down first in the rainy autumn and then by the harsh winter weather.

Held at Moscow in December 1941, it was clear that the war would not be over as quickly as Goebbels had promised his attentive audiences, and food supplies would run too low… far too low to have any to spare for the 'filthy Jews'.

The emphasis then switched from sending Jews to labour camps to work, to exterminating them outright.

If the entire Jewish population of the occupied countries – men, women and children, young and old alike – was to be shipped to the east, again away from the eyes of the German population at large, to be murdered, it would involve a massive logistical exercise, at a time when precious resources were already stretched in fighting a war on two fronts.

There was only one way it could be achieved – and that was with the full co-operation of the German state railways.

THE 'FINAL SOLUTION'

Heydrich arranged a meeting on January 20 in a villa at 56–58 Am Großen Wannsee, in western Berlin's lakeside beach resort, and which the SS had bought for use as a conference centre. Heydrich's conference would be on the Final Solution of the European Jewish question.

Among the delegates was SS Obersturmbannführer Adolf Eichmann, who became the architect of the Holocaust.

Eichmann brought with him a list of the estimated number of Jews in each country in

A burning synagogue during Krystallnacht.

Fire crews were ordered on Krystallnacht to protect only neighbouring buildings not owned by Jews.

Heydrich's wish list: the estimated populations of Jews in Europe presented at the Wannsee Conference.

How the New York Times reported Krystallnacht.

A Nazi anti-Semitic and anti-Soviet poster.

Europe, including countries which the Nazis had occupied, and others which were at war with Germany – such as Britain with its 330,000 Jews, or neutral – such as Spain, Sweden and Ireland.

Estonia was listed as 'Judenfrei' (free of Jews) as since the Nazi invasion, the 1000 or so Jews who had been there had been dealt with by the Einsatzgruppen by the end of 1941.

Eichmann's list was nothing less than a wish list, if not a schedule of death, comprising every one of the estimated 11 million Jews in Europe.

The conference lasted just 90 minutes, and was conducted using veiled terms for the intended fate of the Jews.

Heydrich made his position perfectly clear: "Under proper guidance, in the course of the final solution the Jews are to be allocated for appropriate labour in the east. Able-bodied Jews, separated according to sex, will be taken in large work columns to these areas for work on roads, in the course of which action doubtless a large portion will be eliminated by natural causes. The possible final remnant will, since it will undoubtedly consist of the most resistant portion, have to be treated accordingly, because it is the product of natural selection and would, if released, act as the seed of a new Jewish revival."

EXPEDIENT EXEMPTIONS

He added that during the "practical execution of the final solution", Europe would be "combed through from west to east".

'Evacuated' Jews would first be sent to 'transit ghettos' in the General Government (the part of Poland originally occupied by the Nazis in 1939) from which they would be transported eastward.

Jews over 65 years old, and Jewish First World War veterans who had been severely wounded or who had won the Iron Cross, would be sent to a 'model' concentration camp that had been established at Theresienstadt. Such exemptions were not made for any reasons other than expediency – to reduce the risk of public protest as happened with Aktion T4.

For the purposes of the 'Final Solution', said Heydrich, 'mixed race' Jews – who had two Jewish grandparents – would be considered to be Jews. If, however, they were married to a non-Jew, or had been given written exemption by the state, they would merely be sterilised.

Those with just one Jewish grandparent, or who looked blatantly like a Jew because of their "racially especially undesirable appearance", or simply "behaves like a Jew", would be deported even if they were married to a non-Jew.

If a marriage to a Gentile produced children being raised as Germans, the Jewish partner would not be deported. If they were being raised as Jews, they might still be deported, or "get away" with being sent to Theresienstadt.

I wonder what would have happened if DNA testing had been available to the Nazis. They might well have found that a far greater proportion of the population had Jewish ancestry than hitherto suspected, including maybe some Nazi top brass. Might Heydrich have organised another conference, one to decide on what percentage might qualify someone for deportation and 'special treatment' and whether the set percentage should be universally applied? Would he then quibble for ages about what DNA level constitutes a 'real' Jew, or would cells in their grey matter spark into life and some might just realise how pathetic the question, like anti-Semitism and indeed racism as a whole, really was?

Not a chance, for it seems that Heydrich did not really care about whether Jews or any other 'inferior' humans were his victims.

Four months after his conference, May 27, 1942, Heydrich was attacked in Prague by a British-trained team of Czech and Slovak soldiers sent by the Czechoslovak government-in-exile to kill him. Ambushed in his car at the corner of a road, he died in hospital from shrapnel wounds a week later.

The reprisals were appalling, infamously resulting in the destruction of the village of Lidice and more than 15,000 Czech citizens being either murdered or sent to concentration camps.

Was the assassination worth it? Historians have debated ever since.

Alois Denemarek, whose family were targeted by the Gestapo in the reprisals, said it definitely was.

"Even though it cost the lives of my family, my brother, my mother, my father and hundreds, thousands of other people. But as I always say – that's nothing compared to the losses we would have suffered if Heydrich had been allowed to live," he said.

That is the underlying truth of the Holocaust and its 'junior partner' Aktion T4. First it would have been the Jews. Then the Czech nation as a whole and the rest of the Slavonic peoples, who were also considered inferior by Nazi ideologists. Then trade unionists, certain types of intellectuals, artists, homosexuals, maybe eventually even Germans who were deemed to be just slightly too short, or had ginger hair or some other undesirable characteristic.

By 1942, the Nazis had given themselves a licence not only to kill Jews, but in effect anyone that their party officials chose to personally dislike.

Had they won the war, where would it have stopped?

But Wannsee also highlighted the infernal concoction for which all the ingredients had now been mixed by the Nazis. The age-old hatred of the Jews by now honed to perfection through years of semi-hypnotic and repetitive propaganda: the Aktion T4 premise that euthanasia was a positive force for the greater good of racial purity: the war against the Soviet Union for which a German public had been lulled by Goebbels into patriotic fervour, and which would provide cover of darkness for unimaginable evil… and last but not least, one of the world's most professional and sophisticated railway networks, which would make it all possible.

Hermann Goering, who told Reinhard Heydrich to draw up plans for the final solution.

Nazi Propaganda Minister Josef Goebbels, who whipped up hatred against Jews throughout the Thirties. He had a deformed right leg, the result either of club foot or osteomyelitis, and wearing a metal brace and special shoe because of his shortened leg, walked with a limp. He was rejected for military service in the First World War. If Aktion T4 had been applied through society, might he have qualified for 'special treatment'?

Adolf Eichmann, who masterminded the implementation of the Holocaust.

THE DAWN OF MASS MURDER

A Nazi lesson for all train travellers: a public hanging next to railway tracks leading to Krakow. YAD VASHEM

The mass genocide of European Jews may be deemed to have begun in the summer of 1941, nearly three months before the Wannsee Conference.

Historians have deemed that it began in Lithuania, shortly after the Germans invaded as part of Operation Barbarossa, the invasion of the Soviet Union.

Before the Holocaust, there were as many as 250,000 Jews living in Lithuania, and the Baltic state was considered to be a major seat of Jewish learning, theology and philosophy.

Operation Barbarossa began on June 22, when more than four million Axis troops invaded Soviet occupied territory to the east of Germany. It was the biggest invasion in the history of warfare, and the Eastern Front which it opened up had more forces engaged than in any other conflict the world had ever seen.

The German forces captured three million Soviet POWs, who unlike their British and US counterparts were not covered by the Geneva Convention, and

most were deliberately starved to death in German camps as part of a grand scheme to reduce the Eastern European population to create 'Lebensraum' for Germans.

As we saw in earlier chapters, the persecution of the Jews was introduced gradually in Germany, beginning with the restrictions of civil rights and the passing of the Nuremberg Laws.

As the German army rapidly advanced towards the Russian border, special killing squads followed in its wake. There were the 'Einsatzgruppen der Sicherheitspolizei und des SD', shortened to 'Einsatzgruppen', SS paramilitary death squads which conducted mass shootings. They carried out killings ranging from a handful of people to massacres of tens of thousands, and eventually were responsible for more than a million murders.

They were the first Nazi organizations to begin mass murder of Jews as an organised policy.

They were first recorded in action on the

first day of Operation Barbarossa in the border town of Gargzdai, one of the oldest Jewish settlements in Lithuania. Around 800 Jews were shot by Einsatzgruppe A in what is known as the Garsden Massacre. Added to that figure were around 100 non-Jewish Lithuanians, many of them killing for trying to save their Jewish neighbours.

As the Nazi war machine steamrolled eastwards, mass executions of Jews began within days, if not by German hands, then by sympathetic forces.

On June 25-26, around 1500 Jews were reported as killed by Lithuanian partisans. Killings by Lithuanian Nazi auxiliaries were supported by the German administration.

SS Brigadeführer Franz Walter Stahlecker arrived in Kaunas on June 25 and delivered speeches whipping up anti-Jewish fervour.

Thanks to Nazi propaganda, which as we have seen had built itself on a bedrock of anti-Semitism, Jews were, quite astonishingly, blamed for the excesses of the Soviet communist dictatorship which had

Children from the Lodz ghetto being transported to the Chelmno murder camp in September 1942. During September 1-2, the Gestapo and local police forcibly removed 2000 patients, including 400 children, from all ghetto hospitals. Two days later, Chaim Rumkowksi, the chairman of the Jewish Council of Lodz, addressed an audience of around 1500 in tears and asked them to hand over their children to the Nazis to save the lives of the rest of the ghetto population. By September 12, 15,700 inhabitants of the Lodz ghetto had been deported to Chelmno.

been driven out by the Germans. Jewish synagogues were set on fire, and around 2300 more Jews were murdered in the nights that followed, in the capital Vilnius, Kaunas and in the countryside.

Around 80,000 Jews were killed by October and about 175,000 by the end of the year.

This was before the Nazis introduced their ghetto policies for Jews, or built the murder camps. The Lithuanian Jews were marched to pits and then shot and buried.

The surviving 43,000 Jews were concentrated in ghettos in Vilnius, Kaunus, Šiauliai and Švenčionys and became slave labour to support the German military machine.

Thanks to mass co-operation between the Lithuanians, who had welcomed the Nazi invaders as freeing them from the Soviet rule which had been forced on them through annexation a year before, and the Germans, the genocide rate of Jews in the country, which estimates placed at 95–97%, became one of the highest in Europe. The most notorious Lithuanian unit was the Lithuanian

Sonderkommando Squad from Vilnius which was responsible for the deaths of up to 100,000 Jews, Polish intelligentsia and Russians in the Ponary massacre, which lasted from July 1941 until August 1944. The executions took place next to Ponary (Panerai) railway station; from 70,000 Jews living in Vilnius, only 7000 survived the war, and their culture was destroyed.

Out of approximately 208,000-210,000 Jews in the whole of Lithuania before 1939, an estimated 195,000–196,000 were murdered before the end of the war.

THE TERROR OF LVOV

Holocaust actions began in the Galician city of Lvov in the same week as the Lithuanian genocide.

The German army overran the city, which was then in Poland and is now in Ukraine, on June 30, 1941, and it was discovered that around 1500 inmates (including Jews as well as Poles and Ukrainians) in the city's three prisons had been murdered, and the blame was laid at the door of the retreating Soviets.

The city's Jews were told to take the decomposing bodies from cells and cellars into the prison yards. Nazi propaganda blamed the killings on Jewish commissars (even though Jews had died too) and encouraged local Ukrainians, organised as a militia, to take their revenge.

At least 4000 Jewish men were killed in subsequent anti-Jewish riots known as the Prison Massacre, while the Germans committed further atrocities of their own, including the murder of Polish university professors.

Up to this stage, the victims were still just Jewish men, not women, who were simply beaten. However, as the riots continued, Ukrainian civilians and auxiliary militias began to murder women and children.

These acts, some maintain, marked the physical start of the Final Solution. Furthermore, around 3000 people, again mostly Jews, were murdered by the German military in the municipal stadium.

The Ukrainians had welcomed the Nazi invaders into their city, greeting them with

German Einsatzkomanndo murder a group of Poles in October 1939.

All in a day's work: SS men stand beside corpses of murdered Jews in Chelmno, with the track of the railway that brought them there in the background.

Prisoners from Buchenwald awaiting execution in the forest near the camp. On April 26, 1942, a Polish forced labourer, who worked at Bauern Schmidt's courtyard, was beaten to the point of unconsciousness by a German policeman, Albin Gottwald. Two Poles took revenge on Gottwald and stabbed him to death on a forest path between Poppenhausen and Einoed before escaping. One of them, Jan Sowka, was apprehended shortly after his escape. On May 11, 1942, 19 prisoners from Buchenwald were taken to the place in the woods where Gottwald's body had been found. The Buchenwald SS built three gallows, The prisoners and Jan Sowka were hanged one after another and hundreds of Polish forced labourers were made to watch.

banners and floral arrangements, with the young women attired in traditional Ukrainian folk outfits. Such scenes were typical throughout much of 'liberated' Soviet territory, as the locals saw the Germans as their saviours from the tyranny of Stalin's communism.

Thanks to the ideology of Hitler and the Nazis, they were no such thing. Had Hitler capitalised on the genuine anti-Soviet feeling and befriended those in the Slavonic lands he conquered, rather than persecute them as inferior races when the chance arose, might the outcome of his eastern campaign been different?

Some witnesses, including the few surviving Jews, said it was the Nazis, not the Soviets, who had perpetuated the prison massacre, and used it to whip up the Ukrainians' ancestral hatred for the Jews.

On November 8, 1941, the Germans established a Jewish ghetto which they called 'Jüdisches Wohnbezirk' in the impoverished northern part of the city. The entire Jewish population was ordered to move into it by December 15, 1941, and all Poles and Ukrainians were to move out.

German police also began a series of "selections" in an operation called Action under the Bridge. In this, around 5000 sick and elderly Jews were shot as they crossed under the rail bridge on Pełtewna Street while they were on their way into the ghetto. The Jews called it 'bridge of death'.

The Germans established a Jewish police force of between 500-700 officers called the 'Jüdischer Ordnungsdienst Lemberg', wearing dark blue Polish police uniforms with the star of David. They were armed with rubber truncheons.

The Jewish 'police' were coerced to act as such, and reported to the Jewish National city council known as the Judenrat, which in turn answered to the Gestapo.

The Lemberg ghetto was one of the first to have Jews transported to the death camps as part of Operation Reinhard. Between March 16 and April 1, 1942, 15,000 Jews were taken to Kleparów railway station and deported to the newly-created Belzec extermination camp.

OPERATION REINHARD

Heydrich's Wannsee Conference took place against a background of a rapidly rising death toll of Jews shot during massacres in the east.

Among the worst occurred at Babi Yar, the name of a ravine in the Ukrainian capital Kiev, on September 29-30, 1941, wherein 33,771 Jews were killed in a single operation.

German forces had entered Kiev on September 19. A decision to kill the city's Jews was made a week later by the military governor, Major-General Kurt Eberhard, the police commander for Army Group South, SS-Obergruppenführer Friedrich Jeckeln, and the Einsatzgruppe C Commander Otto Rasch, ostensibly in revenge for guerrilla attacks against the German forces.

The Babi Yar massacre turned out to be the biggest single mass murder for which the Germans and their allies were responsible

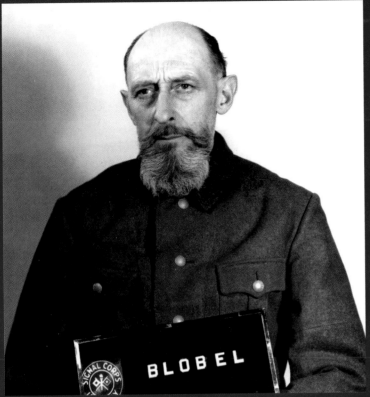

BLOBEL

Paul Blobel, an SS colonel who had won an Iron Cross during the First World War, was mainly responsible for the Babi Yar massacre at Kiev. During Operation Barbarossa, he commanded Sonderkommando 4a of Einsatzgruppe C in Ukraine, where he was responsible for liquidating political and racial undesirables. In June 1942 he took charge of Aktion 1005, with the task of destroying the evidence of all Nazi atrocities in Eastern Europe. Mass graves had to be exhumed, before the bodies were burned. Blobel came up with the idea of lying alternating layers of bodies with firewood on a frame of iron rails. A witness once overheard Blobel laughing as he was driven past the ravine of Babi Yar in Kiev in summer 1942. The witness saw strange movements of the earth, with clumps of earth rising into the air as if by themselves, with smoke billowing forth. Blobel said: "Here lie my 30,000 Jews." He was hanged at Landsberg Prison shortly after midnight on June 8, 1951.

Austrian Nazi Odilo Lotario Globocnik was the lead administrator of Operation Reinhard. On November 9, 1939, Himmler appointed him as SS and Police Leader in the Lublin district of occupied Poland. He was responsible for the destruction of the Warsaw and Bialystok ghettos. Some believe that it was Globocnik who came up with the idea of industrialised murder in purpose-built camps and at a two-hour meeting with Himmler on October 13, 1941, he was given permission to begin work on Belzec extermination camp. The month before, he had met Phillip Bouhler and Victor Brack, who were responsible for the T4 euthanasia programme, which had been using gas chambers disguised as shower rooms to execute many of its victims. Globocnik committed suicide after being captured after the end of the war.

during its campaign on the eastern front. It is also said to be the biggest single killing of the Holocaust.

The Germans placed wall posters around the city ordering all Jews to appear at 8am on Monday, September 29, at the corner of Mel'nikova and Doktorivska streets, together with their documents, warm clothing and linen, in readiness for resettlement. Anybody who failed to comply would be shot.

The Germans could not believe the response to the posters. They had expected no more than 6000 Jews to turn up, but more than 30,000 appeared, all eager to be resettled, having at that stage scant reason to disbelieve the Nazi lie. They were taken by truck to the ravine, where they were all told to undress, and beaten if they refused.

By the time they heard the machine gun fire and realised what was going on, there was no chance to escape.

The Jews were herded into groups of 10 and driven down a corridor of soldiers. When they reached the bottom of the ravine, the victims were seized by members of the Schutzpolizei and made to lie down on top of Jews who had earlier been shot.

A police marksman walked over the corpses and shot each Jew in the neck with a sub-machine-gun.

The Germans buried their victims under thick layers of earth, while their money, valuables and clothing was given to local ethnic Germans and to the Nazi occupying administration.

Other massacres took place at the same site afterwards. The victims would be Ukrainian nationalists, Soviet POWs, Roma and civilian hostages. It is estimated that up to 150,000 further murders were committed at Babi Yar.

Operation Reinhard or Aktion Reinhard was the code name for the Nazi plan to murder Polish Jews in the General Government, the name for occupied Poland.

The big difference between Operation Reinhard and the atrocities going on elsewhere was that it would be far more planned and systematic.

Jews and other undesirables would not be frogmarched to the edge of pits and packed in like sardines after being shot.

Under Operation Reinhard, they would be taken to concentration camps which were equipped with specialist killing facilities. And the railways would prove to be the lynchpin of the Final Solution.

The first Nazi concentration camps were set up in 1933 as straightforward prisons, forced labour camps and for the re-

education of offenders. Their inmates might include socialists, communists, anarchists, homosexuals and Roma or gypsy people, later to be joined by religious groups like bible students and Jehovah's Witnesses who refused to swear a loyalty oath to Hitler or take part in military service.

They were not designed for genocide, but nonetheless, by the outbreak of war in 1939, brutality in them had become worse than institutionalised. Inmates were dying en masse from disease and starvation. Dachau, Buchenwald, Sachsenhausen, Bergen-Belsen and Mauthausen-Gusen: their names were to become etched in history by the suffering of those incarcerated inside.

After Heydrich produced his blueprint for the Final Solution, a new type of camp was designed and built.

Located within the General Government, and again out of sight and out of mind of the German population, some of whom had dared to resist Aktion T4 and succeed against Hitler, these were places built for one purpose only: death on an unimaginable scale.

Bełżec, Sobibor and Treblinka: all of them reached by rail and equipped with their own stations, their purpose was to murder hundreds of thousands of innocent people, and destroy the evidence.

There were also, of course, Auschwitz-Birkenau or Majdanek, which served a double function. Those inmates deemed fit enough to work would become slave labourers until they succumbed to disease, brutality or starvation.

The rest would be murdered in gas chambers, often within an hour or two of getting off the 'resettlement' train to the east.

The murder camp programme was a direct legacy of the discredited Aktion 4. The SS officers responsible for Aktion T4, including Christian Wirth, (a supervisor of all six T4 euthanasia institutions in Germany), Franz Stangl, and Irmfried Eberl, were given the job of setting up the extermination camps.

THE FIRST MURDER CAMP

It was on October 13, 1941, that Himmler verbally ordered SS and Police Leader Odilo Globocnik, who was based in Lublin, to begin building the first Operation Reinhard camp at Belzec.

It was operational from March 17, 1942, just weeks after the Wannsee Conference of January 20, when Heydrich's Operation Reinhard extermination blueprint, which was already being enacted, was unveiled.

The site lay about a kilometre south of the nearest railway station at Belzec, which lies in the Lublin district, 47 miles north of Lvov – how convenient.

A forced labour camp had been set up there in April 1940 for the purpose of building defensive works like anti-tank ditches along what had been, prior to Operation Barbarossa, the border between German and Soviet-occupied Poland.

Its excellent road and rail links made it a perfect choice as the model for further Nazi death camps.

Building work began in early November 1941, using Polish villagers, inmates from the smaller Trawniki concentration camp south of Lublin and eventually Jewish slave labourers.

Wirth, along with SS-Hauptsturmführer Gottlieb Hering, were the two commanders of Belzec. Hering, with an impeccable Aktion T4 record, had been in charge of the Sonnenstein and Hadamar euthanasia centres, while Wirth had been there when the first test gassing of handicapped people took place at Brandenburg.

Around the same time as Belzec was being built, another murder camp, Chelmno or Kulmhof, began operating, from

December 8, 1941, as part of Operation Reinhard. Its victims were to include Polish Jews from the Lodz ghetto, Hungarian Jews, Poles, gypsies, Czechs and Soviet POWs.

By this time there had been complaints about the effect of shooting large numbers of unarmed civilians on the soldiers delegated to carry out the task. In short, their commanders recognised that it was bad for morale. A different form of mass killing had to be devised – one which was far more 'humane'… not for the benefit of the victims, but for those carrying out mass murder.

It was said Chelmno was so successful only two or three people lived to tell the tale. Around 152,000 people died there, with most murdered in gas vans, whereby the carbon monoxide from the exhaust pipe was fed back into the vehicle, often as it was moving.

Chelmno's first victims were the Jewish population of the Polish town of Kolo.

Brought in by rail, they were locked overnight in a watermill and left without food or water. The next day they were taken in trucks to the nearby forest and gassed en route. Their bodies were dumped in deep pits, before the trucks went back to the mill for more victims.

Himmler visiting Mauthausen concentration camp, which was opened on August 8, 1938, a few months after the Anschluss of Austria and Germany, which itself marked the beginning of Hitler's drive through Europe and the brutality and carnage on an industrial scale that followed. Himmler himself chose the site for the camp, because it lay near stone quarries which could provide hard labour for those sent there. While it was not designated a murder camp as such, levels of brutality there were rarely exceeded. For example, the quarry contained the 'stairs of death' up which prisoners were forced to carry roughly-hewn blocks of stone one behind the other: those that were exhausted and fell down created a domino effect crushing the others behind. Also, prisoners who made it to the top were lined up and given the choice of either pushing the one next to him off the cliff edge or being shot. Mauthausen became one of the largest slave labour camp complexes in Axis-controlled Europe and had more than 50 sub camps. It has been estimated that as many as 320,000 people died in them, the average life expectancy being six months.

In late January, 1942, the secretary of the local council, Stanisław Kaszyński, and his wife were arrested and executed three days later for trying to raise public awareness as to what was going on. The mistakes of Aktion T4 would not be repeated.

It may have been Wirth who proposed building fixed gas chambers at Belzec, because he saw that the use of gas vans at Chelmno could not handle the huge numbers of people scheduled for murder under Operation Reinhard.

He decided to run the exhaust from a car engine through pipes into the stationary gas chamber.

GAS SUSPICIONS

Wirth rejected the use of the cyanide-based pesticide Zyklon-B, which was used for the first time in an experimental gassing at Auschwitz on September 3, 1941. Deputy camp commandant SS-Hauptsturmführer Fritzsch oversaw the murder of 600 Russian POWs and 250 Polish prisoners using the gas, and the Nazis were so pleased that they went ahead and built a gas chamber and crematorium by converting a bunker.

However, Wirth was concerned that such large quantities of Zyklon-B, which was produced by private firms, would be needed at Belzec that suspicions would be aroused. Using ordinary petrol to produce carbon monoxide would sidestep that problem.

However, Belzec also had a small gas van, a converted Opel-Blitz post office vehicle, which was used for Jews and gypsies right up until the end of the camp.

The wooden gas chambers were disguised as the barracks and showers of a labour camp, to fool the intended victims.

When they were offloaded from the trains, passengers were forced to run straight to the 'barracks' so they would not have sufficient time to plan a revolt.

A small number of Jews were chosen to carry out manual labour in and around the gas chamber, such as removing and disposing of the bodies, and sorting out the victims' clothing and possessions. They were known here and elsewhere as 'special commandos' or Sonderkommandos.

So many bodies were buried in pits at Belzec beneath a thin layer of soil that when they putrefied, the resulting gases escaped and the earth layer split open. Learning from this experience, crematoria were built in subsequent murder camps.

Soon it became clear that the three gas chambers originally built at Belzec could not cope with the huge number of victims ferried in from Kraków and Lvov. A new concrete block with six gas chambers was built, capable of killing 1000 people at a time. They were copied by the other two Operation Reinhard murder camps at Treblinka and Sobibor.

The last transport of Jews to Belzec arrived in December 1942, virtually all the population of Jews in the surrounding area having by then been extermination.

The last train departed at the end of June 1943. It carried 300 Jews to Sobibor for gassing.

NO DISGUISE

After that, the camp closed. The buried bodies were dug up and cremated so as to leave no trace, while the camp was taken down and fir trees planted to hide what had been there. A building used as an SS HQ, which had belonged to the Polish state railway before the war, remained in situ.

After the German and Ukrainian guards left, local villagers began clandestine visits to the site to dig for gold and valuables left by the Jewish victims. In doing so they dug up human remains... to the great embarrassment of the Nazis, who then relandscaped the site as a farm. A Ukrainian guard and his family were told to live there permanently, to make it seem genuine.

Similar attempts to disguise redundant murder camps were also employed at Treblinka and Sobibor.

But humanity could not and would not ever forget or forgive.

Christian Wirth was a pivotal figure in both the Aktion T4 euthanasia programme and Operation Reinhard. He was appointed as commandant of Belzer murder camp and then Chelmno, and later became inspector of all Operation Reinhard camps. SS Corporal Franz Suchomel, who served in Sobibor and Treblinka, later testified: "I remember that Wirth in brutality, meanness, and ruthlessness could not be surpassed. We therefore called him 'Christian the Terrible' or 'The Wild Christian'." He was killed by Yugoslav partisans on May 26 1944, after having authorised the building of a crematorium at Risiera di San Sabba concentration camp.

Prisoners in the distinctive striped uniforms at Dachau attend the roll call.

One of the gas vans for Chelmno being inspected.

The Babi Yar ravine in Kiev. MARK V

FOURTH CLASS passengers

Nur für deutsche Fahrgäste

Nur für Deutsche on tram No. 8 in occupied Kraków. The slogan Nur für Deutsche ('only for German' signified that certain establishments and transportation were reserved only for Germans. Signs bearing the slogan were posted at entrances to parks, cafes, cinemas, theatres and other facilities. In streetcars and trains, the first car was usually reserved for German administrative and military personnel, Nazi party members and German civilians. Some other nationalities, regarded by the Nazis as subhumans, were allowed to use the remaining cars. Resistance fighters often painted the words 'nur für Deutsche' on graveyard fences or street lamps, signifying a gallows.

From the moment Hitler became Chancellor, the Jews were treated as second class citizens.

Between 1933 and 1943, no fewer than 629 decrees were passed which brought about everything from segregation to outright persecution.

The watershed was, of course, the Nuremberg Laws of 1935. The following year, Jews were prohibited from taking professional jobs, not only removing their influence in education, politics, higher education, and industry, but also taking away much of their ability to stop the rising tide of anti-Jewish measures sweeping the country.

In April 1933, Jews were banned from working in the public sector and those who already were could be sacked. They were also prohibited from the media, the theatre and the film industry. They could not advertise their businesses except in newspapers specifically for Jews. All female Jewish students were expelled from German universities and colleges, along with almost all of their male counterparts.

In 1935, the regime established two classes of citizenship: Germans and German Jews, who had no protection abroad.

The following year, Jews were deprived of the right to vote.

From 1938, German Jews' passports were stamped with a huge red letter J. That year, they were banned from going to theatres and cinemas.

Jews had to pay income tax at the top rate regardless of actual income and Jewish children were barred from attending the same schools as Aryan children.

From March 1, 1938, Government contracts could not be awarded to Jewish businesses. On September 30 that year, Aryan doctors could treat only Aryan patients. Jews had already been banned from being doctors, so how was a Jew able to get medical treatment?

On November 8, 1935, the Deutsche Reichsbahn had issued a directive banning its staff from shopping in Jewish-owned stores. This ban was extended on August 31, 1938, to include any business dealings with Jews and with companies whose policies were influenced by Jewish investors.

In early 1939, Jews were ordered to stay out of central Berlin and some other cities, and a few months later, to move to designated Jewish apartment blocks, which had a large J and the Star of David above each entrance. They could not use public parks or even beaches, and were also banned from keeping pets.

One of the principal reasons for making life increasing difficult for the Jews was the hope that they would leave Germany of their own accord. Of course, the image of wealthy bankers that the Nazis loved to paint about Jews accounted for less than a tiny percentage of the Jewish population, the majority being ordinary people who had to earn a living like everyone else.

From January 1939, Jews were banned from owning their own businesses, a decree which lined the pockets of many a Nazi party member who was able to snap them up for next to nothing.

Continuing on from Krystallnacht, if Jews were attacked, the police did nothing to protect them.

All of these measures were reported around the world, and there was soon little illusion about what was like for a Jew in Hitler's Germany.

Eventually, they were banned from using public transport altogether.

GOEBBELS' 'BRILLIANT IDEA'

Nazi propaganda minister Joseph Goebbels one day had a brainwave.

He looked at the situation in the Deep South of the USA, where white and blacks were segregated on trains, and asked – why don't we do that with the Jews in Germany?

The segregation of races in the United States up to fairly recent times is today considered as nothing less than abominable. Yet it was standard practice in many walks of life, and as with the eugenics practices described earlier, and early 20th century anti-Semitism, hardly set an example for the rest of the world to follow.

In 1890, Louisiana passed the Separate Car Act, a law stipulating that railroads provided separate accommodation for blacks and whites, including different carriages.

Homer Plessy, a man who was seven-eighths Caucasian and one-eighth African by descent, was persuaded by a group of angry New Orleans residents to join their fight against the law. He disobeyed the law by sitting in a whites-only coach, having been classified as coloured.

On June 7, 1892, Plessy bought a first class ticket in New Orleans and boarded a whites-only car on an East Louisiana Railroad train bound for Covington.

The railroad had also opposed the law as it would require it to buy more carriages.

Plessy was asked to move to a coloureds-only carriage but refused, and was arrested by a private detective who had been assigned to follow him, knowing of his intentions beforehand.

In the subsequent court case Homer Adolph Plessy v The State of Louisiana, Plessy argued that the state law which demanded that the East Louisiana Railroad segregated trains had denied him his rights under the 13th and 14th Amendments of the United States Constitution, which prohibit slavery and guarantee the same rights to all citizens of the United States, respectively. However, Judge John Howard Ferguson ruled that Louisiana had the right to regulate railroad companies as long as they operated within state boundaries. Plessy was fined $25, and lost further appeals to the Supreme Court of Louisiana.

Losing the case laid the basis for more segregation laws. Out of it emerged the concept of separate but equal, on the basis that segregation was legal as long as the provided facilities were of equal quality. In reality, however, whites received far superior facilities in many areas of society than blacks.

Indeed, the 'separate but equal' principle became a feature of US society until it was overturned during the landmark Supreme Court decision of Brown v Board of Education of Topeka, Kansas, in 1954. But in the meantime, Nazi Germany had been watching.

Goebbels decided to implement the US model of segregated railway carriages in Germany.

Four weeks after Krystallnacht, it was ordained that in some areas at least, separate carriages must be provided for Jews and Aryans. "It is considered that the time has now come when Jewish travellers should be segregated from Aryans," one US newspaper reported.

However, not only did Goebbels not have his brain in gear, but had not done his sums.

Jews in Germany at the time amounted of only around 0.4% of the population, whereas in the US, blacks made up a far bigger percentage.

There then followed the spectacle of the despised lone Jew having a carriage all to himself and unintentionally being made to feel like a king by the railway authorities, while the poor suffering Aryans were packed in the other coaches, unable to sit down through lack of space, but prohibited from sharing the coach with the Jew purely through Nazi ideology.

In March 1939, a ban on Jews using sleeping and dining cars was implemented, without any public announcement being made. Despite Krystallnacht, the Nazis were still mindful of international public opinion.

However, once the Second World War had broken out, caution in areas like this went out of the window.

On September 18, 1941, at the same time as all Jews were ordered to wear the Star of David, they also had to seek police consent to travel outside of their home cities and towns by rail, but could still use trains in their localities.

In peak periods, Jews had to let others get on trains first. They were allowed just third-class travel, and then only after all Aryan passengers had found seats first.

From April 11, 1942, the Interior Ministry insisted that Jews needed police permission to use any train. Two months later, they were banned from station waiting rooms.

It may seem facetious to mention this in view of what was happening to Jews elsewhere on Deutsche Reichsbahn at the time, but from February 20, 1943, discounted fares were no longer made available to them.

With these measures regarding everyday train travel, the railways helped intensify the humiliation of, and discrimination against, Jews that they were by then suffering from every other corner of German society too. If only it had stayed at just humiliation.

All of these measures humiliated and inconvenienced Germany's Jews, but most were not physically harmed by them.

German troops on leave at HBD Nord in 1942. DR ALFRED GOTTWALDT COLLECTION

GERMAN RAILWAYS AND THE NAZIS

Before Hitler came to power, the Nazi party did its best to enlist support from railway workers. At the same time, its propaganda rants claimed that the state railway was controlled by the US and Jewish stockbrokers.

In 1925, in the Garbolzum in Saxony, the first regional Nazi party cell was established by a railway official. By 1930, it had branches in more than 200 railway offices and depots.

The general director of Deutsche Reichsbahn-Gesellschaft, the national railway company, banned political campaigning by members of any party during working hours.

In many ways, this apolitical stance had a downside when the Weimar government tried to stop the railway hiring special trains to take Nazis to their rallies, giving a 40% discount into the bargain, in a bid to stop them using cheaper road transport. The railway told the Government that it could not refuse, as it had responsibilities as a common carrier.

After Hitler came to power, Nazi political wings appeared all over the Reichsbahn.

They included the Fachschaft Reichsbahn, within the national union for German railway officials, and a workers' version, the Fachgruppe Reichsbahn, in the German Labour Front.

On March 20, 1933, the Fachschaft Reichsbahn reported the railway's senior management to the Chancellor's office for refusing to replace all Jews and Communists from key positions on the railway and replace them with Nazi sympathisers.

When this missive met with no response, the Stormabteilung (SA) brownshirts raided the railway headquarters building and demanded the sacking of the entire board of directors along with all Jews and Freemasons, and the cancellation of all Jewish contracts.

While the Government did nothing, the argument was settled within Deutsche Reichsbahn itself, in liaison with the Nazi party.

Hitler paved the way for concrete action to be taken in this respect with the passing of the law for the Reconstruction of the Professional Civil Service in April 1933.

In the wake of its passing, the railway complied with the earlier Nazi demands about no longer doing business with Jews or employing them.

From June 14, 1933, all leftists would be sacked, and the only Jews allowed to stay on would be those who had joined before the First World War or had served at the front in that conflict. It was Nazi party representatives who took responsibility for the sackings.

Around the same time, there had been street protests whipped up by Nazis against the leadership of the national railway, and its director general Julius Dorpmüller.

The son of a railway engineer, Dorpmüller studied railway and road construction before joining the Prussian state railway administration.

In 1908 he was appointed chief engineer for the German section of the new Chinese Imperial state Tianjin-Pukou railway, but became a refugee when China declared war on Germany.

In 1919 he became departmental head

with Deutsche Reichseisenbahnen German Reich Railways, and after a series of promotions, became the general manager of the nation's railways on June 3, 1926, the day his predecessor Rudolf Oeser died.

At one stage, when a mass protest was taking place against the Reichsbahn board, Hitler stopped his train and telephoned the leaders of the demonstration to say that he had every confidence in Dorpmüller and the rally should be called off.

In September 1934, a compromise which Dorpmüller had proposed with the Nazis was agreed, following months of 'Aryanisation' of the railway. Under the agreement, the Reichsbahn would be left to run its own affairs, but would put into effect the Nazi party's ideological demands while also obeying the regime's military and economic policies. This deal held good until the fall of Hitler.

On February 2 1937, Dorpmüller was appointed as the Reich Transport Minister.

The Deutsche Reichsbahn was a key player throughout German's role in the Second World War.

It supplied the military on both fronts, and once territories had been occupied, it reorganised their own railway networks to suit German needs.

At the same time, it continued to serve the homeland with the needs of everyday passenger and freight transport needs despite the war.

Deutsche Reichsbahn also played the pivotal role in implementing Nazi Germany's racial policies, transporting millions of Jews, gypsies and other 'inferior' people to their deaths in concentration and murder camps.

NAZI IDEOLOGY AND RAILWAY STAFFING

The Ostbahn, or Prussian Eastern Railway, was based around a 460 mile main line linking Berlin with Danzig (Gdansk) and Königsberg (Kaliningrad), and reached the border of the old Russian empire at Eydtkuhnen (Chernyshevskoye).

With the partition of Poland following the signing of the Treaty of Non-Aggression between Germany and the Soviet Union, on August 23, 1939, which led to the outbreak of war a little over a week later, and then the launch of Operation Barbarossa against the Soviets, the role of the Ostbahn became vital.

However, the big difficulty which faced the Nazis was who should run the railways of occupied Poland, at all levels?

The obvious answer is railwaymen, but then the question follows – what race should they be?

Occupied Poland's Governor General Hans Frank reached agreement with the Reichsbahn that German staff needed to be used solely in supervisory and policy-making positions, with locals providing the bulk of the workforce.

Here, the locals were Polish, who were considered racially inferior, and who were to record the second-highest number of holocaust victims after the Jews, who despite their large numbers in the occupied territories, could certainly not be considered for railway work.

Telling the Poles that they were subhuman would not exactly dangle the right carrot for them to work the railways efficiently and effectively.

After the partition of Poland, Deutsche Reichsbahn despatched around 9000 staff to the occupied territory to help run its railways in proper German fashion. That meant that there was one German working on the railways for every four Poles.

Accordingly, Poles were relegated to performing manual tasks and roles where they could not harm the smooth flow of operations.

With a few months, it became clear that not only had the deployment of so many DB staff left the home railways inadequately manned, but there were still labour shortages on the Ostbahn Polish lines, so the indigenous population would have to be used more effectively after all.

Under Nazi ideology, a Pole could not be placed in a position whereby he would be giving orders to a German.

The compromise was that from January 1940, Poles were again allowed to work on the footplates, and hold responsible posts in signalboxes and engine sheds. But at all times, they must be overseen by a German. Bigger facilities would be supervised by three Germans, smaller ones by two, but one German must be on duty at all times.

By May that year, the shortage of manpower became so severe that Polish locomotive crews were allowed to handle Wehrmacht trains, after swearing an oath to Hitler. Not only that, but there were paid the same as German drivers and firemen.

However, the worst was not yet passed. Rationing in the General Government meant that Germans were given priority with food, leaving Polish railway workers malnourished. Eventually, trains were reduced in length because, it was said, firemen did not have enough strength to continually shovel large amounts of coal into ever-hungry fireboxes.

The occupation of western Poland changed the Nazi perspective of the Jewish problem.

For six years since the Nazis came to power, they had done their best to step up persecution of German Jews in every way they had though they could get away with.

Before the war, there were around 330,000 Jews under German jurisdiction. Yet the acquisition of half of Poland brought another two million into the fold.

On September 21, 1939, Himmler ordered Heydrich, his fellow passenger on that record-breaking train in 1936, to gather Polish Jews and concentrate them in ghettos.

The ghetto policy involved packing as many as possible into the worst residential areas of a city, forcing them to live in cramped conditions with little prospect of work and meager food rations, as a precursor to a far worse fate.

The railways began to play their part in what has been described as the greatest crime of all in human history.

Between October 1939 and January 1940, around 80 trains carried more than 90,000 Jews and some Poles from Posen and the Wartheland. While others brought them to ghettos in places like Warsaw, Lublin and Lodz.

On November 9, 1939, passenger train officers of the railways in the east were told to make sure that the railway carried out its duty to relocate these people.

Heydrich, however, was not happy with the efficiency and effectiveness of these early deportation trains, and on December 21, 1939, he appointed Adolf Eichmann to take control of the transportations, to ensure that they were tailored to meet the aims of Nazi racist ideology.

EICHMANN JOINS THE PARTY

Born in Solingen, Germany, on March 19, 1906, Eichmann left high school without having graduated and later became a sales clerk. He joined the Jungfrontkämpfervereinigung, the youth section of Austrian officer Hermann Hiltl's right-wing militia.

On the advice of family friend Ernst Kaltenbrunner, who succeeded Heydrich after the latter's assassination and would be executed for crimes against humanity after the war, Eichmann joined the Austrian branch of the Nazi party and also the SS.

In 1933 when the Nazis came to power, Eichmann was accepted into active duty SS regiments, and promoted to squad leader. He was posted to the administrative section of Dachau concentration camp.

In November 1934, accepted an offer to join Leopold von Mildenstein's 'Jews Section', or Section II/112, of the SD or Sicherheitsdienst, the intelligence and security body of the Nazi party. He later viewed this move as his 'big break'. There, he became a head squad leader and was promoted to second lieutenant in 1937.

On the surface, Mildenstein appeared sympathetic to Jews. He had taken an early interest in Zionism and had attended Zionist conferences to increase his understanding of the movement. He took up the Zionist baton and promoted it as a way out of the Jewish problem in Germany.

The country could achieve the Nazi desire to become free of Jews simply by getting them all to emigrate to Palestine – a win-win situation. His SS superiors liked the idea, and so he was placed in charge of the Jewish Desk at the SD.

A woman about to be murdered by the SS in Belzec extermination camp, the first of its kind in occupied Poland. SS Colonel General Christian Wirth, a former police officer who had played a leading role in the T4 euthanasia programme, was the first camp commander.

Albert Ganzenmüller, the under-secretary of state at the Reich Transport Ministry, who knew full well about the nature of the deportation trains and did not care. He was never brought to justice.

Reich Transport Minister Julius Dorpmüller.

A monument at Belzec murder camp made from track panels. LYSY*

Indeed, some SS officials even encouraged Zionism, as it flew in the face of those who wanted to assimilate Jews with local populations.

Mildenstein was removed from his post in 1936 following an argument with Heydrich, because emigration to the British Mandate of Palestine was not going fast enough.

The following year, Eichmann was despatched to Palestine to see what could be done to speed up the process, but he was refused entry by the British authorities.

By then promoted to first lieutenant, at the end of 1938 Eichmann was chosen to set up the Central Office for Jewish Emigration, and became an advisor on all Jewish matters to the Third Reich.

That included administration of the concentration camps, stealing Jewish property, and the running of transports to take Jews en masse to ghettos and then the murder camps.

In December 1939, Eichmann was made chief of the Jewish Department Referat IV B4 of Himmler's Reichssicherheitshauptamt, the stated duty was to fight all 'enemies of the Reich' inside and outside the borders of Nazi Germany. These enemies were Jews, Communists, pacifists, Freemasons,and Christian activists.

The first chief of the RSHA was Heydrich, who was superseded by Kaltenbrunner in 1943. The organisation had responsibility for the Einsatzgruppen death squads that followed in the wake of the German army as it steamrollered through Poland and Russia towards Moscow.

At the start of 1940, Heydrich, Eichmann and their planning team began drawing up the detailed blueprint for the transports to the east.

A size limit of 1000 people was selected for the deportation trains.

While Deutsche Reichsbahn did not take part in the planning stages, Eichmann maintained close liaison with the state railway. Therefore, there clearly must have been people who knew in its higher echelons what the true purpose of these trains was. How far the knowledge cascaded down the DB tree at this stage is anyone's guess.

At a conference in Leipzig on January 22-23 attended by Eichmann, DB officials made arrangements to carry Jews to the Lodz ghetto.

THE MADAGASCAN ALTERNATIVE

Both ethnic cleansing and German resettlement were key components of Hitler's plans for conquered territories. It was not all about deporting Jews to the east; hundreds of thousands of ethnic Germans and their belongings were brought into the fatherland from occupied countries such as Poland and Lithuania during 1939-40.

In turn, Jews were forced out of certain areas to make way for the incoming Aryans. Deutsche Reichsbahn again provided transport.

Eichmann was also involved with a Nazi scheme to resettle European Jews in Madagascar.

The idea was first proposed by the anti-Semitic orientalist scholar Paul de Lagarde in 1885, and was proposed by others again in the 1920s.

It was not the only scheme proposed to allow the Jews of Europe to achieve their goal of having once again after nearly two millennia in the wilderness a homeland of their own.

In 1903, the British Uganda Programme proposed to give 5000 square miles of the Mau Plateau in British East Africa, an area with a suitable temperate climate, to Jews for relocation, as a response to pogroms in Russia at the time.

However, after investigating the implications, the Zionist Congress turned down the offer, after it was found to be a dangerous country filled with lions and other dangerous creatures.

Some Jews disagreed with this decision, and broke away to form the Jewish Territorialist Organisation to found a Jewish state anywhere they could. A few Jews, meanwhile, did relocate to Kenya, and their families are still there today.

Nazi leaders loved the idea of Madagascar. In May 1940, Himmler wrote: "I hope that the concept of Jews will be completely extinguished through the possibility of a large emigration of all Jews to Africa or some other colony."

DEPORTATION HALTS

Following the fall of France, the island was in the hands of the collaborationist Vichy regime.

German diplomat Franz Rademacher, the son of a railway engineer, was chosen to lead Referat D III, or Judenreferat, in Joachim von Ribbentrop's Foreign Affairs Ministry, and drew up plans for mass forced deportation of Jews to Madagascar. By June 1940, Hitler spoke about the plan to Benito Mussolini and also with Grand Admiral Erich Raeder.

On August 15, 1940, Eichmann unveiled Reichssicherheitshauptamt: Madagaskar Projekt, a blueprint for the resettlement of a million Jews per year over four years, thereby ridding Europe of them once and for all. It would be paid for by seizing all Jewish assets in Europe.

Many leading Nazis thought the plan was infinitely better than deporting more German Jews into Poland. They went as far as halting all such deportations on July 10 and even suspending the building of the Warsaw ghetto.

All that was needed, it seemed, would be a peace treaty in which France would hand over Madagascar to Germany, which would use the SS to police the island, barring its new inhabitants from having any outside business contacts. Then Germany would conquer Britain in Operation Sealion, and the surrendered British Navy would be used to ferry the Jews of Europe to the 'super ghetto' of Madagascar.

What spoiled the plan was Britain, firstly by winning the Battle of Britain, and then maintaining superiority over the high seas, and finally by seizing Madagascar from Vichy forces in 1942 and handing it over to the Free French.

In October 1941, Rademacher became responsible for mass deportations and murders of Serbian Jews, and was also involved in the deportation of Jews from France, Belgium, and The Netherlands.

Operation Barbarossa was the spark for the deportation of Jews to be stepped up. From Hitler's perspective, it was to be not only a territorial war against the Soviets and Bolsheviks, but also an ideological one against Jews and other minorities.

On October 4, 1941, Heydrich and Eichmann approved the railway deportation plan. The very next day, Deutsche Reichsbahn trains began taking German Jews to the east. By November 4, 20 transports carrying 19,827 Jews had arrived in Minsk, where the SS shot them.

Deutsche Reichsbahn supervisors were told to ensure that the trains ran on time.

NO GOSSIP?

Researchers have said that information about the trains was restricted to railway managers and key personnel. That would surely have involved stationmasters, signalmen and drivers at some point. It is difficult to believe that at the lowest rungs of the ladder, details of what was going on would not have spread by word of mouth, such is human nature, and railwaymen's everyday shed gossip.

One operational instruction was that 15 minutes should be left on single-track routes between an ordinary train passing through and a Jewish deportation train arriving.

The German administration in Poland was faced with the problem that these trains were bringing more Jews into ghettos that had already burst at the seams, such as the one in Lodz. These specials were accordingly diverted to Riga and Minsk, and when those cities' ghettos also became full up, the Jews living there were sent even further eastwards, to be murdered in pine forests and other remote locations.

Himmler took the view that shooting was too slow, and would never achieve his goal of a Jew-free continent. A better method of mass killing had to be sought, in order for these trains to be stepped up.

At first, the trains merely conveyed Jews to the misery of ghettos.

However, Himmler ordered the building of the most infamous of all concentration camps anywhere in the world, Upper Silesia near Germany's eastern border.

Its name became a byword for the new depths of depravity into which mankind was to prove that it could sink. Osweicim was its Polish name, but to the Germans and the rest of the world, it is known as Auschwitz.

THE TRAINS OF DECEIT

The site was chosen as it lay at the centre of the Nazi-controlled continent. At the time, Europe was criss-crossed by numerous rail routes, and from the perspective of the

A platform scene with 'Hitler' greeting 'Mussolini' next to a steam locomotive. This is a still from Charlie Chaplin's first talking movie and biggest-grossing picture, The Great Dictator, which satirised fascism. In his 1964 autobiography, Chaplin said that he would not have been able to make such jokes about the Nazi regime had the extent of the Holocaust been known at the time.

The 'new Israel' that never was: the Nazis had a masterplan to send all European Jews to Madagascar, which would then be blockaded so they could not leave the island. The plan fizzled out when it became clear that Britain remained master of the seas and deportation ships could not get through, so Eichmann went ahead with Plan B and the deportation trains to the east. OLIVIER CAPEL*

Coloured waiting room sign from the Greyhound bus station in Rome, Georgia, from segregationist era United States. Despite fighting the worst racist nation in the history of the planet, the US armed forces during the Second World War treated black soldiers differently to their white counterparts.

German army staff motorcar on railway in Southern Germany in 1937. DR ALFRED GOTTWALDT COLLECTION

planners of the Final Solution, all routes led to Auschwitz.

The law demanding that all Jews wore the yellow Star of David came into effect on September 19, 1941, the month before the deportation trains began. By that time, they had become officially ostracized from society, and lived in constant fear, in crowded and often insanitary conditions and had a nightly curfew imposed.

Many of them may therefore have viewed the prospect of a new life in the east being sold to them by their oppressors as harbouring hope for a bright new future.

The deportation process was a major undertaking for the authorities.

Firstly, several local council departments and government offices would have to work in liaison with each other.

The Jews would either have to be forced to gather at an assembly point to board the train, or be encouraged to do so by advertising the virtues of the labour camps in the east where they would earn a good living.

Once an assembly point was selected, police would be marshaled into place.

The gathering could be directed by city officials, with Labour Office representatives collecting the workbooks, and Finance Ministry officers amassing property inventory forms. Revenue Office staff and court officials supervised the state theft of the Jews' property.

Jews selected for deportation were often given a few days' notice at best and told to fill in forms to start their place in the huge cycle of bureaucracy. Others were told to leave at very short notice after SS men kicked down their doors.

They were given a list of items that they were allowed to take with them.

Once they arrived as the gathering point, often days before the train left, their luggage was inspected. Banned items were seized along with anything that weighed more than the limit of 100lb.

Police conducted body searches for hidden valuables, weapons, jewellery and money.

Their identity cards were stamped with the date of their 'evacuation' and their destination.

After this, the Jews were often marched under armed police escort through city and town streets to the railway station. Most would never see their home town again.

The police had been delegated to the job from their normal duties, to which they would return after the train departed. It was said that many carried out their special duties with pride.

Sometimes local people turned out to watch the Jews being led away. Some were filled with compassion, while others simply looked away. Some cheered, and shouted insults which indicated that they knew, albeit vaguely, what was to happen to the deportees.

Others seized the opportunity and queued to buy property which had been taken from the departing Jews. In certain places, auctions of stolen Jewish property proved popular.

Once the train had departed, bureaucracy again swung into action. The seized property had to be accounted for, unused ration cards returned, labour cards filed and the deportation had to be registered in the personal files of those who were on board.

As far as the state was concerned, those heading for the death camps had ceased to exist.

The bureaucracy was not, as was the case in most postwar Soviet Bloc countries, carried out for its own sake, but so that the army of civil servants and other individuals concerned could shirk responsibility.

They could process one small piece of paper and then plead that they were just a tiny link in the chain and in any case were only obeying orders and state laws. Giving these little people the shroud of legality to hide behind in theory left their conscience clear. Yet how many did not know what they were doing?

GANZENMÜLLER: THE MAN WHO RAN THE TRAINS

One man who certainly did, and clearly did not care less, was Albert Ganzenmüller, under-secretary of state at the Reich Transport Ministry.

At the age of 18, while still at school, Ganzenmüller had taken part in Hitler's failed Beer Hall Putsch, an attempt to seize power in Munich in 1923.

He gained a doctorate in engineering, and became an executive with the Deutsche Reichsbahn in 1931. He also joined the Nazi party and the brownshirts around the same time.

In 1938, Ganzenmüller was promoted to Oberregierungsrat, or senior government advisor, and in another upwards move became head of electrical engineering at the DB central office in Munich.

He was assigned to take over the repair of the electric railway network in occupied France in 1940, and then he asked to be transferred to the railway's eastern division in the Ukraine.

He impressed his Nazi bosses so well that Albert Speer, the Minister of Armaments and War Production, recommended that he was promoted to deputy general director of the German State Railways as well as under-secretary. The local party office in Munich wrote that he was "fully reliable politically".

In that post, one of his first jobs was to help organise the deportation trains.

In a response to a complaint from Himmler's personal adjutant Karl Wolff about problems with track maintenance and irregular trains on the line to the Sobibor murder camp, on July 28, 1942, he replied: "A train carrying 5000 Jews has run daily since July 22 from Warsaw to Treblinka via Malkinia; furthermore, another train has run twice a week with 5000 Jews from Przemysl to Belzec.

"The senior management of the eastern division of the railways… is in constant touch with the security service in Krakau. The latter is in agreement that transport from Warsaw to Sobibor via Lublin should

continue while the reconstruction work on this stretch renders such movements impossible."

Wolff replied a fortnight later: "I note with particular pleasure from your communication that a train with 5000 members of the chosen race has been running daily for 14 days and that we are accordingly in a position to continue with this population movement at an accelerated pace."

Early the following year, Himmler personally approached Ganzenmüller to make sure that the removal of Jews to Auschwitz went smoothly.

After the war, Ganzenmüller was detained at an interrogation camp in Italy, but escaped and fled to Argentina. An amnesty in 1952 saw him return to Germany three years later.

The above correspondence between Ganzenmüller and Wolff was discovered in 1957, after which the German authorities began investigating him. It was not until 1973 that he appeared before a court. In Düsseldorf, he faced trial on the grounds that he aided and abetted the murder of millions of Jewish men, women and children.

The case was halted the same year because he was in poor health after suffering a heart attack, and proceedings were discontinued in 1977. Ganzenmüller died in 1996, aged 91, a free man.

Ganzenmüller claimed after the war that he became a member of the Nazi Party because he was unhappy with both the state of the German economy and his own career prospects, but denied that he knew his trains were taking Jews to be murdered – a clear lie. Colleagues, however, including his wartime secretary, did not consider him to be particularly anti-Semitic, but was wholly concerned with his career and used his party membership and obedience to that end.

THE WEB THAT ENSNARED EUROPE

The SS developments in the use of poison gas to kill people in large numbers in static gas chambers gave Himmler exactly what he wanted.

It enabled far more trains to be run from both Germany and occupied Poland to the likes of Auschwitz, Belzec, Majdanek and Treblinka.

Himmler selected the sites for the ghettos, choosing cities with excellent rail connections, and the murder camps, which had to be connected to main lines while retaining their seclusion.

Eichmann was the mastermind behind the deportation operation. He along with local SS officers arranged with the administration of each of the occupied territories for the transport of Jews using local lines.

Once he had drawn up the plan, Eichmann's deputy Rolf Gunther would see that it was carried out.

In turn, Gunther told his deputy Franz Novak about each of the train movements and how many Jews would be on board.

Novak would then liaise with Office 21 in Deutsche Reichsbahn's Traffic Section.

MINSK

German forces occupied Minsk, capital of the Belorussian Soviet Socialist Republic, soon after Operation Barbarossa began. The Belorussian SSR became part of the Reich Commissariat Ostland with Minsk a district capital.

In July 1941, the Germans established a ghetto in the north-western part of the city and forced 80,000 people, including Jews from nearby towns, to move there.

Added to that figure between November 1941 and October 1942 were more than 20,000 Jews from Germany and the Protectorate of Bohemia and Moravia.

Many of them were shot or gassed in special vans when they reached Maly Trostinets, a small village about eight miles to the east. Others were housed in a separate ghetto in Minsk that segregated German Jews from

local Belorussian Jews: even racist policies were applied to the most despised of victims.

Jews were forced to work in factories inside the two ghettos as well as undertaking forced labour, including sweeping snow from the local railway tracks, as pictured here.

In August 1941, Jews established an underground in the Minsk ghetto organiSing escapes

and forming seven different partisan units in the forests outside the city, to which 10,000 fled.

The Germans destroyed the Minsk ghetto in autumn 1943, deporting some Jews by train to the Sobibor extermination camp and killing the remaining 4000 Jews at Maly Trostinets.

DR ALFRED GOTTWALDT
COLLECTION

The head of that section, Paul Schnell, would tell his junior, Otto Stange, who had responsibility for special trains, to arrange for vehicles in which to convey the passengers. Like a fleet manager on any main line railway today, Stange first had to find out what carriages or wagons were available for use.

The buck was then passed to the general operating office of the eastern division, where a schedule plotting the movement of the carriages was drawn up by Karl Jacobi in the passenger coach office with the aid of a deputy, Fritz Fahnrich.

Eventually the jigsaw came together to produce a schedule of death trains over a two or three month period.

The trains for Jews were classified Da if they came from Germany or occupied Europe, while those running within the

Ostbahn territory of occupied Poland were designated PKr, or Pj if they came from outside.

Like one of today's inter-city multiple unit trains, the rakes of carriages that had been assembled were kept together and reused time and time again. Assigned locomotives were changed around every 65 miles.

THE THOUSAND 'SPECIALS'

Between October 1941 and April 1945, during a period of almost 1250 days, far more than a thousand special trains ran with Jews from Berlin and Frankfurt, from Drancy near Paris and in Brussels from Malines, from Westerbork in Holland, Salonika or Rome, and from Berehovo Bilke in the Carpathians and from Białystok.

The network of death train lines spread out like a spider's web, a cancer reaching

into every corner of Europe controlled by the Germans. Every train had to be filled, mostly crammed well beyond capacity, every time a new source of Jews was identified, just to maintain the quotas in the gas chambers.

In the Deutsche Reichsbahn grand scheme of things, the deportation trains were classified as freight extras. That meant that slow journeys could be expected, as priority had to be given to normal goods trains, troop trains, military supplies and coal trains.

Over and above taking Jews to their deaths, Deutsche Reichsbahn also carried Jews and to work in slave labour camps and factories.

The trains also brought in the building materials for the murder camps and equipment such as the crematoria furnaces.

CATTLE TRUCKS

Jews captured in the Warsaw Ghetto uprising in May 1943 are led by German soldiers down Nowolipie Street to the assembly point for deportation. Only Avraham Neyer, seen to the right of his little daughter, survived the camps and later emigrated to Israel.

'They took the Jews to the concentration camps packed into cattle trucks'… so runs the often quoted historical account of the deportation trains.

In reality, unlike Britain, the German railways did not have purpose-built cattle wagons as such. What were used were large wooden boxcars, accessed via a sliding door on one side.

Indeed, these were, among many other general purposes, used for transporting cattle, and there were large hooks and loops fixed to the interior walls for tethering them in place if need be.

Cattle wagons, as seen on the British railway network of the day, would have been sheer luxury to those unfortunates who were sealed into these boxcars, packed in up to 100 a time, mostly without windows and totally lacking food, water, toilet facilities and sufficient space to sit or lie down, never mind the lack of any heating in the plummeting winter temperatures.

The deportation trains were often the slowest on the system. Sometimes the trains could be kept still for hours while waiting for preferential traffic – which normally meant everything else – to pass.

Railwaymen on every system across the globe that was in operation at this time would not have treated livestock in the same way, if not from pure humanitarian grounds, then out of economic necessity, because the animals would probably not have reached the end of the journey alive and compensation would have had to be paid. In this case, however, the treatment meted out

to the Jews on the transports jigsawed in perfectly with Nazi ideology. It must, however, never be forgotten that the death trains were far from being an exclusive Jewish phenomenon.

Among other prisoners on board them could be found gypsies, Sinti and Roma, Slavs, political prisoners, members of any resistance movement, homosexuals... or in fact anyone whom the Nazis considered too different for their liking.

'THIRD CLASS' PASSENGERS

However, the deportation trains did not start out by using boxcars or 'cattle trucks'.

The first 'special trains' (the Nazis always had 'code' words to cover up their true intentions) were made up of ordinary passenger coaches. In some cases, there would be one or two carriages attached to the rear of a normal service passenger train and uncoupled at a set point.

These carriages would be locked and blanked off from the rest of the train, so that the 'ordinary' passengers would not gain access and see what was happening at first hand. Indeed, survivors have told that when their train passed through bigger cities, they were ordered to close the windows and curtains.

On some of these special transports, the passengers were told that if they opened the windows even fractionally, they would be shot.

Sometimes there would be bars across the windows to prevent escape. In the case of third class four-wheeled carriages,

there would be two armed policemen on board, normally standing on the front and rear balconies.

While the Deutsche Reichsbahn had 66 'prison cars' in its fleet, these were clearly nowhere near enough to accommodate anything near the planned number of deportees, and in any case they were in regular use for their intended purpose, whereas carriages could easily take 25 or more people to a concentration camp.

Still, the prison cars, which had been introduced in Germany around the turn of the century to take suspected criminals between prisons and the courts, were also pressed into service and were used when the first concentration camps were set up after Hitler came to power. Designed to handle to up 30 prisoners with up to four to a cell, they were attached to normal timetabled trains.

DEPORTATION FROM SCHLESWIG-HOLSTEIN

In a booklet entitled In Memory of the 70th Anniversary of the Deportation of the Jews from Schleswig-Holstein, published by the Landeszentrale für politische Bildung, 'special trains' from Kiel which used ordinary carriages are described.

Jews from Pinneberg, Ahrensburg and Elmshorn were ordered to go to Kiel, the location of the local Gestapo headquarters.

Jews were brought to the station there in lorries. Once their assets had been seized, their train fares were deducted. Indeed, no matter how bad the conditions on the death trains were, it was normal practice that the

Jewish passengers had to pay their way, whether they had agreed to travel or not.

Survivor Josef Katz from Lübeck recalled: "At about 11am two large omnibuses of the Lübeck Strassenbahn Gesellschaft pulled up; quickly the 90 of us are boarded...

"Two special train carriages stand ready at the Lübeck station. They are heated passenger carriages.

"Slowly we leave the station, and soon the towers of the city are no longer to be seen in the mist of a grey winter's day. In Oldesloe, we are told, we will be coupled to a transport from Hamburg. The Gestapo officer accompanying us says that we are destined for Riga.

"In the meantime the Jewish Aid Society of Hamburg has distributed travel rations to us in the compartments.

"Slowly the train with 1200 Jews rolls out of the Oldesloe station hall, accompanied by the good wishes of the members of the aid society on the platforms.

"At the next stop, the doors of the train are locked. 'Green Police' with weapons on their shoulders now take over the guarding of the train. Now a different wind blows. We are now forbidden to look out of the window or to make contact with the free people on the station when the train halts."

Bettina Goldberg from Flensburg/Berlin wrote: "...In Schleswig-Holstein two transports were prepared. The second departed on July 18, 1942, with 37 persons – via Hamburg – to Theresienstadt; the first though had departed, on December 6, 1941, with 133 persons to Riga – Jungfernhof. In total there were 964 people on this transport, the majority being those who had lived in Hamburg.

"On December 4, the Carlebach family (this refers to Rabbi Carlebach) together with 747 further Hamburg Jews, including at least 41 who had moved there from Schleswig-Holstein, had to report to the Sammellager at Moorweidenstrasse 36.

"From here the 753 men, women and children were taken on the morning of December 6 by lorry under police guard to the Hannöverschen Bahnhof at Oberhafen (now a disused goods depot).

"There, third-class passenger coaches stood ready for them. The destination was not told to those concerned."

The train ran first to Bad Oldesloe, where there was a short stop, for the two smaller transports from Kiel and Lübeck were to be coupled on. The Lübeck transport comprised, as far as is currently known, 34 men, 56 women and two children under 10, a total of 92 persons, of whom 86 came from Lübeck itself, four from Bad Schwartau and two from Ratzeburg. Nineteen of these people were already over 65 and therefore technically should have been spared deportation, but it appears that local officials treated this rule rather flexibly and none of their superiors ever complained. In the Kiel transport there were also 11 people who were over 65. So far as is known this group comprised 41 persons – 21 men, 18 women, one child under 10 and one infant; 38 came

City police frogmarch Jews to the station at Brandenburg an der Havel for deportation in 1942.

A typical passenger train at Berlin Anhalter station. One or two carriages would have been added to send Jews to concentration camps. DR ALFRED GOTTWALD COLLECTION

from Kiel itself, while the rest had been brought there from Ahrensburg, Rendsburg and Elmshorn.

As the Gestapo, Stadtpolizeistelle Kiel, informed the Landrat in Pinneberg on November 15, 1941: "The amount for the rail journey from the place of residence of those concerned to Kiel was to be deducted from their (confiscated) property."

Following the marshalling of the transports from Hamburg, Lübeck and Kiel in Bad Oldesloe, the overfilled and sealed coaches went off to the east.

The journey lasted three days and three nights and the destination was the marshalling yard of Skirotava in the south of Riga. The deported were therefore now in the Reichskommisariat Ostland, which included the occupied Baltic states of Latvia, Estonia and Lithuania as well as parts of White Russia (Belarus).

The train guards had told the Jews that they were to be brought to the Riga ghetto. However, the mass murder in the Rumbula Forest of 27,500 of the 30,000 persons already there, Latvian Jews, took longer than planned and so there were not enough places for the new arrivals in the ghetto.

It was only the following transport, with 1011 persons on board from Cologne that arrived a day later, that was directed straight

to the ghetto. The Schleswig-Holstein Jews instead went to the makeshift concentration camp, Jungfernhof, where there were already 3000 people from previous transports from Nuremberg, Stuttgart and Wien.

This transport arrived via Danzig at the goods yard in Riga on December 9, ironically the day on which the Wannsee Conference had originally been scheduled to take place; it was postponed, as already described, to January 29, 1942, because of the Japanese attack on Pearl Harbour on December 7 and because the USA entered the war two days after that.

Up to that point, while the Nazis had wished to eliminate all Jews in the occupied territories, the orders at that time did not include those in Germany, the so-called Reichsjuden.

The USA's entry into the war, however, was interpreted by Hitler as the result of a world Jewish conspiracy, despite the anti-Semitism in the States described in a previous chapter. From this point on, the Fuhrer considered the murder of all Reichsjuden to be acceptable.

When the Jews reached Skirotava, German security guards and Latvian Hilfspolizei drove them with whips and clubs in order to make them run. They left behind their luggage, which was the guards' intention, with the promise of rich pickings for their persecutors.

The Jews trudged on foot through snow and ice to the camp several kilometres away. Six days before, they had been living in their own homes albeit under the punitive racist restrictions imposed by the Third Reich. Now they were on a former farm surrounded by barbed wire fences, living in the middle of winter in unheated cowsheds and barns with no toilet facilities and no warm water in a foreign country.

Jungfernhof, which lay just over two miles from Skirotava station, was little more than a holding pen that was used until the inhabitants who had not died from the cold and hunger could be shot. It was commanded by Rudolf Seck, a 33-year-old former farmer, who treated the unwanted prisoners on 'his' farm with great brutality.

Most inmates were shot on March 26, 1942, at a pit in the Bikernieki birch forest four miles north of Jungfernhof, to which they were taken by lorry on the pretext of being brought to work at a (non-existent) fish factory at the Dumanünde. The 'fish' was a deliberate SS 'joke', as the victims were to be packed like sardines in mass graves. Around 1800 people were shot on this day by 10 Latvians under SS officers, including some 90% of the Jews from Schleswig-Holstein.

The leader of the commando was Viktor Arajs, aged 32 at this time, a former law student and a policeman, who built up a group of Latvians which murdered around 45,000 people, firstly in Latvia and then in Belarus.

In 1943, with defeat starting to loom on the distant horizon to the east, Himmler ordered the removal of all trace of mass graves and a unit, Sonderkommando Sk-1005-B, was formed, tasked with excavating

and burning or destroying the human remains, and these men removed traces at Bikernieki and Salaspils.

It is believed that out of the 3986 Jews from Germany and Austria who came on the transports to Jungfernhof, 3838 were murdered. Of those taken from Schleswig-Holstein, only five men and three women survived the war.

KEEPING TO TIME: MORE IMPORTANT THAN GIVING PASSENGERS WATER

A lady survivor of a transport to Riga, Hilde Sherman, was deported from Mönchengladbach station along with her husband and his family. First stop was Düsseldorf, where around 1000 Jews were gathered together and beatings by the SS began. She and others were forced to strip naked and all their possessions were taken away. One man was clubbed to death simply for asking an SS guard when the train was due.

Hilde boarded a passenger carriage, and the doors were locked from the outside, although they could still look out of the windows. While the passengers had bread, they had no water and soon their thirst became unbearable.

At Insterburg on the prewar Polish border with Lithuania, the train stopped and the passengers were permitted to disembark and collect snow for drinking.

Finally, the train arrived at Skirotava, and amid more scenes of raw brutality, the passengers were told to get off, but the last to leave were forced to clean the carriages with their bare hands. They were forced to walk around 16 miles to the ghetto as Latvians looted their possessions. A police officer named Salitter, who was involved with this particular deportation train, appeared – according to his later account –

to have shown some spark of humanity when he allowed mothers who had become separated from their children to move into the carriages where they were.

He recorded: "In order to supply the Jews with water, it is essential that the Gestapo get in touch with the Reichsbahn and co-ordinate one-hour stops every day at a railway station in the Reich.

"Because of the timetable, the Reichsbahn was reluctant to comply with the transport commander's wishes.

"The Jews are usually on the road for 14 hours or more before the transport leaves and have used up all the drinks they had taken with them. When they are not provided with water during the trip, they try, in spite of the prohibition, to leave the train at every possible spot or ask others to get them water.

"It is also essential that the Reichsbahn prepare the trains at least three to four hours ahead of departure, so that the loading of the Jews and their belongings can be conducted in an orderly fashion.

"The Gestapo has to make sure that the Reichsbahn place the car for the guard detachment at the centre of the train. This is essential for the supervision of the transport."

The cost of the deportation trains was shared between the Deutsche Reichsbahn and the police. Most documents relating to them, even down to which locomotives were used to haul them, were systemically destroyed towards the end of the war to eradicate any traces of guilt.

WHEN HUMAN BEINGS BECAME FREIGHT

It was when the transports were intensified during the later years of the war and there were not enough coaches to go round, coupled with the increasing fear that the occupants would realise their fate and try to escape, that boxcars became standard. If, as we are continually told, the German public of the day did not know about the death

German Jews board the carriages of a deportation train to Riga's ghetto at Bielefeld station in December 1941.

Jewish families wearing the mandatory Star of David waiting to board a deportation train comprised of boxcars.

camps, the Jews had started to become well aware of their fate.

The boxcars, which appeared en masse on the special trains in the second half of 1942, also kept the 'freight' out of the gaze of outsiders, some of who might speak out just as they did over Aktion T4.

Deutsche Reichsbahn, like its British counterparts of the day, had a wealth of assorted freight wagon types distributed over its system, for the railways were still far and above the principal means of carrying goods. Many of the boxcars used in the deportation trains had been seized from railways in occupied countries.

Not only were deportees carried in the boxcars; regular German soldiers occasionally rode in such vehicles too, but with benches placed along the inside walls and sufficient room to move.

Each ordinary deportation train might accommodate 1000 prisoners, with up to 12 armed policemen guarding each train, travelling in the elevated brakeman's compartment, a standard feature on continental freight trains, or in a separate passenger carriage with all the comforts you might expect.

There was also a 'half and half' system. For example, from May to September 1942, one special weekly train was scheduled to run from Vienna, each carrying 1000 Jews in third-class passenger carriages as far as the Wolkowysk yard in eastern Poland, with a second-class car for the guards. Once there, the Jews transferred to boxcars for the remainder of the trip to Minsk, where many

were shot. The passenger cars were cleaned and then returned empty for loading. This practice was mirrored by many of the deportation trains during 1941-42.

Albert van Hoey, aged 20, from East Flanders in Belgium, was a member of a small underground group and was arrested one Sunday in 1944 on his way not to a synagogue but to a church.

His memories of his journey in one such cattle truck were recounted in the book Verschleppt zur Sklavenarbeit by Gerhard Hoch and Rolf Schwarz (Alveslohe, 1985) as follows: "On August 8, 1944, we were taken from the Nieuwe Wandeling prison in Ghent by bus to Antwerpen. Four SS men, armed with guns, guarded us. For several hours we were cooped up in the prison at Beginenstrasse, Antwerpen.

"In the evening, under heavy guard, we were taken to the East station. During the whole night and the following morning prisoners were brought from other Belgian prisons and camps to the train.

"Around 1pm on August 9, 1944, our trip to misery began; around 800 men and several hundred women, separated from each other, crammed into cattle wagons with the label 'terrorists'.

"In bright sunshine we left Antwerp in the direction of the Netherlands; some kilometres from the border I managed to send a message, wrapped in a knotted handkerchief, through the window mesh, pushing it out. It comprised bits of newspaper cuttings stuck together on to paper with cooked potato and some

scratched notes. This message was picked up by a German patrol which collected others too; it was then taken secretly by a Belgian woman worker and sent on to my family. This was the only news they got of me until the end of the war. The journey into hell had begun.

"Some prisoners received packages with some food from the Belgian Red Cross. We could not, however, swallow anything as our throats were dried out. There was nothing to drink and the tropical heat meant suffocating closeness because of the wagon being so overfilled. We had to defecate in the wagon and so there was a dreadful, overpowering stench of excrement and sweat. There was not enough room to sit down and so we had to bear the whole journey standing.

"So the journey continued via Rosendaal, Breda, Eindhoven, Venlo, Kaldenkirchen; at this border station there was an appell – a roll call. They screamed at us, shouted and stamped around, so that any hope we may have had that things might get better disappeared.

"The night passed with repeated stopping and starting. We passed through the dimly lit stations of Neuss and Düsseldorf. On August 10 we passed Kassel, Erfurt and Weimar.

"Then came the junction for Buchenwald. We had never heard of this place. During some of the pauses the SS men had thrown stones at us if we showed our faces behind the mesh in the windows. We were already half mad when we arrived at Buchenwald at about 4pm.

"Everything that we possessed was taken from us, including the Red Cross packets. Then we had to take off all our clothing in order to be deloused under the shower, always 10 together, fully naked. All body parts with hair were shaven. I almost fell unconscious but was just able to hold myself upright. Then each of us was handed a pile of lumpy clothes. They looked so utterly impossible that even in our misery we had to laugh on seeing each other – for it was even possible that someone did not recognise their own brother. Then we had to stand in line and were given our numbers – I got number 75623.

"It was almost night when we were brought to our temporary quarters – 800 men in two tents which were full of fleas. Luckily it was a warm night and the tents were partially open.

"We newcomers found ourselves in a camp with 50,000 prisoners, a real town of barracks... During the first days we had to work in a nearby quarry and carry heavy stones under our arms into the camp.

"On Sunday we were moved to Block 57 – in a wooden barrack that was divided into 16 'boxes'. Each box served as the eating and sleeping space for 54 prisoners. They were formed with three-storey bunks, in each 'bed' of which nine people had to lie – this was only possible if one lay head to feet and feet to head, like herrings in a tin. Each bed was about 2-4m metres wide.

"The block was full of fleas and lice and for 800 men there were only 100 bowls. Carrying the heavy stones, injections against all sorts of illnesses and the hours-long appell – these filled our days during this 'quarantine' period.

"After one such appell, there was a great sorting out... the greater portion of the newcomers were to go on a transport. I was included. The prisoner clothing we had worn until now was to be handed back and instead we got the zebra (striped) uniforms. Our numbers were sewn into it with metal wire.

"On August 23 our train set off – 400 Belgians and 100 prisoners of other nationalities. Again we were packed into cattle wagons.

"Burning heat and dreadful thirst made the journey into a nightmare. And now above all I had diarrhoea, dreadful cramps and an apathy as a result. Where were we going? No one told us.

"After 30 hours of rail journey for only 120km we were in Blankenburg (Harz), 12km south of Halberstadt. In groups of 100 men, in rows of three, guarded by armed SS men, we had to march many kilometres to an empty spot surrounded with a three-metre-high barbed wire fence and a series of high watchtowers.

"There was standing already a wooden barrack for the SS and 42 Hitler youth tents. In each tent there were 12 prisoners. We slept on straw with our heads pointing out and our feet in the middle. Luckily it was still summer."

He was indeed one of the luckier ones and was delegated to mere hard labour.

The same book also described the conveyance of Soviet prisoners of war by train to the death camp at Heidkaten near Kaltenkirchen. They were told they were being taken for medical treatment. These men were taken by the Elmshorn-Barmstedt-Oldesloer railway, in the luggage van of normal passenger trains and accompanied by up to five guards, to a halt which was named Hoffnung. Translated, that means hope. It was anything but.

One witness recalled seeing the POWs marched off the train, many too weak to walk. These people simply fell down into the roadside ditches or fell to the ground and could not get up again. They were beaten to death or shot.

Transports of sick Soviet POWS refilled the camp every week. German guard soldiers from the camp waited at the halt with a two-wheeled flat cart and brutally

Jewish women being deported from the Warsaw ghetto in open trucks.

A Deutsche Reichsbahn type Opole freight car, built between 1938 and 1942, and now owned by the Friends of the Historic Harbour Railway EV at Bremer Kai in Kleiner Grasbrook, Hamburg. CLAUS-JOACHIM DICKOW*

An original boxcar used for death camp transports is preserved at Fort van Breendonk in Belgium. JOJAN*

A traditional British cattle truck like BR 12T B 891054, pictured in Bewdley on the Severn Valley Railway, bears little resemblance to the sealable boxcars often described as such when referring to the Nazi deportation trains. ROBIN JONES

dragged those who could not walk on to it, often stacking them.

During 1941, as well as shipping Jews to their deaths, Deutsche Reichsbahn also carried them and other prisoners to work in slave labour camps and factories.

IC Farben was building a synthetic rubber plant at Dwory near Auschwitz, and between July and December 1941, nearly 160,000 prisoners were ferried between the camp and the work site in captured boxcars, each carrying 100 prisoners at a time.

ESCAPE FROM TREBLINKA

Avraham Kaszepicki, who had served in the Polish army and was deported from the Warsaw ghetto to the Treblinka murder camp on August 25, 1942, later told how the SS men arrested him and fellow workers in a honey factory in the city.

They were marched with hundreds of other Jews to the nearest railway station, Ukrainian and Latvian guards whipping the crowd into submission as they were herded on to boxcars. Avraham recounted: "We were moving closer to the boxcars. Already we could see elderly people stretched out on the floor of the first car, half-unconscious.

More than 100 people were crammed into our car. The ghetto police closed the doors.

"When the door shut on me, I felt my whole world vanishing. Some pretty young girls were still standing in front of the cars, next to a German in a gendarme's uniform (the train escort).

"The girls were screaming, weeping, stretching out their hands to the German and crying: 'But I'm still young! I want to work! I'm still young! I want to work!' The German just looked at them and did not say a word. The girls were loaded into the boxcar and they travelled along with us.

"After the doors had closed on us, some of the people said: 'Jews, we're finished!' But I and some others did not want to believe that. 'It can't be! They won't kill so many people! Maybe the old people and the children, but not us. We're young. They're taking us to work'.

"The cars began to move. We were on the way. Where to? We didn't know. Perhaps we were going to work in Russia." However, some of the elderly people remained sceptical, as soon as the train started

moving, they started to recite the prayer for the dead."

Avraham continued: "It's impossible to imagine the horrors in that closed, airless boxcar. It was one big cesspool. Everybody was pushing toward the window where there was a little air, but it was impossible to get close to the window.

"Everybody was lying on the ground. I also lay down. I could feel a crack in the floor. I lay with my nose right up against that crack to grab some air. What a stench all over the car! You couldn't stand it. A real cesspool all over. Filth everywhere, human excrement piled up in every corner of the car. People kept shouting: 'A pot! A pot! Give us a pot so we can pour it out the window'. But nobody had a pot."

The train came to a halt in the middle of nowhere and an armed guard boarded to rob the occupants of the boxcar of money, watches, jewellery, everything that was not well hidden. Two prisoners managed to jump off the train, which was immediately

Women and children deportees leaving the boxcars of a newly arrived transport train at Auschwitz. Within hours most of them will probably have been murdered.

stopped so that the Germans could shoot them. Those in the boxcar were so desperate that they paid Polish railwaymen 500 to 1000 zlotys, a small fortune, just to get half a pint of water. The Poles were being oppressed by the Germans. Had Hitler won the war, those Poles would almost certainly have been the next to beg for water on the way to their deaths.

"Those who had been able to get some water got no great pleasure from it," said Avraham. "One person cried that his father had fainted; another that his mother had passed out and a third that his child was unconscious, and so the water was divided into such small portions that no one got much benefit from it. Various important people, professors and doctors, were riding in our car. They took off their shirts and lay on the floor gasping.

"As I started to drink my water, a woman came up to me and said that her child had fainted. I was in the middle of drinking and simply couldn't tear the cup away from my lips. Then the woman sank her teeth into my hand with all her might to get me to stop drinking and leave her some of my water.

"I wouldn't have minded being bitten again, just as long as I could have more water. But I left over some of the water in the cup and saw that the child got to drink it."

By 7am, the sun had risen and the temperature inside the boxcar became stifling. Men and women lay half naked as they struggled to breathe. After stopping for several hours, again without food or water, the train reached Treblinka late that afternoon. By that time, several of the passengers were dead.

Aravham was later told that when some other death trains had reached Treblinka, all the occupants of the boxcars were dead on arrival.

A gate was opened to let the train into the camp and immediately closed behind it again. Ukrainian guards then used whips to drive the occupants out of the boxcars before they had a chance to put their clothes

back on again. Within hours, the women and children, and many of the men, had been gassed and their bodies reduced to piles of ashes in the crematoria.

To hide the true nature of Treblinka, the local passenger station to the north of the camp was closed from August 27, 1942.

A typical train bound for the camp from the Polish city of Czestochowa might consist of 58 boxcars with two third-class passenger cars for the guards. The trains without people weighed 600 tons and the occupants added another 200 tons.

Some trains to Treblinka carried up to 7000 people.

Avraham was one of those selected to work at the camp. Eighteen days later, he managed to escape by hiding himself in stolen clothes which were sent back to Lublin in a boxcar. For him alone, the train brought freedom.

He returned to the Warsaw ghetto where he joined the ZOB (Jewish Fighting Organisation). He was killed in the Warsaw ghetto uprising in April 1943, but not before he had given his testimony in detail about the Nazi atrocities in Treblinka. His testimony was written down in Yiddish and rediscovered in December 1950 by Polish construction workers. The original document is now preserved in the city's Jewish Historical Institute.

THE WAVES OF DEPORTATIONS

Despite the worsening persecution of Jews and the launch of Operation Reinhard following the Wannsee Conference, there was no standard pattern to the Holocaust at its height. The killing of Jews developed in different ways in different areas.

At the start, the Nazis were far less cautious about killing Russian Jews, of whom around 1.5 million died, than their German counterparts. Adolf Eichmann laid down guidelines as to which Jews could be murdered and which would, for the time being, receive a degree of lesser 'special

treatment' due to their political, national or other circumstances.

For instance, Spanish Jews were protected, as although the Franco government was sympathetic to the Nazi cause and he had been aided by the Germans in the Spanish Civil war, Spain did not take part in the Holocaust and remained ostensibly neutral throughout the war.

The German police and the SS had to follow Eichmann's guidelines to the letter, although they were not known to the Jews. However, the more intense the Holocaust became, the more lax the guidelines became.

For instance, at the outset, the deportation of people in their sixties was banned, because they could not work.

The original idea was to exterminate Russian and eastern European Jews and then deport the German Jews to fill their places in the ghettos before using them as slave labour.

However, by June 1942, the transit concentration camp in Theresienstadt in Czechoslovakia had elderly German Jews brought in. Inside this camp, which doubled up as a ghetto, there developed rivalry between German and Czech Jews for the scant resources available.

After a few months of staying in the ghetto, the German Jews were sent onwards by train to Minsk, Treblinka or Auschwitz, where they were murdered. Around 2000 people left this place by train on a one-way journey to the East each week.

Until the sliding door of the boxcar was open, the deportees packed like sardines inside would suffer days of darkness. ROBIN JONES

The interior of the boxcar in the German Museum of Technology. Around 100 people were packed into such wagons for a journey which could last several days without food or water. ROBIN JONES

Hooks for securing cattle lined the interior walls of the boxcars. Around eight animals could be tethered in each wagon. ROBIN JONES

The Minsk ghetto was a prime early destination, but during the winter of 1941 the army commander there told Himmler he needed the trains for food and military hardware, not the delivery of yet more Jews. Accordingly, the Minsk-bound deportation trains were diverted to ghettos in Riga, Kowno in Lithuania (where the Jews were shot by locals) and Poland.

There was a three-week pause in the deportation trains at Christmas 1941 because the special trains were needed for army holiday transport. But the trains to Riga began again in January.

Many observers wonder how the Germans had the resources to bother with deportation trains when they were fighting a war.

As it was, the German railway network, which like that in Britain was far bigger and more intensive than today, had plenty of spare capacity.

When a renewed offensive against the Red Army began in the summer of 1942, the programme of deportation trains was interrupted again.

The last German Jews to be deported were those who had enjoyed some degree of protection because they worked for the military, in factories producing armaments and the like.

They were replaced in February and March 1943 by Russian forced labour. The removal of the last Jewish factory workers became known as the 'factory operation'.

In one bizarre incident in October 1941, Himmler admonished a local commander in Riga who had killed 15,000 – because several thousand of those had been German. Killing Latvian and Russian Jews was acceptable, but at that stage, not the Germans.

There were also frequent clashes between the Nazi ideologists and the military pragmatists. Jews working as slave labour in a factory would be transported to a death camp at the whim and behest of the former. Then when supplies to the front line fell short, the army commander would demand to know where they were, only to be told there was a blip in production because all the workers had been liquidated.

The deportation of German Jews resumed again in March 1942; this time they were despatched to Lublin in Poland, but German local leaders pleaded with the Nazi hierarchy not to send any more as they had plenty already. Hans Frank, the Governor-General of occupied Poland's 'General Government' territory, finally agreed to take more when the death camps at Belzec and Sobibor near Lublin were ready for the local Jews. At least 40 'resettlement' trains packed with German Jews then arrived in Lublin.

By May 1942, however, Himmler realised that nobody was coming to take the German Jews, maybe paying ransom for them to be allowed out of occupied territories, so he ordered the deportation trains containing them to go straight to the death camps. In the middle of 1943, Himmler declared Germany to be 'Judenrein', free of Jews. There were still two main groups,

however. Firstly, there were the 'submarines', Jews who had managed to go underground into hiding. Then there were around 10,000 German Jews in mixed marriages, who were not allowed to be deported. However, if they committed a crime, no matter how petty, they could still be placed on the special trains. There were Gestapo agents watching their every move and waiting for an excuse to pounce.

These were among the last Jews living in Germany.

OPEN WAGONS

Towards the end of the war, open goods wagons were used. Designed to carry coal, iron ore, timber, stone or agricultural produce that was weatherproof, they were pressed into service for bringing prisoners to the camps. Even the guards travelled in the open if no brake compartment was available.

The sides of some wagon types used in this way were less than 2ft high, because they were designed to drop down for quick unloading of bulk ore.

The prisoners had to stand in the open ore wagons, because the floor was built at a slant to permit rapid unloading. Survivors recall that some prisoners fell over the short sides and on to the tracks, often with fatal consequences.

In the open wagons, often a can was passed around as a communal toilet and the passengers sometimes relished holding it just to gain some warmth from the fresh urine.

Needless to say, many prisoners froze to death while being conveyed in the open freight wagons in winter.

Deutsche Reichsbahn was based a few hundred miles from Britain, where railwaymen had been feted as national heroes as railway history reached its zenith in the Thirties. Looking at just a handful of these stories of those who were made to suffer on the special trains, paying a ransom for a cup of water given half the chance, it might as well have been light years away.

Dr Alfred Gottwald of Deutsches Technikmuseum in Berlin, who has produced seminal texts on the deportation trains, explained: "The social system was one of ordering and obeying.

"There was some resistance by railwaymen, but it was not on the job. The honour of railwaymen is seen as operating the railway, not obstructing it.

"They might have given food to Jews in hiding or given some other private help like that."

HUMANITY HITS BACK

There is only one known attack on a Holocaust deportation train, and that was staged by three young resistance fighters in Belgium, from where around 25,000 Jews and 350 Sinti and Roma were sent to the camps, with just 1205 surviving.

All of the deportation trains passed through Boortmeerbeek station. The 20th transport on April 19, 1943, was halted two miles north of the station by the trio, who had not realised that it was the first one to use boxcars rather than carriages. As such, it was far better protected, both in terms of guards and also opening the doors to let the deportees out.

The three managed to wrench open the door of one boxcar so that 17 Jews escaped. Just before the German border, another 214 managed to get away. Out of those who fled, 87 were rounded up and sent to Auschwitz, but the rest survived.

Their rescuers, who were also able to flee, had been friends since their schooldays. They were led by Jewish doctor Youra Livschitz, who was arrested but managed to get away. Betrayed, he was arrested a second time and shot in February 1944.

A second, Robert Maistrau, was later arrested and survived both Buchenwald and Bergen-Belsen, while the third, Jean Franklemon, was also detained and survived Sachsenhausen concentration camp.

A memorial plaque and a monument can be seen at Boortmeerbeek station. The plaque bears the inscription 'Friend who passes by, pay deference to these heroic hands which saved those who were sent to hell by evil powers'. Initiated by the Jewish Museum of Deportation and Resistance and Maurice Tzwern, whose mother fled the train, it was dedicated on April 19, 1993, the 50th anniversary of the attack.

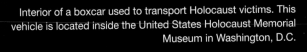

Interior of a boxcar used to transport Holocaust victims. This vehicle is located inside the United States Holocaust Memorial Museum in Washington, D.C.

TERMINUS!

At a very distant glance, it could be a busy seaside station on a summer Saturday, packed with families with babies and young children and their luggage, eager to be directed to the bus to their hotels. However, the uniforms, the boxcars and then the trademark gateway tell all. This was the selection on the ramp outside Auschwitz-Birkenau, where SS monsters such as Josef Mengele decided at a glance who was to live, or die within hours in the nearby gas chamber.

The Nazi killing machine went to extremes to keep the true nature of the destination of the deportation trains hidden from those it forced to ride on them in beyond inhuman conditions.

The element of deception was maintained as best it could be, from the moment the deportees boarded the train to the seconds when the deadly Zyklon B pellets were thrown into the gas chambers.

As highlighted in the previous chapter, long before the death camps were reached, it had become clear to those in the boxcars that neither the authorities nor railway staff gave a damn about the fact that some of them were dying because of the abhorrent conditions.

It does not take much of a leap of faith to move from that position to realise that those who suffered in this way would be in no fit state to start work in the well-paid labour camps of the east where they had been promised new lives, and it was more likely than not that those ordering the deportation had much worse in store.

All the deportation trains had to do was reach a terminus, and when it arrived, those on board were relieved when the huge wooden doors were pushed back, air was released into the miniature 'Black Holes of Calcutta' that each wagon had become and they were allowed to disembark.

In many cases, those who had arrived at death camps thought they had merely reached another railway station. The Nazis in some cases went to great lengths to adjust the surroundings to lull their latest consignment of victims into a false sense of security.

At the extermination camp of Treblinka, for example, a façade had been built to make the disembarkation ramp look just like a country station, compete with clock – only if you had hung around long enough would you have perhaps noticed that the hands did not move.

Many did not know what to expect. As the transports increased, rumours had begun to percolate 'back down the wire' about the camps. Many of the new arrivals would clearly fear the worst. Others would delude themselves with the lies that the Nazis had told about promises of a better life ahead, if only to cling to a last glimmer of hope.

Wehrmacht NCO Wilhelm Cornides in August 1942 recorded in his diary that a railway policeman in Rzeszow in south-eastern Poland had told him that a marble plaque with golden letters was to be erected on September 1 because then the city would be free of Jews.

The railway policeman also told him that "trains filled with Jews pass almost daily through the shunting yards, are despatched immediately on their way and return swept clean, most often the same evening". He added: "Some 6000 Jews from Jaroslaw were recently killed in one day."

Cornides then took an ordinary passenger train from Rzeszow to Chelm, where he observed: "At 10 minutes past noon I saw a transport train run into the station. On the roof and running boards sat guards with rifles. One could see from a distance that the cars were jammed full of people. I turned and walked along the whole train. It consisted of 35 cattle cars and one passenger car.

"In each of the cars there were at least 60 Jews – in the case of the enlisted men's or prisoner transports these wagons would hold 40 men, however, the benches had been removed and one could see that those who were locked in had to stand pressed together.

"As soon as the train halted, the Jews attempted to pass out bottles in order to get water. The train, however, was surrounded by SS guards, so that no one could come near.

"I talked to a policeman on duty at the railway station. He answered: 'Those are probably the last ones from Lvow. That has been going on now for three weeks without interruption. In Jaroslaw they only let eight remain, no one knows why'."

The policeman said they were going to Belzec for 'poison'.

On another journey, also documented on the www.holocaustresearchproject.org website, Cornides spoke to another railway policeman who said: "In the railway documents these trains run under the name of resettlement transports," adding that after the murder of Heydrich several transports containing Czechs had passed through. He was in no doubt about the one-way nature of those trains.

The train passed Camp Belzec which was next to the railway line. A woman passenger happily pointed it out.

ODOUR OF DEATH

Cornides wrote in his diary: "A strong sweetish odour could be made out distinctly. 'But they are stinking already,' said the woman. 'Oh nonsense it is only the gas,' the railway policeman said laughing.

"Soon, the sweetish odour was transformed into a strong smell of something burning. 'That is from the crematory,' said the policeman.

"A double track led into the camp. One track branched off from the main line, the other ran over a turntable from the camp to a row of sheds some 250 metres away.

"A freight car happened to stand on the turntable. Several Jews were busy turning the turntable – SS guards, rifles under their arms, stood by."

He recorded another conversation with a policeman in the town hall restaurant in Chelm on September 1, 1942, after asking how the Jews were killed. The policeman answered: "Someone tells them that they must be deloused. Then they undress and enter a room into which at first a heatwave is let in, and thereby they already have received one small dose of gas.

"It is enough to act as a local anaesthetic. The rest then follows and then they are immediately burned."

The policeman said that the Jews were killed because they spied for the Russians, operated the black market and rigged prices.

JOURNEY'S END

On the arrival of each transport, much the same pattern of procedure followed at every camp. This is what happened in the biggest, Auschwitz, first at the initial camp and then also after the railway line was built into the larger Birkenau camp with its infamous 'Ramp' platform.

There would be SS officers and doctors, who would form the new arrivals into lines. Women, children, the sick and the elderly would be told to move into a line to the left, and the fit and able into another to the right.

The air would be full of shouting and screaming amid scenes of untold distress as horrified family members were suddenly parted from each other without warning or explanation, before they could gather their breaths from the train ride to hell.

In some cases, the SS guards at this stage would try to keep brutality to the minimum, if only to stifle awareness of what was to follow, maintain the deception to the end and eradicate the risk of a revolt by prisoners who would by then realise that they had nothing to lose.

In other cases, deportees would be shot there and then for no apparent reason; dogs would be set on them or they would be kicked and beaten if they did not get into line.

The left line, which comprised the bulk of the incoming transport, would be marched off from the station to a 'shower block', often built next to or a stone's throw from the railway. The interior of the building would look exactly like it was meant to be inside, complete with dummy shower heads. History, of course, records its real purpose, and those who were told to strip naked, leaving their clothes and possessions behind, and had their heads shaved so that their hair could be recycled for the German war effort would within a few seconds of the door behind being closed and locked be dead.

The gas killed relatively quickly, but it was not necessarily instantaneous. Victims, finally realising that there were no showers, frantically clambered over each other, trying to find a pocket of air. Others would claw at the doors until their fingers bled.

Yet when compared to the many-faceted torments which were to face those not selected for the gas chamber outright, those quick deaths might be considered even fortunate.

Once everyone in the room was dead, special prisoners who had been spared a similar fate for a few weeks, maybe months, and known as Sonderkommandos, would enter the gas chamber and remove the bodies, which would then be searched for gold and then placed into the crematoria. That would often be the fate of those who had merely been rendered unconscious by the gas.

The belongings of those who had been gassed were seized and sorted in the Camp Kanada (Canada) warehouse for shipment back to Germany. Camp Kanada symbolised wealth to the prisoners, and also the guards, who at times faced Gestapo inquiries for pilfering and corruption.

Those boxcar passengers who had been sent to the right during the selection on the ramp went through a dehumanising process that would permit their survival for as long as they were deemed of benefit to Germany.

They were given a genuine shower and underwent a delousing process. Their clothes and personal belongings were also stolen from them and their hair was shaved completely off before they were given the infamous trademark pyjama-style striped prison outfits and a pair of shoes, usually the wrong size.

Each new arrival was then formally registered and had their arms tattooed with a number. They would then be set to work, either maintaining the camp as a forced cog in the wheels of the death machine, or shipped out as slave labour to nearby factories and other industrial sites.

Within days, if not hours, the new prisoners would have found out about the fate of their families after they last saw them in the left line at the railway ramp. Many could never recover from the shock to their system and either committed suicide or resigned themselves to wasting away.

WHO CREATED HELL ON EARTH?

The brick gateway to the purpose-built death camp Auschwitz-Birkenau II with a railway track leading into it is the defining image of what lies way beneath the depths of human depravity and is instantly recognisable the world over.

Yet who build this landmark of pure evil? Yes, slave labourers carried out the actual physical construction of the gateway and the camps, but who supplied the bricks?

In one sense, it was a local brickmaker. There again, you might also say it was the rest of the world.

The foundations of the Holocaust were laid not by Hitler, Himmler, Heydrich or Eichmann, but by centuries of illogical hatred against a dispersed and homeless people whose only 'crime' was in being different to the indigenous populations of where they settled. Every generation that passed without that purposeless hatred being wiped away simply added more 'bricks'... as did those who seized on the theory of eugenics.

Then there was the rampant anti-Semitism in places such as the United States, home to motor magnate Henry Ford with his printed diatribes against Jews; the Pope, who signed the Concordat with the Nazi Party in 1933 rather than using his influence to the full to condemn the known Nazi excesses; the endless stream of propaganda from Dr Goebbels and Julius Streicher's rantings that appeared in each edition of *Der Stürmer*.

The septic mixture that had brewed over the centuries finally boiled over when the Nazi Party provided the catalyst. Never before had such an ideology had at its disposal one of the greatest gifts of all bestowed on the human race – the railway... not only to create a nightmare beyond anyone's worst dreams, but to normalise and legitimise it in the minds of many.

This is how that gateway – and the hell that burned 24/7 behind it – came to be built, and that infernal railroad laid right up to its ever-hungry entrance.

And the opinion of this author is that the big lesson, surely, is that it is our sole responsibility, we the people, to ensure that another like it never rises from the ground. Will we take on that responsibility... or will future history show that we shirked it?

WHY OSWIECIM?

It was SS General Erich Julius Eberhard von Zelewski who was the initial driving force behind the building of the original camp, later known as Auschwitz I, in order to relieve overcrowding in Polish jails. Given responsibility for much of Silesia as higher SS and police leader, his subordinate, SS-Oberführer Arpad Wigand, came up with the idea of using the site of the former Polish artillery barracks, with its excellent rail links, in the Zasole suburb of Oswiecim (Auschwitz) in January 1940.

Walter Eisfeld, the former commandant of Sachsenhausen concentration camp, was sent to inspect the site, and a decision was taken to build the new camp by late February.

The first commandant was Rudolf Höss, who was already a convicted murderer and a staunch Nazi from the early days of the party. In Mecklenburg on May 31, 1923 Höss and members of the Nazi Freikorps beat suspected communist Walther Kadow to death on the wishes of the local farm supervisor, Martin Bormann, who later acquired infamy as Hitler's private secretary.

Höss was sentenced to 10 years' imprisonment, but Bormann only one. Höss was released in July 1928 as part of an amnesty and joined the Artaman League, a German nationalist back-to-the-land movement that promoted clean living and a farm-based lifestyle. On August 17, 1929 he married fellow member Hedwig Hensel and they had two sons and three daughters between 1930-43.

His deputy at Auschwitz was to be SS-Obersturmführer Josef Kramer, who had served at Dachau, Sachsenhausen and Mauthausen, and was later placed in charge of Bergen-Belsen, where he became known as the Beast of Belsen. Like Höss, he was to be hanged for war crimes, a far cleaner death than was meted out to their victims.

The Nazis evacuated the surrounding area, including 17,000 Polish and Jewish residents of the western districts of Oswiecim, plus people who were living in a shanty town by the old barracks and the residents of eight local villages, creating an empty zone of 15 square miles. A Camp Interest Zone was established to isolate the camp from the outside world.

FIRST ARRIVALS

The designers of Auschwitz came up with a blueprint for the most streamlined mass killing centre that the world had ever seen, and it was all made possible because of its railway connections.

The first prisoners were 30 German

criminals from Sachsenhausen concentration camp who arrived in May 1940 and were intended to act as functionaries within the prison system.

The first deportation transport comprised 728 Poles, including 20 Jews, and arrived on June 14, 1940, from the prison in Tarnów; they were housed in the former premises of the Polish Tobacco Monopoly until the camp next door was ready.

The prisoner population afterwards soared and by March 1941 had reached 10,900, largely comprised of Polish intelligentsia and underground resistance members.

The SS, which was of course in charge of the camp, did not want to do all the dirty work and chose trusted prisoners to act as their subordinates to supervise other inmates. These were known as 'kapos' and were often equal in brutality to those who gave them their orders.

A class system was introduced among the prisoners, with each category having to wear special marks on their clothing. At the bottom of the rung were Jews and Soviet prisoners of war.

At first, all of the prisoners had to work in neighbouring armaments factories, except on Sundays, while being fed on a well below subsistence regime. Many were worked to death, while others were locked in cells in Block 11, the Punishment Block, and left to starve to death, the idea of Höss's deputy Karl Fritzsch, or they were asphyxiated in rooms with no air.

THE 'DISCOVERY' OF ZYKLON B

Fritzsch never received a normal school education and for many years had worked on ships on the Danube. After joining the SS, he was posted to Dachau.

At Auschwitz, he quickly gained a reputation for sadism and brutality. On July 29, 1941, it was found that three prisoners were missing. Fritzsch sentenced 10 remaining prisoners to be locked in cells and starved to death.

One of the condemned, Franciszek Gajowniczek, was heard by fellow prisoner and Franciscan priest Maximilian Kolbe to cry: "My poor wife! My poor children! What will they do?" Kolbe immediately asked the SS if he could take Gajowniczek's place, and it was agreed. The priest survived the other condemned men and after being incarcerated for two weeks, was murdered with an injection of carbolic acid.

Miraculously, Gajowniczek survived Auschwitz and was eventually freed by the Allies. He was a guest of Pope John Paul II when Kolbe was canonised on October 10, 1982.

Not just satisfied with killing people, Fritzsch loved to inflict psychological torture. On the first Christmas Eve at Auschwitz, a Christmas tree with electric lights was set up in the main square. Beneath it, instead of presents, the Nazis displayed the bodies of prisoners who had died while working or who had frozen to death at roll call, which had been deliberately prolonged to cause maximum suffering in plummeting

With the boxcars in the background, women and children stand on the arrival platform at Auschwitz II, known as the ramp. There it was decided who would be immediately gassed, or became a slave labourer with a life expectancy of a few months. This picture is part of the Auschwitz Album – a unique photographic record of the arrival and selection procedure and which may have been taken by two SS men. The images follow the processing of Hungarian Jews in early summer 1944.

An everyday scene at Auschwitz-Birkenau in the summer of 1944 saw incoming Jews awaiting the selection process. In the background waits Crematorium II.

Jewish women and children being unwittingly sent to their deaths in Crematorium II pass Crematorium III on the far side of the railway tracks.

An hour from death: a Jewish woman carries a little boy towards the Auschwitz gas chambers. At the first Nuremberg Trials, surviving senior Nazi figures rushed forward in the dock to deny any knowledge of the atrocities in the camps after the court viewed images of children marched to their deaths. A newspaper reporter stood up and shouted out for them all to be taken outside and hanged there and then.

Women and children deemed unfit to work by the likes of Mengele stand in a small grove at Auschwitz, awaiting their turn in the gas chambers.

Little children hand in hand and their mothers are marched towards the gas chambers.

Elderly Jewish men and women who had been selected for death (but did not realise it) await their imminent fate next to the boxcars they arrived in.

temperatures. He also banned the singing of Polish carols.

However, Lagerführer Fritzsch's 'finest' moment of all came when he came up with the idea of using Zyklon B gas, a highly lethal cyanide-based pesticide derived from prussic acid, for mass murder, carrying out his first experiments on 600 Russian POWs and 250 Polish inmates in the bunker of Block 11 while Höss was away in late August 1941. When Höss returned, Fritzsch impressed him with more successful trials.

Ironically, after he was transferred to the Flossenbürg concentration camp, he was arrested during an internal SS investigation into corruption, and an SS court charged him with – of all things – murder. As his punishment, he was sent to fight on the front line, but his eventual fate remains unclear.

Höss oversaw the subsequent conversion of a bunker into a gas chamber in which 60,000 people were murdered during 1941-42, before SS troops converted it into an air raid shelter for their own use.

THE RAIL NETWORK OF EVIL

This first camp was followed by Auschwitz II-Birkenau, a purpose-designed extermination camp, which was needed because Auschwitz I was overflowing.

Building work started in October 1941, and its first gas chamber, which was ready the following March, was 'The Little Red House', a brick cottage converted into a murder facility by ripping out the inside and bricking up the walls. It was operational by March 1942. A second brick cottage, 'The Little White House', was then similarly prepared.

Höss later testified that Himmler had personally ordered him to prepare Auschwitz for the Final Solution. He said that Himmler had told him: "If it is not carried out now, then the Jews will later on destroy the German people," and explained: "He had chosen Auschwitz on account of its easy access by rail and also because the extensive site offered space for measures ensuring isolation."

Indeed, the superb rail connections enjoyed by Oswiecim made Auschwitz the hub of a continental-wide railway network based on an ideology of undiluted evil. As country after country fell, trains carrying Jews, gypsies and other hated people poured into the camp from every corner of occupied Europe, with just one goal – mass murder.

With more and more trains heading for Auschwitz, in early 1943 the Nazis decided to greatly increase the site's killing capacity. Crematorium II, which had been designed and built as a mortuary, with morgues in the basement and ground-level furnaces, was converted into a gas chamber. This meant fitting a gas-tight door on the morgue and adding vents for Zyklon B and ventilation equipment to remove the gas.

By March it was operational, and was quickly followed by the building of three further crematoria, just in time as Operation Reinhard reached its peak.

By that time, there were around 6000 SS members working at the camp.

NOT ENOUGH FOR HIMMLER

On January 20, 1943, Himmler wrote to Albert Ganzenmüller of the Transport Ministry, frustrated at the lack of progress on Operation Reynhard, and pleading for more trains. In desperation, when he received no immediate response, he rang his under-secretary of state for transport personally on February 3.

Himmler need not have worried, for meetings between the SS and the Deutsche Reichbahn to plan the next phase of deportation trains were well under way. Between January and the end of March, more than 60 special trains carrying 96,450 people steamed into Auschwitz from Poland, Belgium, Germany, France, Czechoslovakia, The Netherlands, Bulgaria and Greece.

That June, around 100,000 Jews were removed from the ghettos and work camps in Bialystok and ferried by train to their deaths at Auschwitz and Majdanek extermination camps, and between June and March 1943, a further 21 trains took 53,519 Jews to Treblinka.

Place such figures in perspective. The atomic bomb dropped on Hiroshima has been estimated by some researchers to have killed around 90,000 people. The populations of the modestly-sized English cities of Worcester and Bath are respectively around 93,000 and 90,000. Imagine if their entire populations were wiped off the face of the earth within eight weeks.

Despite compliance in Operation Reinhard, the deportation trains were not a big money-spinner for the railway: in fact, some experts have said that it probably just about broken even once its costs had been taken into account.

The Deutsche Reichsbahn billed the SS for the cost of operating the trains, but offered 'special discounts' for bulk travel.

The SS was charged half of the standard Third-class fare reserved for groups of over 400 people.

It was not just the blood of the deportees that was on the hands of the Reichsbahn. The property stolen from the victims was taken away from the murder camps and from possessed Jewish properties in freight trains for use elsewhere in Germany, where clothes in particular helped address shortages in the years of wartime austerity. It has been said that second-hand Jewish clothes were worn by much of the Fatherland's population at this time.

From the occupied lands in the west, 735 trains with 29,436 freight cars filled with furniture stolen from the homes of deported Jews were run to Germany. It has been said that the railway itself kept the contents of 1576 of these boxcars for itself.

One boxcar alone taken away from a murder camp was said to contain 3000kg of women's hair. Himmler had approved the use of human hair to make clothes. A highly-effective insulating material, it was woven into socks for U-boat crews, keeping them warm in a particularly cold environment. Horsehair was also used. It is known that a factory at Roth south of Nuremberg used such supplies to make insulated cables.

The railway line served another purpose at Auschwitz. It divided the men's camp from the women's.

These camps were set up for those who were not sent immediately to the gas chambers following the selections on the platform, and who were to be worked to death.

It was said at both Auschwitz and other concentration camps that female guards and overseers could exceed the unbridled brutality of their male counterparts.

Auschwitz produced at least two examples who stood out at least above the rest as they revelled in their power of life and death over the unfortunates who came into their realm.

The daughter of an Austrian shoemaker, Maria Mandel was either personally responsible or involved in the deaths of more than 500,000 female prisoners after rising through the ranks to become commandant of the women's camp and satellite camps under Höss in April 1942.

She took part in the selections of prisoners for the gas chambers and also oversaw beatings and floggings.

It was said that she stood at the entrance to the camp as incoming prisoners disembarked from the trains. Any who even dared to turn their head and glance at her was taken out of the line and never seen again.

When one prisoner, 22-year-old Mala Zimetbaum, was set to be publicly hanged for managing to escape with her Polish boyfriend Edek Galinski, she managed to cut her arms with a hidden razor blade in a suicide attempt to beat the gallows. It was Mandel who informed the rest of the camp that Berlin had ordered her to be burned alive in the crematoria instead.

Yet before she joined the SS at the age of 26 in October 1938, Mandel was nothing more than an ordinary office worker. In terms of career ambition, she was a nobody. In fairness, there appears to be no record of a blemish against her either.

In Chapter 1, we asked what made ordinary railwaymen, whose close counterparts across the North Sea in Britain were being fêted as national heroes for their enginemanship skills, turn into an army of accomplices to mass murder. Duty to the railway, obedience to orders and fear of reprisals have been given as reasons or excuses.

Yet the same pattern of blind indifference was not only apparent throughout much of the rest of Third Reich society, but Nazi ideology offered a new platform in which non-achievers, losers and no-hopers were given power, which in cases like Mandel became obscene absolute power for power's sake. It was akin to a beggar winning a Lottery payout, and splashing out on everything possible in an orgy of excess, but without any semblance of conscience or pity.

It was said that Mandel chose 'pet' Jews for herself, holding them from the gas chambers until she tired of them, and then selected a replacement.

It was Mandel who came up with the idea of having a Camp Orchestra, and in June 1943 ordered Polish music teacher Zofia Czajkowska to assemble it from female prisoners, who were then spared the gas chamber.

At first, the women's orchestra played at the gate when the work gangs went out, and when they returned. However, when the number of trains arriving at Auschwitz increased, the orchestra was posted to the entrance by the railway tracks, their melodies contrasting sharply with the sounds of the steam locomotive.

There, they played classical music to ease the minds of the fearful boxcar passengers who were being herded through the gate. This tactic maintained the lie that the prisoners were merely going to a better life in work camps in the east, right up to the last minute. Czajkowska was eventually replaced as conductor by Alma Rosé, the niece of composer Gustav Mahler. Reportedly, Mandel was not adverse to culture herself, and enjoyed hearing the orchestra play Madame Butterfly.

She also became fond of a young SS girl, Irma Grese, who had at one time worked in an SS hospital as an untrained nurse. Later assigned to work as a telephone operator in the Ravensbrück concentration camp, she arrived at Auschwitz-Birkenau in 1943, at the age of 20, was placed in charge of the road construction work unit, and was soon promoted to a camp overseer.

Grese acquired the nickname 'the beautiful beast' because of her own shocking levels of brutality. Also taking an active and regular role in selections for the gas chamber, she would beat inmates for no reason and walked around the camp with dogs and a whip, which she used on the faces of good-looking Jewish women prisoners. After Auschwitz was evacuated, she continued her sadistic activities at Ravensbrück and Bergen-Belsen. Both Grese and Mandel were hanged soon after the war.

PLATFORM'S SMILING SATAN

Waiting to greet the new arrivals on the platform ramp at Auschwitz was the most evil creature ever to grace a railway station with his presence.

Goebbels' anti-Semitic posters had for years caricatured the 'sinister menace to the world' presented by the typical 'base and ugly' Jew who inadvertently always resembled Fagin.

Yet here among the SS uniforms on the crowded ramp was the complete antithesis to the despised Jew: a handsome, youngish and decorated military officer, smartly dressed, with a calm demeanour, sober – unlike other SS officers at the platform – and with a pleasant and inviting smile.

His name was Dr Josef Mengele. His 21 months at the camp made his one of the most reviled names in history. If that brick gateway was indeed the doorway to hell, then here was Satan incarnate.

The theories of eugenics and racial purity brought millions of people on a one-way train ticket to Auschwitz. Exactly those same theories brought Mengele to this terminus too.

Born on March 16, 1911 in Günzburg, Bavaria, in 1935 Mengele graduated with a PhD in anthropology from the University of Munich. In January 1937, at the Institute for Hereditary Biology and Racial Hygiene in Frankfurt, he became the assistant to Dr Otmar Freiherr von Verschuer, a leading eugenicist who was obsessed with 'racial hygiene' and who was the director of the Kaiser Wilhelm Institute of Anthropology, Human Heredity, and Eugenics and the Institute for Genetic Biology and Racial Hygiene. He also had an interest in twins.

Early geneticists considered, with scant scientific proof to back up their belief, that research into twins was like a Rosetta Stone which could unlock secrets about human evolution. They assumed that the environment affected both identical twins in exactly the same way over an extended period of time. They were wrong, for observation shows that a mutation might affect the development of one of the twins early on, but not appear in the other.

In 1908 Fischer had visited what is now Namibia to study the mixed-race offspring of German or Boer fathers and African women and he recommended they should not reproduce. He also was involved in medical experiments on the Herero tribe. He was clearly influential , for in 1912 interracial marriage was banned in German colonies.

During Aktion T4, Fischer and others at the Hadamar Clinic oversaw the compulsory sterilisation of the 'Rhineland Bastards', children fathered by Africans serving as French colonial troops after the First World War, but with German mothers. The clinic's director was von Verschuer, under whom Mengele had studied.

After graduating in medicine, Mengele joined the SS in 1938. Conscripted in 1940, he asked to join the Medical Service of the Waffen-SS, the combat arm of the SS. He distinguished himself as a soldier in Ukraine, being awarded the Iron Cross Second Class in June 1941.

The following January, he dragged two German soldiers from a burning tank and was awarded the Iron Cross First Class. While on the Eastern Front, Mengele himself was wounded, and was declared medically unfit for combat. He was delegated to the Race and Resettlement Office in Berlin, where he joined up again with his teacher von Verschuer.

In May 1943 he was posted to Auschwitz with the aim of carrying out genetic experiments on the inmates, and had been allocated funding to do so.

He saw himself as leading the way for the future of the Aryan race. If he could find out the secrets of heredity, it would ensure that future German children would all be blonde and blue-eyed Nordics, with any deformity stamped out.

FINGER OF FATE

Under von Verschuer, Mengele had come to believe that twins held the key, and Auschwitz would allow him to take as many off the railway ramp at selection time as he wanted for research purposes. What matter, when they were as good as dead the day they boarded their train? In his laboratory, they would survive for much longer than if they had been sent in the left line straight to the gas chambers.

He regularly took his turn on the ramp as the selector, and in his calm, cool way, appeared to relish the power it game him over life and death. A slight wave of his finger or riding crop would send the next arrival in front of him to the left line or the right.

Camp survivor Oliver Lustig, a Romanian Jew, remembered such scenes: "In his prime, over the age of 30, tall, slender and dignified, SS Captain Dr Mengele would come to each selection dressed as if he was attending a ceremony: freshly shaved, his uniform impeccably ironed, his boots shined, and wearing fine buckskin gloves.

"Pedantic, meticulous, never in a hurry, he would lightly hum a tune and with a serene face, almost smiling, he would indicate, barely moving the index of his right hand raised at shoulder level, who should step out of line, out of life. He moved his finger naturally, calmly, detachedly, like a film director signalling an actor to exit the scene."

Meanwhile, the SS guards would call out for twins on his behalf, and when pairs were discovered, he would become very excited.

Snatched from their parents, screaming and without warning or explanation, the chosen pairs would be led away by soldiers. They were taken to a genuine shower block, and allowed to keep not only their own clothes but also their hair, before they were tattooed with a special number.

Afterwards, they were taken to a special 'twins' barracks' where measurements were taken and their statistics recorded. After that, they were taken for inspection by Mengele.

After roll call outside their barracks every day, Mengele again appeared to inspect them. He often brought them sweets and chocolate, and occasionally played with them. Some even called him 'Uncle Mengele'. The conditions in which the twins were kept were among the best in Auschwitz.

Then lorries came to take them off for their special assignments… in Mengele's series of laboratories.

Each pair of twins was forced to undress and lie beside each other so that comparative measurements could be made. Large quantities of blood were taken from them on a daily basis. Experiments involving mass transfusions of blood from one twin to another were carried out. Chemicals would be injected into their eyes, often causing severe and painful infections, and even permanent blindness. Mengele's aim: To see if brown-eyed children could be Aryanised to make them blue-eyed Germans.

The children underwent painful injections without explanation. Diseases such as typhus and tuberculosis were given to one twin and not the other: when the victim died, the other was killed also, so that a

The 'Himmelstrasse' or 'road to heaven', along which victims walked to the gas chamber in Sobibor. Sources say that around 250,000 Jews were murdered in Sobibor, famous for a mass escape of 600 slave labourers on October 14, 1943, of which 50 evaded recapture. Shortly after the revolt, the Germans closed the camp and planted pine trees to hide their crimes. JACQUES LAHITTE*

comparative autopsy could be done on both. The surviving twin was murdered with chloroform or phenol injections straight into their heart.

Some of the twins had been stabbed with a needle that pierced their heart and then were injected with chemicals which caused near immediate blood coagulation and death

Surgery was carried out without anaesthetic. Limbs were amputated and sexual and other organs removed.

At least one case was reported whereby Mengele tried to create a pair of Siamese twins by stitching a pair back to back. They died in indescribable pain within days.

Eyes, blood samples and tissues would be sent off to von Verschuer for further study. Mengele himself kept jars full of twins' eyeballs on a shelf in his laboratory.

Another area of macabre research by Mengele was dwarfism, and short people would be hauled off the trains: In one case, Mengele had had his eye on a family of dwarves, and pulled them out of the gas chamber just before the door was due to be closed and the Zyklon-B pellets thrown in.

Auschwitz survivor Alex Dekel later said: "I have never accepted the fact that Mengele himself believed he was doing serious work – not from the slipshod way he went about it. He was only exercising his power.

"Mengele ran a butcher shop – major surgeries were performed without anaesthesia. Once, I witnessed a stomach operation – Mengele was removing pieces from the stomach, but without any anaesthetic. Another time, it was a heart that was removed, again without anaesthesia. It was horrifying.

"Mengele was a doctor who became mad because of the power he was given. Nobody ever questioned him – why did this one die? Why did that one perish? The patients did not count. He professed to do what he did in the name of science... but it was a madness on his part."

Railways had given so much to humanity over the previous 130 years, and now they were taking people to endure new levels of suffering that even some of the worst despots in history would not have countenanced.

It gets worse, if that could ever be humanly possible. Several Auschwitz survivors alleged that Mengele had 300 children burned alive in an open pit.

In Mengele, the Complete Story, a book by Gerald Posner and John Ware, a Russian prisoner at Birkenau named Annani Silovich Perko gave a sworn statement made to the Moscow state prosecutor in September 1973 as follows: "After a while a large group (of SS officers) arrived on motorcycles, Mengele among them. They drove into the yard and got off their motorcycles. Upon arriving, they circled the flames; it burned horizontally. We watched to see what would follow. After a while, trucks arrived, dump trucks with children inside. There were about 10 of these trucks. After they had entered the yard, an officer gave an order and the trucks backed up to the fire and they started throwing those children right into the

In August 1944, members of the Sonderkommando at Auschwitz-Birkenau managed to secretly photograph the extermination process of the prisoners, and four photographs survive. This one shows women prisoners running naked, presumably to the 'shower block'.

Auschwitz commandant Rudolf Höss, who gave a highly-detailed and full and frank testimony of the mass murders at the camp – both during the Nuremberg Trials and in his memoirs written prior to him being hanged on April 16 by the Poles, immediately adjacent to the Auschwitz I crematorium.

Josef Mengele in SS uniform, possibly at Auschwitz.

Maria Mandel, the sadistic commandant of the Auschwitz women's camp.

Nazi anthropologist Wolfram Sievers.

Elisabeth Klein, murdered because the Nazis wanted her skeleton for a museum.

A surviving gas chamber at Auschwitz. AHP

Preserved furnaces in an Auschwitz crematorium. AHP

One of the mountains of victims' shoes at Auschwitz. AHP

An Auschwitz survivor's painting of children being thrown on to a fire.

Discarded canisters of Zyklon B gas, AHP

Auschwitz prisoners go no further. AHP

A floral tribute at the end of the railway line leading into the entrance to Auschwitz-Birkenau camp. AHP

fire, into the pit. The children started to scream; some of them managed to crawl out of the burning pit; an officer walked around it with sticks and pushed back those who managed to get out. Höss and Mengele were present and were giving orders."

Hitler, Himmler, Reinhard and Stalin were monsters because of the enormity of the orders they issued, but never then carried out themselves. If only a handful of the reports about him are to be believed, Mengele personally did much worse than even mass murder, with his own hands. Never mind the experiments that the world never heard about, because no witnesses survived to tell of them.

He was said to have sent more than 400,000 people to the gas chambers. Out of 1500 pairs of twins who fell into his clutches, only 100 could be found after the war.

Another individual in Auschwitz who defiled the title 'Doctor' in every which way was Carl Clauberg, who looked for cheap ways to sterilise women, such as using X-rays or injecting liquid acid into their uteruses without anaesthetic. It is believed he experimented on 700 women.

With the Red Army advancing, Clauberg moved to Ravensbrück concentration camp to continue his experiments on Roma women and was captured there in 1945 by the Soviet forces.

Put on trial in the USSR, he received a 25 year sentence but served only seven years due to a prisoner exchange. Back in West Germany, he outraged survivors by boasting of his scientific achievements, and was arrested in 1955 to face more charges. He died from a heart attack before his trial could start.

Mengele and Clauberg were by no means alone, for grotesque medical experiments were being carried out at many other concentration camps, each of them also a similar insult to the term 'science'.

With Mengele, however, the devil looked after his own, or perhaps himself. Eventually taken prisoner by the Americans under a false name, he was released in June 1945 and worked as a farmhand in Bavaria, before fellow Nazis helped him flee to Argentina, where he became acquainted with deportation train organiser Adolf Eichmann amongst many others. In Buenos Aires, Mengele practiced medicine and performed illegal abortions, at least one of which was fatal.

The capture of Eichmann by the Israeli secret service Mossad in May 1960 saw him flee to Paraguay with a passport in the name of José Mengele. He later moved on to Sao Paulo in Brazil, where he lived with Hungarian refugees Geza and Gitta Stammer. Under the name Wolfgang Gerhard, he spent the last seven years of his life in a bungalow.

It was said once that he underwent an operation for abdominal pains, and surgeons found the inside of his gut thick with tiny particles of hair bristles. Throughout his life in South America he had chewed his moustache constantly through nerves, wondering when the hand of justice would finally tap him on the shoulder as it had done with Eichmann. Maybe a quick death on the gallows would have ended his suffering much sooner. Maybe he deserved his years in exile in torment.

It was not to be. Despite the efforts of the likes of Nazi-hunter Simon Wiesenthal, it was nature which took the matter in hand. Mengele died on February 7, 1979, in Bertioga, Brazil, where he either drowned or suffered a stroke, while swimming in the Atlantic.

It remains an indelible stain on the history of each of the countries that gave Mengele refuge that they allowed him to live there, or some may say, even live at all.

The Nazis' persecution of gypsies was nothing new: Bavarian police had begun amassing a registry of Roma people in 1899, and a commission was later set up to coordinate police action against them in Munich.

However, when Hitler came to power the floodgates of hatred were opened on the wandering people of Europe, who like the Jews were classified as 'racially undesirable'.

The problem they faced here was defining who was or was not a 'gypsy'. (Note: This word is now often considered an insult, the people themselves refer to 'Roma' and 'Sinti'. But we shall use it here simply because it was the term used at the period in question.)

It was easier with Jews, because of their ancestry and the availability of religious records. Yet Roma had been Christians, and therefore in that respect alone 'jolly good sorts', for centuries, and so the records did not show who was of Romany descent.

Drawing on their expertise in the by-now barely-if-at-all 'science' of Eugenics, the Nazis looked to the measurement of physical characteristics to decide. They enlisted the aid of Dr Robert Ritter, a child psychologist at the University of Tübingen, a specialist in criminal biology, a discipline which holds that genetics determines criminal behaviour.

In 1936 Ritter was appointed director of the Ministry of Health's Centre for Research on Racial Hygiene and Demographic Biology at the University of Tübingen, and began a racial study of the estimated 30,000 Roma living in Germany in order to classify them by racial types.

His interviewers blackmailed the Roma who they met, threatening to send them to concentration camps unless they identified their relatives and their last known residence, in order to compile a registry of all German gypsies.

Ritter decided that Roma, having originated in India, were once Aryan, just like the Germans. However, over centuries of travelling from their ancestral home in India they had been corrupted by interbreeding with 'lesser' races.

DEGENERATE BLOOD
He declared that 90% of all German Roma were therefore carriers of 'degenerate' blood and criminal characteristics, and advocated forced Sterilisation. The remaining pure-blooded Roma could then, just like native Americans, or 'Red Indians', in the US, be placed on a reservation and studied further. Himmler later took up this idea, but the regime would not allow it.

The Nazis as a whole did not care about the differences between the gypsies, and in parallel with the persecution of Jews, they stepped up measures against Roma, who were also affected by the Nuremberg Laws, the Law for the Prevention of Hereditarily Diseased Progeny, and the Law against Dangerous Habitual Criminals, and many were indeed sterilised.

Before the world's attention turned on Germany for the 1936 Olympic Games, police rounded up all Roma in Greater Berlin along with their wagons and took them to Marzahn, to an open field located near a

cemetery and sewage dump in the east of the city, restricting their ability to travel in and out. Later, they were used as slave labour in armaments factories. As with the Jews, the Roma were now on the route to genocide.

Many were sent to concentration camps such as Bergen-Belsen, Sachsenhausen, Buchenwald, Dachau, Mauthausen and Ravensbrück, and made to wear badges to identify their category. Just as the Jews had the Star of David, Roma wore black triangular patches, the symbol for 'asocials' (prostitutes, beggars, chronic alcoholics and homeless vagrants), or green triangles, indicating 'professional' criminals.

In May 1940 the SS and police deported around 2500 Roma and Sinti from Hamburg and Bremen to Lublin, but the Nazi authorities in Poland objected to receiving more, and the shipments were suspended. As a result, gypsy camps such as Marzahn became long-term holding pens, and conditions grew more squalid by the day. The camp had only three water pumps and two toilets, and disease was rife. Local residents then demanded the deportation of the gypsies on health and security grounds, and police passed their complaints on to Himmler.

In autumn 1941 the German police deported 5007 Sinti and Lalleri gypsies from Austria to the Jewish ghetto in Lodz, where half died within a few months due to inadequate food, fuel and medicines. German SS and police transported the survivors to Chelmno in early 1942, and there they joined the Jews being murdered in the previously-mentioned gas vans.

Eventually, whole gypsy populations would be herded on to the trains to Auschwitz-Birkenau, Belzec, Sobibor and Treblinka, if not murdered locally en masse in the conquered territories to the east.

In December 1942 Himmler ordered the

The 'station sign' at Treblinka.
DAVID SHANKBONE*

Memorial stone at the site of the ramps at Bergen station, from where tens of thousands of prisoners were marched to Belsen concentration camp. BERNICOURT*

The symbolic 'remains' of the railroad in Treblinka, where 870,000 people were murdered, including 800,000 Jews.

The infamous sign over the entrance to Auschwitz. JENNIFER BOYER*

Auschwitz in the 21st century is one of the biggest tourist attractions in Poland, attracting a record 1,405,000 visitors in 2011. PIOTR DRABIK*

A group of tourists ponder over the preserved boxcar outside Auschwitz-Birkenau camp. AHP

deportation of all Roma from the expanded Germany. He made exceptions, however – on racial grounds. Those of 'pure gypsy blood' were excused, as well as those who had assimilated into everyday life and no longer behaved like gypsies, and those who had fought in the German military. The police, however, in many cases paid little attention to these get-out clauses when rounding up Roma – even deporting serving Wehrmacht solders while they were home on leave.

Most Roma, Sinti and Lalleri from 'Greater Germany', around 23,000, ended up in Auschwitz II, where the SS was kind enough to set up a special 'Gypsy Family Camp' for them.

For Mengele, as well as other 'medical' researchers in Ravensbrück, Natzweiler-Struthof and Sachsenhausen, Christmas had come early. There were guinea pigs galore to be had for his personal crusades against human decency in the name of his very non-scientific 'science'.

Needless to say, conditions in the gypsy camp deteriorated, with many inmates dying from typhus, smallpox or dysentery, while others were brought in by the trains and sent straight to the gas chambers, including 1700 Roma from the Bialystok region.

THE SS BACKS OFF

The camp commandant decided in May 1944 to murder all the gypsies, and accordingly SS guards sealed off the family camp. But the Roma had been forewarned and had armed themselves with shovels and iron pipes.

In this instance the SS backed off. The solution was to deport around 3000 fit Roma for labour at Auschwitz I and other camps during the summer.

There is nothing better than a soft target for a fully-fledged member of the SS, and once the fit men had gone, on August 2, the remaining 2898 elderly men, women, children and sick inmates were targeted, forcing them on to lorries taking them to the gas chambers with the aid of starving Alsatian dogs. Virtually all of the inmates in the camp were gassed within a day, while a few stray children who had managed to hide met the same fate within days. In all, 19,000 Roma were murdered at Auschwitz.

In occupied countries outside 'Greater Germany', the SS tended to regard 'pure' gypsies as harmless, but those of mixed race as dangerous and candidates for the deportation trains. The level of brutality differed from country to country, but again underlined the fact that the Holocaust was never an exclusive phenomenon.

Out of just under a million Roman in Europe before the war, it is believed that as many as 220,000 were murdered by the Germans and their Axis allies.

The murder of the Roma by the Nazis is known in the Romani language as 'The Porajmos' or 'The Devouring'.

Among Ritter's assistants at Tübingen had been Eva Justin, the daughter of a railway official, and who qualified as a nurse and psychologist. She also spoke Romani, thus earning the trust of Roma and Sinti people. As part of a dissertation on half-Romani children who had been raised in orphanages and foster homes away from their parent culture, she extensively measured the facial and physical characteristics of Roma.

After she had finished her studies, the 41 children she had used were sent to Auschwitz. Some of the children were used for Mengele's experiments and most were gassed.

It was said that Mengele's assistant once gathered together 14 pairs of Roma twins during one night. Mengele placed them on his polished marble dissection table and put them to sleep, before killing them instantly with a chloroform injection. He then dissected the bodies, making a note of each piece.

Justin gained her doctorate in 1944, and after the war was employed as a child psychologist, working with – who else – Ritter in Frankfurt-am-Main. A 1948 inquiry into Ritter's Nazi activities was closed because of lack of evidence, and he died three years later. A 1958 investigation into Justin's work for him was closed after it was decreed that a prosecution could not be brought because of a Statute of Limitations.

No doubt there are those who might think the pair not only should have been barred from working in any medical profession ever again, but should have appeared before a war crimes tribunal and suffered the consequences.

THE FINAL DEATH TOLL

To record accurately every aspect of the hell that was Auschwitz-Birkenau and its system of satellite labour camps, let alone the other Nazi killing fields, would surely take a library of encyclopaedias.

Deliberate starvation and malnutrition, savage beatings at the mere whim of guards, daily selections for the gas chamber of those who became too ill to work, taking out every 10th person at period intervals and murdering them, working inmates to death through exhaustion, relentless acts of degradation at every opportunity, all of these might even begin to make those nightmarish deportation journeys seem like a relative paradise in comparison, if anyone still had a will to care.

In total, around 1.1 million Jews were deported to Auschwitz, the bulk by rail.

SS and police authorities deported approximately 200,000 other victims to Auschwitz, including 140,000-150,000 non-Jewish Poles, the 23,000 Roma, 15,000 Soviet POWS and 25,000 others including Czechs, French, Lithuanians, Yugoslavs, Italians and Germans and Austrians themselves.

At least 960,000 Jews were murdered in Auschwitz, with 74,000 Poles making up the second-biggest contingent of victims.

Gassing continued until November 1944, at which point Himmler, nervous about his own position after the war, ordered the SS to dismantle the killing apparatus, and this was done the following January.

The railways had made it all possible. Yet as the Red Army, the eventual liberators, approached, many of the remaining inmates were forced at gunpoint to march hundreds of miles in sub-zero temperatures to other camps in Germany, on foot.

NIGHT AND FOG

One group of Jews in Auschwitz found themselves a protected species while they were imprisoned there. When a typhus epidemic swept through the camp, they were placed in the hospital's quarantine ward for their well-being. The Nazis had decreed that

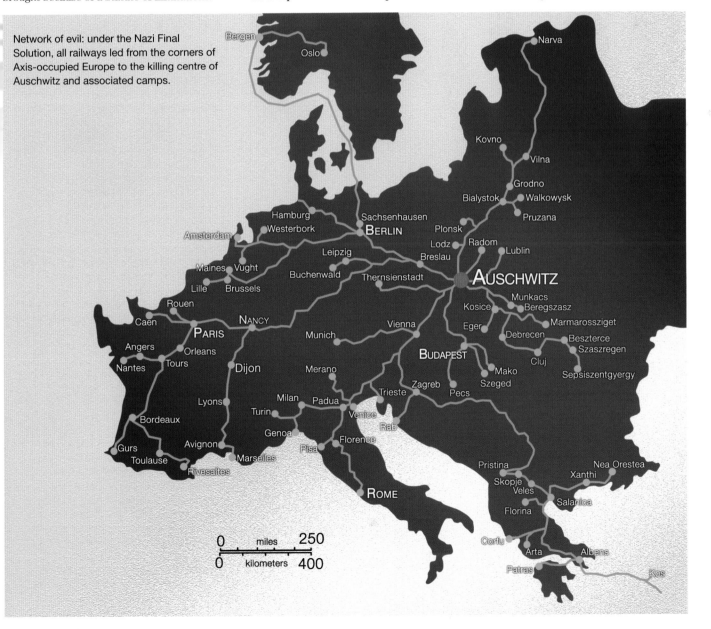

Network of evil: under the Nazi Final Solution, all railways led from the corners of Axis-occupied Europe to the killing centre of Auschwitz and associated camps.

The preserved remains of the Sobibor murder camp's terminal station. A narrow gauge railway was laid from the station to the burial pits, on which a small train from a local sawmill pulled tipper trucks, containing the victims who had died on the deportation trains to the camp. JACQUES LAHITTE*

The village station at Sobibor, the second death camp to be constructed as part of Aktion Reinhard, after Belzec. In March 1942 a short spur line from the station to the camp was built, complete with a ramp where the doomed deportees disembarked. It was screened from the station by a 'green fence' interwoven with branches so that passengers at the station could not see what was going on.

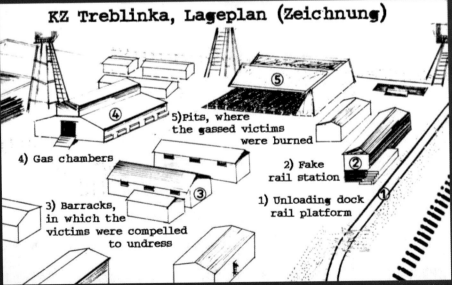

Sketch plan of Treblinka, as drawn by its commandant Franz Stangl. Here, victims were gassed with carbon monoxide generated by diesel engines from Red Army tanks that had been captured during the war. Like Mengele, Stangl fled to Brazil after the war, and after being extradited to West Germany to stand trial for mass murder, he was found guilty on October 22, 1970, sentenced to life imprisonment, and died of heart failure in prison in Düsseldorf on June 28, 1971. He said: "My conscience is clear. I was simply doing my duty."

no harm was to come to them… in Auschwitz.

However, this 'elite' set was destined to be taken to the relatively-obscure Natzweiler-Struthof concentration camp in the Vosges Mountains close to the Alsatian village of Natzwiller in France, and the town of Schirmeck, just over 30 miles south west from Strasbourg. It was the only concentration camp established by the Germans in modern-day France.

This camp had a special purpose – 'Nacht und Nebel' – 'Night and Fog'. Certain prisoners would be taken there and literally wiped off the face of the earth, as if they had never existed, simply disappearing forever into a black hole. Nobody would ever know of their fate.

The select group from Auschwitz had been chosen for one of the Nazis' most bizarre and depraved schemes of all – they were to be turned into grotesque museum exhibits.

Himmler gave the go-ahead for a collection of Jewish skeletons to be created – not from dead people, but from the living.

The project involved the creation of an anthropological display to show the world just how inferior a race the Jews were, and how they were sub-humans, or 'Untermenschen'.

The collection was to be housed at the Anatomy Institute at the Reich University of Strasbourg, where the corpses were prepared.

In charge of the operation was SS-Hauptsturmführer August Hirt, who was a chairman at the university during the war. He worked hand in glove with the 'Ahnenerbe', which was a Nazi think tank founded on July 1, 1935 by Himmler as a 'study society for intellectual ancient history', but in reality to research the anthropological and cultural history of the Aryan race, and to drum up evidence that prehistoric and mythological Nordic populations had once ruled the world.

Hirt worked with Wolfram Sievers, the Reichsgeschäftsführer, or managing director, of the Ahnenerbe from 1935 to 1945, Rudolf Hermann Brandt, personal administrative officer to Himmler and the son of a railway worker, and Bruno Beger, a German racial anthropologist who took part in Ernst Schäfer's 1938 journey to Tibet, backed by Himmler who believed that the Aryan race originated there and wanted proof. Beger also helped the Race and Settlement Office of the SS to identify Jews.

Originally, Jewish commissars in the Red Army who had been captured on the Eastern Front were to be used for the collection. However, this demonic trio began the collection with skeletons from prisoners at Dachau.

In February 1942 Sievers sent Himmler a report which read: "By procuring the skulls of the Jewish-Bolshevik Commissars, who represent the prototype of the repulsive, but characteristic sub-human, we have the chance now to obtain a palpable, scientific document.

"The best, practical method for obtaining

and collecting this skull material could be handled by directing the Wehrmacht to turn over alive all captured Jewish-Bolshevik Commissars to the Field Police. They in turn are to be given special directives to inform a certain office at regular intervals of the number and place of detention of these captured Jews and to give them special close attention and care until a special delegate arrives.

"This special delegate, who will be in charge of securing the 'material' has the job of taking a series of previously established photographs, anthropological measurements, and in addition has to determine, as far as possible, the background, date of birth, and other personal data of the prisoner.

"Following the subsequently induced death of the Jew, whose head should not be damaged, the delegate will separate the head from the body and will forward it to its proper point of destination in a hermetically-sealed tin can especially produced for this purpose and filled with a conserving fluid.

"Having arrived at the laboratory, the comparison tests and anatomical research on the skull, as well as determination of the race membership of pathological features of the skull form, the form and size of the brain, etc., can proceed. The basis of these studies will be the photos, measurements, and other data supplied on the head, and finally the tests on the skull itself."

In 1943 Hirt had 79 Jewish men, 30 Jewish women, two Poles and four Asians, who may have been Soviets, set aside at Auschwitz for 'special treatment'.

Beger chose them for their perceived stereotypical racial characteristics. The initial selections and preparations were carried with the aid of SS Obersturmführer Dr Hans Fleischhacker, a German anthropologist.

The Auschwitz contingent was transported to Natzweiler-Struthof on July 30, 1943. Here they were gassed, by Josef Kramer, the future commandant of Belsen-Bergen camp where he was dubbed the 'Beast of Belsen'. The murders took place on August 17 and August 19 that year. It is said that one prisoner was shot as he tried to escape being gassed. It was conjectured that the Asians were killed by the use of mescaline as a poison in an experiment by Hirt.

Kramer later testified: "I led about 15 women to the gas chamber. I told them they were going to be 'disinfected'. With the help of some of the SS guards, I got them completely undressed and pushed them into the gas chamber. When I closed the door they began to scream. I put some of the crystals that Hirt had given me into the funnel above the observation window. I would watch everything that was going on inside through it. The women continued to breathe for half a minute and then fell to the floor. I turned on the ventilation, and when I opened the door they were lying dead on the ground, full of shit. I told some of the male SS nurses to put the bodies in a truck and take them to the Institute of Anatomy at 5.30 the next morning."

Once these victims had been murdered, anatomical casts of their bodies were made. Then the bodies were stripped of flesh and reduced to skeletons.

Following D-Day, as the Allied forces approached Strasbourg, some of those involved began to worry that the corpses might be discovered.

Sievers sent a telegram which read: "The collection can be defleshed and rendered unrecognisable. This, however, would mean that the whole work had been done for nothing – at least in part – and that this singular collection would be lost to science, since it would be impossible to make plaster casts afterwards."

The remains of the victims were found at the university after France was liberated.

War correspondent Meyer Levin said: "The world had vaguely heard. But until now no one of us had looked on this. It was as though we had penetrated at last to the centre of the black heart, to the very crawling inside of the vicious heart."

Brandt and Sievers were hanged in Landsberg Prison on June 2, 1948 after being convicted at the so-called Doctors' Trial in Nuremberg, while Hirt shot himself. Beger was convicted by a West German court as late as 1974 as an accessory to 86 murders but, despite getting a light three year jail term, he did not serve any of it.

Amongst the many people who vanished at Natzweiler-Struthof were four captured women agents of the British Special Operations Executive, Diana Rowden, Vera Leigh, Andrée Borrel and Sonya Olschanezky, who were given lethal injections of phenol during a medical 'assessment' the day they arrived, on July 6, 1944. Borrel regained consciousness and fought to the last to avoid being placed in the crematorium along with the bodies of her three dead colleagues, but despite scarring the face of the camp executioner as he placed her in the oven, she could not escape.

Both the doctor who administered the injections and the executioner were later executed by the Allies for war crimes.

At this point, I have a question to ask of all those readers who insist that it is a harmless bit of fun to dress up in Nazi uniforms, whether you are Prince Harry at a fancy dress party in 2005 or a re-enactor at a railway family event, or who are considering voting for a minority far-right party with Nazi sympathisers among its supporters, maybe in protest at the main parties for not doing enough, 'as it will not do any harm because they will never get in'.

Are you still here?

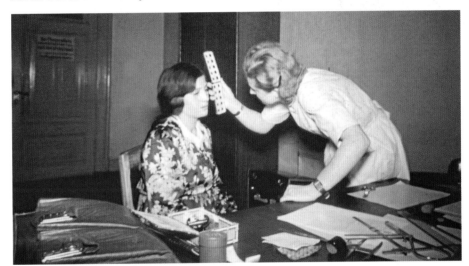

A research assistant at the Third Reich's Centre for Research on Racial Hygiene and Demographic Biology in 1938 compares a gypsy woman's eye colour to a chart as part of a racial survey of all gypsies living in Germany.

The first Nazi camp for gypsies was at Marzahn near Berlin.

BERLIN GHOST STATIONS
THE GHOSTS OF GLEIS 17

On the eastern outskirts on Berlin lies Grunewald station, a popular choice for commuters.

A subway leads beneath the station to a tree-lined small square with a few shops and a fruit stall.

The station, like many others in the modern world, has over the decades been pruned back and although still sizeable, is now much smaller than it was back in the Forties.

To the immediate east of the square, and now enshrouded in trees, is Grunewald's former Gleis 17 (Platform 17), which back then handled mainly freight traffic.

It has now been restored as a Holocaust memorial because it was from this platform that tens of thousands of Jews from Berlin were herded on to trains bound for the camps.

On October 18, 1941, the Reich Main Security Office began deporting Jews from Berlin, in cooperation with the Reich Ministry of Transport, on which it placed total reliance.

The same day, a special Deutsche Reichsbahn train steamed out of Grunewald with 1000 Jews on board, bound for the Łódź Ghetto.

Before the Jews boarded the train, city police helped the SS to gather the men, women and children together in the synagogue in Levetzowstraße in the Moabit district.

These intrepid heroes of the Third Reich then chased them down the road to Grunewald by foot.

From July 1942, these trains from Grunewald also went directly to the murder camps as well as the ghettos in Łódź, Kaunas Minsk, Riga and Theresienstadt.

Anhalter station near the heart of the city along with the Putlitzstrasse freight terminal were also used for special trains from 1942 onwards.

At first, as in many places elsewhere, carriages were used to make up the trains.

The last deportation train from Grunewald's Platform 17 ran in March 1945.

It is estimated than 55,000 Jews from Berlin and surrounding areas who left on these trains were murdered. That figures comprises around third of the city's entire Jewish population in 1933.

After the war, both the Bundesbahn in West Germany and the Reichsbahn in East Germany did not want to review the pivotal role played by Deutsche

Reichsbahn in Holocaust. In 1985, both German states celebrated the 150th anniversary of the railway, since the arrival of Der Adler, but neither seemed willing to even mention the darkest years.

After reunification, both state railways were amalgamated into Deutsche Bahn AG.

It was only then that it was decided to erect a memorial to remember the innocent victims of the perverted creed that waged war on humanity wherever it suited.

The railway's board agreed to erect a central memorial at Grunewald station marking the deportation transports handled by a willing and compliant Deutsche Reichsbahn.

A competition was held to design a memorial, the entries to be judged by a panel including Ignatz Bubis, chairman of the Central Council of Jews in Germany, Heinz Dürr, chairman of Deutsche Bahn AG, Professor Gottmann, director of the Museum of Transport and Technology, Jerzy Kanal, chairman of the Jewish Community in Berlin, and Dr Salomon Korn, an architect in Frankfurt-am-Main.

The winning design came from the architect team Hirsch, Lorch and Wandel based in Saarbrücken and Frankfurt-am-Main.

The memorial comprises 186 cast steel objects arranged in chronological order and set in the ballast next to the edge of

Anhalter station in the early days of the Third Reich.

A 1900 view showing the front facade of Anhalter station.

The ruined façade of Anhalter station. Nearly 10,000 Jews passed through those entrances before boarding the deportation trains.

Platform 17. Each of the objects lists the date of a transport, the number of deportees, the point of departure in Berlin and the destination.

No trains now depart from Platform 17. Vegetation has been deliberately left to grow between the rails to show that none ever will again.

The 180 yard platform had been demolished so it was rebuilt as part of the memorial, which was formally unveiled on January 27, 1998.

A path leads around the site, which is just yards away from the 'live' main line.

Anhalter station, once a major terminus in Berlin, nearly half a mile south of Potsdamer Platz, closed in 1952, but the ruin of its great entrance survives.

Opened on July 1, 1841, as the terminus of a line to Jüterbog, it became the focal point of a network from where services ran to Leipzig, Frankfurt-am-Main and Munich, eventually expanding into the biggest and grandest station in continental Europe when it was opened by Kaiser Wilhelm I and Chancellor Otto von Bismarck on June 15, 1880, after having been designed by architect Franz Heinrich Schwechten.

Hitler's plan to turn Berlin into the world capital Germania would have seen Anhalter station superseded by two new termini, Nordbahnhof (North Station) and Südbahnhof (South Station). Albert Speer, Hitler's chief architect before he became Minister of Armaments and War Production, would have taken Anhalter, by then cut off from its approach tracks, and turned it into a swimming pool.

However, during the war Anhalter was used to deport 9600 Jews, in groups of 50 to 100. Here, boxcars were not used: the Jews were deported in ordinary passenger coaches which were marshalled into regular trains departing according to the normal timetable.

It is believed that 116 of these special trains left Anhalter, all going to the Theresienstadt concentration camp in Czechoslovakia before being sent on another and final train to the murder camps.

The monumental station was badly damaged in a bombing raid on November 23, 1943, that left it incapable of handling long-distance trains, and after two further heavy attacks in February 1945, which left the building in ruins, no public trains ran at all.

The Nazi ideologists' raw obsession with murdering Jews was relentless. With the Red Army steamrollering its way towards the city, you might have thought that even the most hardcore Hitler fanatic might have had something better to do, staring the likelihood of a crushing defeat in the face.

Grunewald station as it was during the Second World War.

Ruined infrastructure which formed part of a goods terminal that for a brief period in history also carried people. ROBIN JONES

The tracks are still there, but no trains will ever depart from Platform 17 again. ROBIN JONES

Flee, save your own skin, melt away into the crowd, or maybe take up a gun and fight the Soviets.

None of these. On March 27, 1945, just six weeks before the final surrender of Berlin, and just over a month before the Fuhrer committed suicide, a final deportation train from Anhalter took 42 Jews to Theresienstadt. It was said that Adolf Eichmann wanted to be kept busy murdering harmless people by the million so he would not himself be sent to fight armed soldiers on the Eastern Front.

US servicemen dismantled what was left of Anhalter station's roof in March 1948, and a limited train service restarted. However, the growing friction between the city's occupying forces ended all that. Anhalter was served by trains arriving from places in Soviet-controlled East Germany, but lay in

West Berlin. Accordingly, on May 17, 1952, the Soviets diverted all remaining trains to a station in their Eastern Sector, the Ostbahnhof, and Anhalter was closed forever, despite a blueprint being drawn up for a modern station on the site.

The station was finally demolished in 1960 despite protests, but the ruined central façade was allowed to remain, and indeed has been restored several times since.

Nearby stands a memorial display board honouring the Berlin Jews taken from here

and elsewhere to their deaths. On the Putlitz Bridge overlooking the Putlitzstrasse freight yard, a modern stainless steel memorial to the Jewish deportees was completed in 1992.

What if the worst had happened, and Britain had fallen? Which London stations would have infrastructure preserved as a memorial to the tens of thousands of deportees who would never return?

Would a time have ever come when we would have ever been free to create such memorials?

Signpost to the Grunwald Holocaust memorial

The Platform 17 Holocaust memorial which takes the form of steel edging into which the number of Jews deported on a particular day and the name of their destination are cast. ROBIN JONES

In 1991 the Polish artist Karol Broniatowski created this concrete block embedded with human silhouettes representative of the passage the Jews took to the Grunewald goods yards tracks for deportation. ROBIN JONES

Flowers and candles left at the side of the tracks in memory of the tens of thousands who left Platform 17 on the way to their deaths. ROBIN JONES

CHAPTER NINE

HITLER'S SPECIAL TRAIN

Another and genuinely 'special' train ran over the rail networks of the Axis-occupied countries.

It was the 'Führersonderzug', or 'Führer's Special Train'.

Adolf Hitler used the 15-coach train to travel between his 13 headquarters, including the underground bunker at the Reich Chancellery in Berlin. Before its introduction, there had been a peacetime version.

The wartime special train itself, introduced in 1939 and codenamed Amerika or Erika, was used as a fully-fledged headquarters. Indeed, it can be regarded as the first of his field headquarters, as at the outbreak of war, there were no permanent headquarters built for him.

This train was used by Hitler during the attack on Poland. Later, Hitler and his ally Benito Mussolini met each other several times at the station on the Brenner Pass – through the Alps, along the border between Italy and Austria – arriving there in their own special trains. On March 18, 1940, Hitler was the guest in Mussolini's train as he wanted to muster up support for his planned invasion of Western Europe.

The first permanent installation which became a Führer Headquarters was the Felsennest, near Bad Münstereifel, which was used by Hitler during the Battle of France in May 1940.

The train was used during the Balkans campaign in spring 1941, which ended with the capture of Crete by German and Italian forces on June 1, giving Hitler the significant strategic advantage of direct access to the Mediterranean. Based at Mönichkirchen in Austria during this operation, FHQ (Führer Headquarters) Frühlingssturm (Spring Storm), the campaign was overseen from the train.

A tunnel south of the station was prepared to accommodate the train in the event of an air

Adoring crowds greet Hitler aboard his special train.

One of the locomotives which pulled Hitler's train was Class 01 Pacific No. 01 150-2, seen at Regensburg on a Hof train in the summer of 1973, its last year of service. The BR 01s were the first standardised express passenger steam locomotives built by the unified German railway system. A popular heritage locomotive, on October 17, 2005 it was badly damaged in a fire at Nuremberg/Gostenhof depot. 8474TIM

raid. Apart from short walks to a small hotel next to the station, Hitler did not venture from his train which was parked beyond the station platform. Indeed, he celebrated his 52nd birthday there.

Afterwards, it was not used again as a headquarters, but Hitler continued to use it throughout the war when he travelled between Berlin, Berchtesgaden, Munich and other static headquarters.

Two days before Operation Barbarossa (codename for Germany's invasion of the Soviet Union), Hitler arrived at the Wolfschannze or Wolf's Lair – his massive headquarters fortress in East Prussia – abroad his private train on June 24, 1941. It was there that on July 22, 1944, Claus von Stauffenberg's courageous but ill-fated time bomb attack, designed to kill Hitler, was enacted.

Führer Headquarters were designed to work as command facilities for Hitler, providing communications facilities, conference rooms, safety measures, bunkers, and guard facilities. The special train was no different.

The train included a special Flakwagen armoured anti-aircraft train flatbed car with two anti-aircraft guns – most often a pair of Flakvierling cannon batteries – one at each end of the car. These batteries were not only the primary German light anti-aircraft gun, but by far the most numerously produced German artillery piece throughout the Second World War.

The Flakvierling was a common fixture on trains, and on Hitler's command train,

pairs of them were mounted on either end of a "camelback" flatbed car and then covered to make it look like a boxcar. It was reported that the batteries were never called into action while the special train was in use.

In addition, there would be two locomotives delegated to the train.

Behind them would run two baggage cars; the Führerwagen for Hitler's own use; the command car or Befehlswagen, including a conference room and a communications centre equipped with a short-wave radio transmitter; a Begleitkommandowagen, for the accompanying Reichssicherheitsdienst, his SS bodyguard which later provided protection for other high-ranking Nazi leaders; a dining car; two carriages for guests; and two sleeping cars.

There was also a press wagon, where Hitler received and read newspaper reports, but never invited journalists aboard.

The train was codenamed Erika, and later Brandenburg.

Serving Hitler's Bavarian mountain retreat at Obersalzberg, above the town of Berchtesgaden, where Martin Bormann oversaw the construction of a huge complex of buildings for top Nazis, a doorway led from the platform at the local station so the Fuhrer could walk into his personal reception area.

However, it was not only Hitler who had his own train.

There was the 'Ministers' Train', used by Foreign Minister Joachim von Ribbentrop

and Heinrich Himmler. Ribbentrop had another called 'Westfalen' while Himmler used 'Steiermark', also called 'Heinrich' or 'Transport 44'.

The chief of the Armed Forces High Command Sonderzug had a special train called 'Afrika' or 'Braunschweig'. The Armed Forces Operations Staff had a command train called 'Atlas' or 'Franken'.

Hermann Goering, well known for his love of model railways, had a special train known variously as 'Asien' or 'Pommern'.

The supreme commander of the Navy had a train called, appropriately, 'Atlantik' or 'Auerhahn', while 'Enzian' was the Sonderzug of the command train used by the chief of the intelligence branch of the Luftwaffe.

'Robinson 1' carried the chief of the Command Staff of the Luftwaffe, while the chief of its General Staff rode in 'Robinson 2'.

Hitler last used his private train on January 15, 1945, when he left the Führer Headquarters at Adlerhorst at 6pm and arrived back in Berlin the next day. He would never leave the city again.

The Wehrmacht later destroyed his personal carriage, but the others survived in regular use until the 1960s, and one can be seen inside the Deutsches Dampflokomotiv-Museum (German Steam Locomotive Museum) in Neuenmarkt, Upper Franconia, in northern Bavaria. It formed part of a special train that was used in 1955 by West German chancellor Konrad Adenauer on his historic visit to Moscow.

Hitler's special train, which was also used as his headquarters.

Inside the Deutsches Dampflokomotiv-Museum stands saloon car No. 10242, which served as the dining car in Hitler's train. It was built in Munich in 1937. DDM

DAY OF THE
KRIEGSLOKS

PKP Ty2 Kriegslok 2-10-0 No. 7173 passes Castor with a
Santa special on December 15, 1991. BRIAN SHARPE

Few pictures survive of the deportation trains, and the records of their movements, let alone the rolling stock. These are scant and deliberately so. As a prelude to the postwar years when almost everyone in German society had no knowledge of the death camps from the top down, records were destroyed to place a tourniquet on the truth of what had really happened.

With regard to locomotives, the image that immediately comes to mind are the huge austerity Class 52 Kriegsloks (war locomotives). The no-nonsense powerful 2-10-0s were built to a basic, raw and starkly brutal design with little refinements and huge smoke deflectors their most prominent feature.

The Kriegsloks, however, came on stream towards the latter stages of Operation Reinhard, and undoubtedly hauled many of the deportation trains.

Before them, a variety of seasoned freight locomotives were used: Class 55 0-8-0s, 55.1 or 56 2-8-0s, 57 0-10-0s and 58 2-10-0s.

The Class 55s emerged as Prussian G8.1s between 1913-21, and became the biggest class of state railway locomotives in Germany, with more than 5000 built. Over 1000 were still in use after the war, with the >>

Did this Kriegslok ever haul trains to Auschwitz? It was certainly shedded in the locality during the war. No. Ty-406 was built at Sosnowiec by Orenstein & Koppel in 1943, as works No. 13821, DRB No. 52.4770. Now preserved, it is pictured at Konotop in 1998. Konotop was in Germany until 1945 and a border station. TREVOR JONES

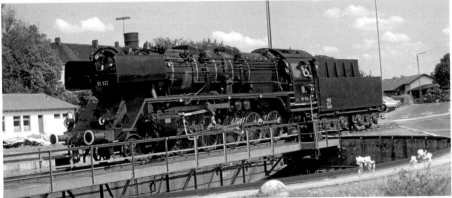

After modernisation, steam was banned by Deutsche Bundesbahn until the 150th anniversary of German railways in 1985 when limited operations were allowed on two routes from Nuremberg. Preserved Class 50 No. 50.622 stands on the turntable at Amberg on June 5, 1985. BRIAN SHARPE

No. 7173 departs from Peterborough Nene Valley station on March 30, 1991. BRIAN SHARPE

>> last being retired at Christmas 1972.

The Class 58s had originated as Prussian State Railways Class G12 during the First World War, when the advantage of standard locomotive classes was shown. At the time, each state railway had its own locomotive types, but if they were fighting a unified war, and there had to be bespoke train movements across Germany, there was a great disadvantage from a servicing and maintenance point of view.

For military purposes, a fast, powerful, freight locomotive without a high axle load was needed.

Nearly 1500 of them were inherited by Deutsche Reichsbahn, where some continued in service until 1953, with others in East Germany soldiering on until the late Sixties.

The Class 57 tender engine (Prussian G10) could be found all across the German system. They fulfilled much the same duties as the Class 55 0-8-0s because of the better weight distribution could work on all sorts of lines. They lasted well into the Sixties, however, the 'modern' locomotive which took prominence throughout the latter stages of the war was the Kriegslok.

It was a wartime development of the pre-war Class 50, using fewer parts and expensive scarce materials to speed production, reducing maintenance time and labour needs.

Additional design changes gave the engines and their footplate crews better protection against the cold winters experienced on the eastern front. They were designed by Richard Wagner, the chief of design in the design office of Deutsche

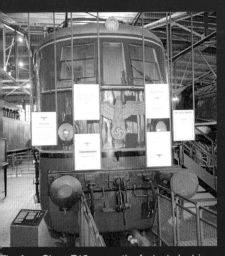

The four Class E19s were the fastest electric locomotives of the Deutsche Reichsbahn. They reached a maximum speed of 112mph, but were designed for speeds up to 140mph, and were the most powerful single frame locomotives in the world of their time. E19 01, now housed inside the Deutsches Technikmuseum, is displayed in its original 1938 red livery with Deutsche Reichsbahn Nazi era badge. ROBIN JONES

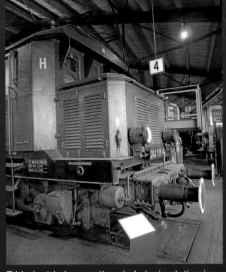

E44 electric locomotives in Leipzig station in 2009. The E44s were the first major class of German electric locomotives and were a dazzling success in the 1930s. A total of 174 were built during World War Two as Kriegselektrolokomotiven. This example is displayed inside the Deutsches Technikmuseum in Berlin. ROBIN JONES

Preserved Kriegslok 2-10-0 No. 52-4966-9 inside the Deutsches Technikmuseum. ROBIN JONES

Reichsbahn from 1922 -42.

In 1936, Wagner was given a gold medal of service by the Society of British Locomotive Engineers. He is well remembered for the standard smoke deflectors on Deutsche Reichsbahn locomotives, but this aspect was just part of a much greater achievement.

During the war, the German locomotive builders were merged into the Gemeinschaft Grossdeutscher Lokomotivhersteller, a subdivision of the Hauptausschuss Schienenfahrzeuge founded in 1942. As a result of combined resources, Germany was able to build more than 6700 Class 52s. Indeed, by sheer volume of numbers, they became one of the biggest locomotive classes in the world.

In charge of HAS were Reich transport minister Julius Dorpmüller and Albert Speer, Hitler's architect and the minister for munitions and armaments.

A variation of the Kriegslok was the large Class 42, of which nearly 900 were built. Their design featured improvements to the driving and running gear. It was intended to build high numbers of these locomotives, but those plans died with Hitler.

Wagner came up with an engine that was durable and efficient, but unlike his British

Kriegslok No. 50-740-8 in Bahnhof Mayen-Ost on May 20, 2006. LOTHAR SPURZEM

Class 52 Kriegslok No. 8080-5 taken at Jaworzyna Slaska in Poland on Saturday, September 29, 2012. It is double heading a German steam special from Cotbus & Berlin, which visited Poland that day. Built in 1944 as No. 52.5015 and no doubt used on military trains of one sort or another, like others in the 1960s, many of the Class 52 Kriegsloks were rebuilt with a larger boiler and renumbered in a 52 8000 series. The locomotive is owned by Lokschuppen and based at Löbau. TREVOR JONES

Deutsche Reichsbahn Class 50 No. 50.3645 heads a freight train near Wegeleben, DDR on March 13, 1981. These 2-10-0s were built from 1939 as standard locomotives for hauling goods trains, and was one of the most successful designs produced for the Deutsche Reichsbahn. It was produced as part of the Nazi preparations for the Second World War, and regarded as a provisional war locomotive or Übergangskriegslokomotiven. Despite wartime losses, a large number remained in service in 1945, and 2159 of them were taken over by the Deutsche Bundesbahn. BRIAN SHARPE

counterparts, did not consider a high power-to-weight ratio a priority. His Kriegsloks therefore had a low axleload of 15 tons and could haul 40% more freight than the Prussian locomotives they superseded. They could haul 4000 tons at 50mph effortlessly.

Yes, they became a trademark of Nazi domination of the continent in the later years of the war, and a symbol of totalitarian brutality beyond its worst excesses. Yet it was obviously not the machines that were evil, but those who used them for their own purposes.

After the defeat of Germany, many war-ravaged countries eagerly seized Kreigsloks to help them rebuild their own railway system. Norway seized 74 which the Germans had taken to that country during the collaborationist Vidkun Quisling regime, as war reparations. Around 100 were built for Romanian State Railways, and more than 150 were used by the Bulgarian State Railways. Around 10 were built specially for Turkey, which took more than 40 second-hand examples on after the war.

Poland had more than 1000 Class 52 and ran them until the Nineties. Communist East Germany used around 800 and even Austria ran examples in service until 1976. Hungary continued using examples donated by the Soviets as war trophies into the Eighties.

Turkey and Bosnia also ran them long after many other European countries had modernised.

They were popular with railway authorities in the eastern countries, because of the Wagner design making them easy to maintain, while delivering power.

In Britain, examples of such locomotives may be the imported USATC S160 2-8-0s, which ran in service during the later war years, and the UK's own War Department Austerity 2-10-0s, several of which lasted well into the British Railways eras, with others sold for use abroad.

One Kriegslok ended up in Britain, run for many years in service on the Nene Valley Railway at Peterborough, a line which can handle rolling stock built to the wider continental loading gauge.

Not all Kriegsloks were steam, however.

Germany gave the world the electric locomotive, back in 1879, where the first electric railway was demonstrated at the Berlin Trades Fair. It is now displayed in the Deutsches Technikmuseum in Berlin.

It was the invention of Ernst Werner von Siemens (1816-1892), who in 1847 with Johann Georg Halske, built the first electrical long-distance telegraph line in Europe and established a telegraph link between Ireland and America.

In 1881, a pioneer electric tramway near Berlin was built.

Siemens was considered the greatest inventor of his age, and today his name is used as the unit of electrical conductance, the siemens.

In 1911, the first long distance electrification in Germany, the Bitterfeld-Dessau line, was opened.

With the start of the Great Depression,

Class 01 Pacific No 01.118, which dates from 1934, heads a short railtour working in January 1986. This class comprised the first standardised steam express passenger locomotives built by the unified German railway system. The idea of standardisation was that it would reduce maintenance costs. Built in 1934, No. 01118 is the only one to have been operational without interruption until today. BRIAN SHARPE

the German railways were starved of investment, yet still sought to modernise. Electrification was seen as the way ahead, but the cost of building and maintaining the existing types of electric locomotives had to be reduced.

Three sample locomotives were built, one of which was Bo-Bo No. E44 001, constructed by Siemens-Schuckert SSW at its own expense in the hope of winning orders from the Reichsbahn.

This locomotive, which began trials in February 1931, is said to have taken German railways into the modern age as far as electric traction was concerned, with individually-powered axles in bogies outside the main frames. and led to a series of different types being developed for batch building.

Still in the depression, a pair of prototype Co-Co freight locomotives of class E 93 were ordered in 1932. This type proved to be so

successful that Deutsche Reichsbahn commissioned AEG and Siemens/Krauss Maffei to develop a more powerful version, in the form of Class E94, the Kriegselektrolokomotiv. The first, No. E94 012, which had a top speed of 56mph, was entered into service on September 4, 1940.

It is unclear as to whether deportation trains were hauled by these or any other electric locomotives.

A Prussian G 8.1 freight locomotive No. 55.3345, at the Bochum-Dahlhausen Railway Museum in Germany around 1980. TOBIAS NÜSSEL*

THE SOFTEST TARGETS OF ALL

The monument to the tens of thousands of women, children and babies at Ravensbrück overlooks the lake. ROBIN JONES

Fürstenberg has welcomed visitors for around a century. An attractive small town, it took off as an inland resort following the building of the Prussian Northern Railway.

Lying on the shores of the Schwedtsee Lake, today a haven for weekend boaters, it still attracts daytrippers from the capital, which is just an hour away by train.

I arrived with my companion on a sweltering September day in a heatwave. Beneath an azure sky, the sunshine brought out the best of the pastel hues of the historic though unostentatious buildings.

The place is very pleasant and the type of place you would dream of either living or owning a second home in. We walked into a welcoming wayside cafe for a few soft drinks to cool down. Just up the road, the signposts told us we were entering the equally delightful village of Ravensbrück, which is almost a suburb of Fürstenberg.

I stopped to stroke a passing ginger cat. The lady of the house came out and using sign language and halting English was proud to tell me that she had three cats in all.

I replied I had four and we struck up a friendly conversation.

It was a sharp contrast to the scenes 60 or more years ago when the townsfolk of Fürstenberg and Ravensbrück turned their backs on incoming train passengers.

Nobody wanted to see or hear, let alone speak to the long lines of women being marched from Fürstenberg (Havel) station to the concentration camp designed to house some of the softest Nazi targets of all – woman and children.

HIMMLER'S CHOICE

Himmler selected this very attractive lakeside location for the camp in late 1938, because it was easy to reach but also somewhat out of the way, surrounded by water and forests. He also owned the dismal swampland site on which it was built. Ravensbrück was the only major Nazi concentration camp for women.

At the end of 1938, 500 prisoners from the Sachsenhausen concentration camp were taken to Ravensbrück in order to build the new camp. A total of 14 barracks, a kitchen and an infirmary were erected, as well as a small totally isolated camp for men.

The camp complex was surrounded by a high wall with electrified barbed wire on the top and guarded by watchtowers.

The first prisoners arrived in Ravensbrück on May 18, 1939. Not a Jewish transport, it comprised 860 German women and seven Austrian women from the Lichtenburg women's concentration camp in Saxony. They were followed 11 days later by 400 gypsy women from Austria while on September 28, 1939, the first Polish women arrived.

Following the outbreak of the Second World War, women from 20 different European countries were brought by train to Ravensbrück, including several convoys of Russian women in 1942.

The prisoners were organised into categories, each with a distinctive coloured triangle, often indicating their nationality.

Political prisoners, resistance fighters and Soviet prisoners of war wore red triangles, Jehovah's Witnesses wore purple triangles, 'asocials' which included lesbians, prostitutes and gypsies had black triangles, and criminals – including those who broke Nazi laws – wore green triangles.

Jewish women had yellow triangles, but if they were also political prisoners they wore a red triangle and yellow triangle that formed a Star of David or a yellow stripe on top of the red triangle. A letter within the triangle indicated the prisoner's nationality.

As would be expected, the general conditions were as bad as the other concentration camps, with deliberate starvation to death, beatings and torture, attacks by dogs, hangings and shootings on a daily basis.

Barracks designed for 250 women later housed 2000, with three to four to a bed and thousands of others lying on the floor without blankets. There were plagues of lice and disease was rampant.

When 500 Jewish women arrived by deportation train from Hungary in autumn 1944, they were placed in a huge tent with a straw floor because the camp was so cramped. Many quickly died.

RAVENSBRÜCK GETS ITS OWN STATION

Until August 1942, all deportation trains to Ravensbrück ran to Fürstenberg (Havel) station, which also received goods supplies for the concentration camp, including Red Cross parcels.

A maximum of 50 women were taken in a carriage to Fürstenberg. Some were ordinary passenger coaches with the doors locked, while others were Deutsche Reichsbahn's special prison coaches.

Many were inmates of prisons all over Germany, and at the start, Sinti and Roman gypsies made up the largest number of Ravensbrück prisoners, but it became used for an increasing number of Polish political prisoners or slave labourers, who by the end of 1941 made up about a quarter of the population.

About 100 yards to the north of the station there was a siding with a loading ramp. It was said that the deportation trains arrived there at night if possible so the residents would not see what was happening.

The occupants of the passenger carriages and boxcars were driven out by uniformed female guards with wolfhounds. At least two dogs had to be provided for transports of 50 prisoners or more, according to Ravensbrück regulations. The prisoners were then ordered to march the two miles to

Ravensbrück inmates toil at the end of a narrow-gauge railway, with the tipper truck presumably pushed there by hand.

the camp on foot, in the case of Jewish women, or were taken there by lorries with canvas roofs.

Fürstenberg resident Georg Dietrich Zollner said: "They told us again and again that the prisoners were criminals, thieves and murderers."

Deportee Annette Eekman later recounted: "People on the side of the road turned away and hid their children as we marched by. That was also very unpleasant. As if we were dangerous human beings."

Anneliese Ahlgrimm, the daughter of the Ravensbrück builder who erected massive chalet-style houses for the camp's SS guards, said: "If any one of the Fürstenberg residents pretends that they did not know what was going on in the concentration camp, they are obviously lying. It happened right in front of our eyes."

On August 15, 1942, a railway station built to directly serve the camp was opened at the end of a short branch off the Fürstenberg (Havel)-Templin line.

It comprised just one platform, with no roof. Its purpose was to take prisoners directly to the camp out of sight of townsfolk. Plans to extend the line into the camp itself never came about.

From this new Ravensbrück station, it was a short walk to the eastern gate of the camp.

The prisoners were expected to line up in fours. They were then marched to the camp baths. As the Red Army made progress on the eastern front, the SS began transferring prisoners from the concentration camps of Majdanek, Stutthof and Auschwitz-Birkenau to Ravensbrück. Prisoners from the Soviet Union, France, Hungary and Slovenia began arriving en masse in 1944.

Romanian Jew Sara-Tuvel Bernstein was sent to Ravensbrück in a locked carriage in the autumn of 1944 after being forced to march from Nazi-occupied Budapest to the Austrian border. Her deportation train took two weeks to reach its destination.

"No woman was allowed to leave the train – except as a corpse," she recounted. "Some died of thirst, the tightness and the stench."

The camp population contained hundreds of children, who suffered mercilessly at the hands of the overseers.

Newborn babies would be immediately separated from their mothers and drowned or thrown into a sealed room until they died, often deliberately in front of the mother.

There are witness statements to the burning alive of children in the crematorium. Others, it was claimed, were buried alive, poisoned, strangled, or drowned.

Among the children sent to Ravensbrück were Czechs from Lidice, a village that had been completely destroyed by the Nazis in revenge for the assassination of Reich Protector Reinhard Heydrich. Others arrived with their Polish mothers after the collapse of the Warsaw Uprising in 1944. Most of them died from starvation.

The uprising prompted mass transports from the Polish capital, with 12000 women arriving at Ravensbrück.

Trains also played another key role for the Nazis at Warsaw – with 300 carriages loaded with plundered valuables also sent to Ravensbrück for sorting. These valuables were stored by the SS in eight huge wooden barracks. The loot included pianos, jewellery, quality dresses, carpets and household items.

Freight trains also brought in raw materials for the camp's own workshops, such as furs for making coats. An order had been passed on January 5, 1942, ordering all Jews to hand in their furs and woollen clothes to their local police station. Other fur coats came from Auschwitz.

On February 2, 1944, 958 alighted from a deportation train of boxcars from France at Fürstenberg, many members of resistance movements. Some had already been sentenced to lifelong forced labour and others to death.

THE ABSENCE AND DESTRUCTION OF HUMANITY

As at Auschwitz, Nazi doctors carried out grotesque medical experiments on prisoners, mostly again with no scientific basis, or simply killed them outright by lethal injection. Girls as young as eight were sterilised by direct exposure to X-rays, while pregnant women were aborted by force.

The principal Josef Mengele counterpart at Ravensbrück was Karl Franz Gebhardt. Gebhardt served as chief surgeon of the staff of the Reich Physician SS and personal physician to Himmler.

When Heydrich was injured by an anti-tank grenade in the assassination attempt on May 27, 1943, Gebhardt was sent to Prague to treat him.

As history records, the grenade inflicted shrapnel wounds but did not kill him outright. Hitler's personal physician Theodor Morell suggested to Gebhardt that he should treat Heydrich with sulfonamide, an early antibiotic, but the advice was refused. Accordingly, Heydrich died from sepsis on June 4, 1942, eight days after the attack.

It was said that Gebhardt's refusal to prescribe sulfonamide contributed to Heydrich's death, but he remained stubborn. He did not like the new science of antibiotics and insisted that infected battlefield wounds could be treated in the time-honoured ways.

He arrived at Ravensbrück and carried out a series of experiments on Ravensbrück prisoners, partly in order to justify his diagnosis of Heydrich.

The legs of prisoners were broken and deliberately infected, so he could show that antibiotics were useless in treating gangrene.

He also attempted to transplant the limbs from camp victims to German soldiers wounded on the eastern front.

The Ravensbrück experiments were slanted in Gebhardt's favour; women in the sulfonamide-treated experimental group received little or no nursing care, while those in the untreated control group received better care.

Gebhardt and 22 other doctors stood trial in the so-called Doctors' Trial at Nuremberg.

On August 20, 1947, he was found guilty of war crimes and crimes against humanity and sentenced to death and was hanged on June 2, 1948, in Landsberg Prison in Bavaria.

What is particularly disgraceful is that two of his surgical assistants later returned to civilian life to practise medicine.

Fritz Fischer was sentenced to life imprisonment but this was reduced to 15 years in 1951 and he was released in March 1954. He regained his medical licence and resumed his career at the chemical company Boehringer Ingelheim.

Herta Oberheuser was the sole female defendant in the Doctors' Trial, where she was sentenced to 20 years in prison.

The court heard that she took part in bone, muscle and nerve regeneration and bone transplantation experiments carried out on 86 women, including 74 Polish political prisoners, in the camp.

She also murdered healthy children with oil and evipan injections before removing their limbs and vital organs.

In other cases, Oberheuser wounded patients to replicate injuries to soldiers and then put wood, rusty nails, slivers of glass, dirt or sawdust into the wounds.

However, she was released for good behaviour in April 1952 and became a family doctor in Stocksee, Schleswig-Holstein.

However, she was sacked in 1956 after a Ravensbrück survivor recognised her. Yet it took another two years for her licence to practise medicine to be revoked.

Elisabeth Marschall, the head 'nurse' at Ravensbrück, selected prisoners for execution, oversaw medical experiments and decided who would be shipped off to Auschwitz. Following the Hamburg Ravensbrück Trials on May 3, 1947, she became the oldest female Nazi to hang, at the age of 61.

The most feared guard of all was Dorothea Binz, who supervised the bunker where women prisoners were tortured and killed. She was said to have beaten, slapped, kicked, shot and whipped women continuously. The camp fell silent when she appeared, carrying a whip in one hand and the leash of an Alsatian on another. Aged just 27, she was hanged on the same day as Marschall.

Resistance fighter Germaine Tillion, who later wrote books about the camp, said that the guards came from all walks of German life and included opera singers, qualified child carers, tram conductresses and retired teachers in their ranks.

Like the prisoners who came by train, the new guard recruits were shocked when they first arrived at Ravensbrück and saw the brutality of the seasoned guards, many of who were personally trained by Binz.

Tillion said that there seemed to be a 50:50 split between the guards who took a special pleasure in persecuting weak, sick or frail woman and those who beat prisoners for the sake of violence itself or to please other SS guards.

Daily work in the camp included hauling a huge stone roller to press stones into the earth to make a road by a 12 to 14-strong team of barefoot women, whose feet were cut to ribbons by the jagged edges of the stones, with ropes cutting into their shoulders. The idea was to work the women to death. If one fell down, the roller was pulled over them.

Until late 1944 or February 1945, depending on reports, when the population of the camp had risen to 80,000, there was no gas chamber at Ravensbrück itself. Women who were deemed too weak to work were sent either to the 'youth camp' at nearby Uckermark, where they were gassed in mobile vans, or to Auschwitz itself.

Every two or three weeks, the SS commandant and SS doctors selected women for the 'transport to Mittweida', an SS code phrase for gassing. Women had to lift their skirts over their hips and run in front of the SS guards and doctors. Those with swollen feet, injuries or scars or those simply too ill or too weak to run were immediately selected for 'recovery' period in Uckermark, a synonym for being locked in cells without food or medical care until they died.

By April 1945, it is believed that up to 6000 women died in the Ravensbrück gas chamber, mainly Hungarian Jews, Poles and Russians.

The thousands murdered in Ravensbrück included the 25-year-old French Princess Anne de Bauffremont-Courtenay; four members of Britain's Special Operations Executive, Denise Bloch, Cecily Lefort, Lilian Rolfe and Violette Szabo; Elisabeth de Rothschild (the only member of the Rothschild family to die in the Holocaust) and Olga Benário, wife of the Brazilian communist leader Luís Carlos Prestes.

SLAVING FOR THE GREAT ELECTRIC RAILWAY BUILDER

A high proportion of Ravensbrück prisoners were sent to work in local SS labour camps and factories, marched out of the front gate in the morning and back again at night. Prisoners had to work day and night until they died from weakness and illness.

Large numbers of female prisoners were transported to one of the Ravensbrück satellite camps after only a few weeks in the main camp. By 1944, trains were taking many of these straight to labour camps.

One of the biggest employers of slave labour from Ravensbrück was none other than the Siemens Electric Company, the same that had invented the world's first electric train and became a railway locomotive builder in its own right.

Today, Siemens is one of the biggest global brands in electrical engineering.

A Siemens factory was built near to the camp and women were forced to work 12 hour shifts on meagre soup rations making electrical components for V1 and V2 rockets.

The selected workers had to rise at 4am, stand on the camp road until 7am in all weathers and then walk the two kilometres to the Siemens factory wearing clogs, often having to wade through the lake when it was swollen in flood. Eventually, with the camp bursting at the seams, in 1944 someone in the SS had a brainwave – build an extra barracks

Heinrich Himmler inspects female guards during a visit to Ravensbrück.

Dr Alfred Gottwaldt of Berlin's Deutsches Technikmuseum helped set up the memorial wagon at Ravensbrück camp. These tracks were laid by the Red Army. ROBIN JONES

Preserved tipper trucks inside a surviving factory block. ROBIN JONES

Prisoners at work in a Ravensbrück sewing shop.

The Ravensbrück crematorium. The gas chamber erected in the last few months of the war is said to have been based in a wooden building on the far side. ROBIN JONES

These imposing staff houses provided the occupants with a far better standard of living than most ordinary Germans of the day might have enjoyed, and therefore were an incentive to join the SS as camp guards. ROBIN JONES

The preserved ovens inside the crematorium. ROBIN JONES

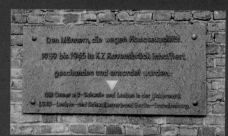

Memorial to lesbian victims of the Ravensbrück regime. ROBIN JONES

A loading bay on the short branch line which served the camp. ROBIN JONES

complex next to the Siemens factory to save all the bother and increase production.

Inmate Margaret Buber-Neumann had the dubious honour of suffering two deportations – firstly to Siberia under Stalin and then, following extradition to Germany, to Ravensbrück and its Siemens factory. She recalled that the civilian engineer in charge of the factory would think nothing about reporting workshy inmates to the guard and would write a letter full of derogatory comments to the concentration camp authority. "I discovered that this zeal was primarily driven by a desire to boost his career and a fear of the front line," she recalled.

Some women managed to obtain garlic and rub it into their fingers, and when they touched the copper coils and relays they were forced to make, rendering them useless. There were many other acts of subtle sabotage. All of them risked being sent to the punishment block and the degrading tasks that were meted out to them by the sadistic guards, including mixing excrement with crematorium ashes using their hands to make high-quality dung.

Researchers have found evidence of more than 90 Siemens slave labour camps, with 15,000 forced labourers in Berlin alone. It is said that up to 100,000 men and women toiled at a Siemens plant at Auschwitz to provide electricity for the camp.

A historical website set up by Siemens itself states: "Following its invasion of Poland in 1939, Germany embarked on a gradual

Sculptures representing women who starved to death in the camp factory blocks. ROBIN JONES

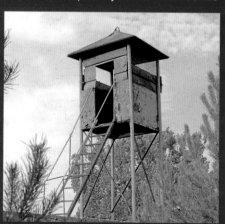

A watchtower overlooked the railway line at the eastern side of the camp. ROBIN JONES

transition to a war economy. The state restricted and even prohibited the production of certain civilian goods and requisites, and military conscription led to a widening shortage of labour. As a result, an increasing number of foreign civilians – men and women – were employed in manufacturing.

"Initially, they chose to work of their own free will. Later, though, many were forced into labour. They worked throughout German industry – in the manufacturing sector, in public services and in agriculture. By the winter of 1941-42, the German economy had become entirely dependent on forced labour.

"In late 1944, at the height of the Second World War, Siemens' total workforce of 244,000 included some 50,000 people who had been put to work against their will. The overall number of men and women who served as forced labour at Siemens during the war years was, however, higher."

In September 2002, following a huge public outcry, Siemens abandoned plans to register the trademark 'Zyklon', the same name as the Zyklon B poison gas used in the death camps, for a range of home products, including gas ovens.

TRAINS BETWEEN THE LABOUR CAMPS

Other women were despatched to work in armaments factories.

Ukrainian prisoner Markia Ged recalled: "On December 26, 1943, I was transported along with 100 other women to Peenemünde in a livestock wagon. The train started at 11am in Fürstenberg and after three hours, our carriages were uncoupled from the train and left on the railway in the middle of nowhere. It was freezing, –18°C.

"After approximately five hours, they attached our carriages to another train. This procedure was repeated at least eight times.

"Finally we arrived in Peenemünde in the morning of December 28, 1943. We were totally stiff and feeling sick because of the hunger. Then we were brought into a gigantic subterranean hall where a lot of men were already working on machines.

"Men and women died like flies. After one year, there were only 24 of us left out of the 100 women from the beginning. They sent us back to Ravensbrück."

Ravensbrück had 70 sub-camps used for slave labour that were spread across an area from the Baltic Sea to Bavaria.

By September 1944, there were 7.6 million foreign civilian workers and prisoner of war labourers in Germany, most of who were forced. By 1944, slave labour made up one quarter of Germany's entire workforce and the majority of German factories had a contingent of prisoners.

The Nazis also had plans for the deportation and enslavement of Britain's adult male population in the event of a successful invasion.

FREEDOM TRAINS

Ravensbrück received around 25,000 more prisoners in 1945, any from other camps which were being cleared. With Germany already suffering chronic food shortages, there was little to spare for the prisoners.

Himmler had by then realised the tide had turned against Nazi Germany and despite the enormity of his crimes, was deluded enough to believe that he could cut a deal with the Americans and maybe stay on in some form of administrative capacity after Hitler had been defeated. The Jew hater extraordinaire began issuing orders to subordinates to ease off on the Jews, and Count Folke Bernadotte, vice-president of the Swedish Red Cross, convinced him to allow the International Red Cross to rescue some prisoners from Ravensbrück and other camps and bring them to Sweden.

The Swedish Red Cross was first allowed to rescue Scandinavians on March 5, followed by women from France, Poland and the Benelux countries.

Through the intervention of the Swedish section of the World Jewish Congress, Bernadotte requested that Jewish prisoners also be sent to Sweden. Surprisingly to many, Himmler agreed.

Between April 22-28, about 7500 women including 1000 Jews were taken out from Ravensbrück either on trains or by the Red Cross 'White Buses'. They were taken by sea from Copenhagen to Malmö in neutral Sweden, given clothing, food and medical attention and were sent to recuperate in different locations before returning to their homelands.

However, with the Red Army advancing in the last months of the war, the SS decided to hide as much of the Ravensbrück atrocities as possible, exterminating witnesses. In March 1945, just weeks before the war ended, 130 babies and pregnant women were gassed.

The women still able to walk were ordered out of the camp on a death march on April 27-28, leaving behind 3000 who were too weak or ill.

The Soviets liberated the camp on April 30, 1945, and a Russian scout unit freed the survivors of the death march a few hours later.

More than 132,000 women and children were imprisoned at Ravensbrück, out of whom 92,000 died.

REMEMBERING THE TRAINS

SS guards and former prisoners with administrative positions at the camp were arrested at the end of the war and tried at the Hamburg Ravensbrück Trials from 1946-48. Sixteen of the accused were found guilty of war crimes and crimes against humanity and sentenced to death.

After the war, parts of the camp were used by the Red Army for military purposes until 1993. New barracks were built for the Soviet troops stationed in the camp as part of the Soviet Union's Cold War anti-missile programme.

In 1954, the sculptor Will Lammert was commissioned to design a memorial site between the crematorium, the camp wall and Schwedtsee Lake.

An enlarged version of his Tragende (Woman with Burden) sculpture was placed on a pillar overlooking the lake, where Jehovah's Witnesses had to dump ashes from the crematorium.

In 1984, the Museum of Anti-fascist Resistance was established in the former SS headquarters and was later replaced by two permanent exhibitions about life in the camp and its victims.

The former accommodation blocks for the female guards are a youth hostel and a youth meeting centre.

On April 16-17, 2005, a ceremony held to commemorate the 60th anniversary of the camp's liberation was attended by more than 600 survivors from all over the world, but mostly from eastern Europe.

To coincide with this event, a new, permanent outdoor exhibition was opened to the east of the camp, on the theme of the deportation trains to Ravensbrück.

Its central exhibit is a single refurbished goods wagon on a long siding that led from the public railway. The boxcar was built in France for the Paris-Lyon-Mediterranee Railway and was one of thousands of vehicles forcibly loaned to the German network during the war. It is not known whether it ever formed part of a deportation train.

The exhibition's information boards describe the origins of the transports and how they developed over time and explain the different types of train, where they arrived and the part played by the local residents. The wagon is within sight of rotting wooden sheds where the loot brought in by the SS was stored.

North of the camp perimeter, the disused line from Fürstenberg to Templin is now used purely for pleasure purposes. You can hire a draisine, a pedal-operated light auxiliary rail vehicle, based somewhat on bicycle technology, to ride up and down the track.

The memorial to the British victims of Ravensbrück. ROBIN JONES

The barracks at Ravensbrück. Only the outlines of the foundations can be seen today.

"I don't look like Fagin... ...so why pick on me?"

Steven Frank, who survived the deportation trains as a young boy and now gives living testimony to the horrors of the Third Reich.
ROBIN JONES

Steven Frank, the son of a Dutch Jewish lawyer, was born in Amsterdam in 1935. His family were secular Jews. They knew about their faith, but did not attend synagogues or keep a kosher household.

At the age of five, he recalled, he saw soldiers wearing jackboots marching through the streets.

By the age of eight, young Steven was also aware that he suddenly had a problem – but could not put his finger on it: "I became aware for a reason I could not understand that I was different from all other children in my street.

"I was no longer allowed to play in the park: my father could not take public transport to work. I couldn't go into the swimming pool or the zoo, while my friends went inside."

In short, he was Jewish.

The reaction to him was strange indeed,

because The Netherlands had always been known for its religious tolerances. That is, until the Germans invaded... and imposed the Nuremberg Laws of 1935.

From then on, a Jew of any description, whether practising or lapsed, was a Jew, and was treated accordingly.

Eventually, under arguably one of the most inhuman and deliberately degrading pieces of legislation passed by anyone, anywhere in modern times, they could be executed merely for not wearing the yellow star of David if they ventured outdoors. Steven still has the faded star he wore as a child during these years.

Steven could just not understand why the sudden change, and why so many places were out of bounds to him. Yes, he was Jewish by birth, but he was otherwise exactly the same as them in every other way. What had he done wrong?

"I did not look anything like Fagin or Shylock, and could not understand why I was told I was any different to my friends," he said.

His father Leonard Frank, the son of a doctor, had been awarded the Dutch equivalent of a knighthood. His mother was the daughter of professional musicians who migrated to England at the turn of the century. When the Second World War broke out, the Franks had the chance to flee to Britain, but decided to stay. His father was the legal member of a board that governed

one of the most advanced Jewish mental hospitals in the world, and wanted to stay and continue his responsibilities there.

Steven's father was brave enough to speak out publicly against the Nazi authorities and wrote letters on behalf of arrested Jews asking for them not to be deported to the east.

After joining the Dutch resistance, his father arranged the issue of false papers to enable people to escape across the border to the safety of Switzerland.

Several Jewish families they knew fled into hiding, and some were even hidden at the Franks' house, despite the huge risk involved. Steven's father and mother were determined to resist the deportations in whatever little way they could find.

However, in 1942 Leonard was betrayed to the Nazis and arrested in his office in Amsterdam. In the morning he had ridden off to work by bicycle, as by then Jews were not allowed to use other forms of transport, but he never returned home.

He was tortured at a prison in Amersfoort before being sent to the Nazi transit camp at Westerbork. This was not a concentration camp in the worst sense of the world, but a waystation whereby arrested Jews and other people who the Nazis did not like were gathered together to be sent by train to the east, in conditions that may have been bad by everyday standards, but deliberately not

sufficiently appalling to raise serious alarm.

From Westerbork, Steven's father was deported to Auschwitz where he was gassed in January 1943.

Not knowing this, his wife tried desperately to find out about his fate, but in vain. Following his arrest, three non-Jewish friends risked their own positions by asking the occupying authorities for clemency on his behalf, citing his many good works. One of the men was Arnold D'Ailly, a banker who after the war went on to become the mayor of Amsterdam.

THE BARNEVALD HAVEN

It was no use. However, the Germans did allow Leonard's wife and three sons to be placed on the 'Barnveld List'.

There they joined around 600 other Dutch Jews who had been selected to live because they were regarded as beneficial to their nation, while around 110,000 others in The Netherlands were shipped to the east and murdered.

The Barneveld list was started by a Hague bureaucrat who had managed to obtain agreement from the Nazis to save two notable Jews and their families from deportation.

News of his actions spread through the country, and others wrote letters pleading to be added to the list. They included doctors,

Westerbork inmates wave off fellow prisoners as they depart for the east, in carriages as opposed to the later boxcars or 'cattle trucks'.

Westerbork prisoners being loaded into the boxcars of a deportation train, like the one Steven Frank rode on.

scientists, artists and teachers.

However, they were not allowed to stay in their own homes but sent to an internment camp which had been set up inside the 19th century mock Tudor castle De Schaffelaar at Barneveld, hence the list's name and the group formed from it.

Safe for the moment, the Jews formed a community of their own within the red brick castle.

Many brought their home furnishings and dishware with them. The women were constantly having their hair styled in the latest fashions and washing every day was no problem. It goes without saying that compared with the conditions of those sent to the East, it was heaven.

However, the castle became more and more crowded, and food had to be rationed.

Steven, his mother and two brothers arrived there in 1943, and stayed for nine months. Then one day in September 1943, German soldiers arrived and gave each occupant half an hour to pack their belongings. Then they were all taken by train to Westerbork.

THE DEPORTATION CAMP

"Auschwitz made of wood," is how Steven describes Westerbork after all these years, because of the similarity of the barrack huts to those in the pictures of the death camp.

He recalled that it was surrounded on three sides by a moat filled with stagnant water.

The railway line which brought inmates in and out ran through the middle of the camp.

Disease was rife in the camp – scarlet fever, diarrhoea and jaundice. "It was a pretty grim place," said Steven. "We did not starve but the food was monotonous."

The camp had been built in 1939 as Centraal Vluchtelingenkamp Westerbork in the north-eastern Netherlands, about six miles north of Westerbork itself.

The pre-invasion Dutch government had intended it for refugees, mainly from Germany but also from Austria, Czechoslovakia and Poland, and mostly of Jewish faith, who were fleeing the excesses which followed in the wake of Kristallnacht.

However, after the Nazis occupied The Netherlands, in a reversal of roles at the end of 1941, they turned it into a deportation camp for Jews, Gypsies and later also for women from the Dutch resistance. Around 15,000 Jews were there at any one time.

Measuring 500m x 500m, the camp was surrounded by a barbed-wire fence and seven watchtowers. The initial 24 large wooden barracks built later became 107, each designed to hold 300 people.

The cost of this building work and of the camp's maintenance was funded from the proceeds of stolen Jewish property, to the tune of 10 million guilders for 1942-43.

The transfer of Jews from Amsterdam to Westerbork began on the night of July 14-15, 1942, and the first transport left for

Auschwitz on the following day.

On July the Dutch railway company Nederlandse Spoorwegen received an order for the construction of a three mile railway branch line into the camp. This was actually built by the prisoners themselves.

Surprisingly, the day-to-day operation of the camp was left in the hands of German Jews, as they spoke the same language as the commandant, and this did change even when the majority of the inmates were Dutch.

Aged eight, Steven was becoming streetwise very quickly, especially after a spot of typical Jew-baiting, when guards made fun of him after setting an Alsatian on him because he played too close to the perimeter fence. "I can still hear the guards laughing," he recalled.

THE ONE-WAY TICKET

Between July 1942 and September 1944, almost every Tuesday a cargo train packed with 1600 inmates left Westerbork for Theresienstadt, Auschwitz-Birkenau, Sobibór or Bergen-Belsen.

They had been organised by Adolf Eichmann's IVB4 office. Those on board would not be coming back.

The Nazi commandant left the make-up of the transports to the Jewish camp leadership. Select inmates, such as foreigners or veteran servicemen, were exempt from transportation.

Jews who had been caught in hiding in The Netherlands were categorised as 'convict Jews' and were sent to Barrack 67, the punishment block. The convict Jews were not permitted to keep their own clothes and had to wear blue overalls and wooden clogs. Both men and women in Barrack 67 had their hair shaved, received no soap, were given less food than other prisoners and were assigned to the hardest labour parties. Furthermore, they were more often than not the first to be chosen for transportation on the next train for Poland.

Steven remembers that on the day before each of the Tuesday departures, a list of all the passengers' names would be posted. People began pleading to be taken off the list as soon as they saw their name there.

Many inmates tried their best to get jobs in the camp so that they would avoid being

Castle De Schaffelaar at Barneveld provided a temporary official 'safe haven' for Jews, but it was not to last. MICHIELVERBEEK CC

Jews arriving at Westerbork in 1942.

Westerbork transit camp, which Steven Frank described as a 'wooden Auschwitz'.

sent on the transports.

Boards on the side of the carriages showed where they were going, although few realised exactly what the word meant. Auschwitz.

At first, the transports were made up of passenger carriages, but later freight wagons used for transporting cattle were used.

Steven said: "I remember the steam trains when they were at a standstill, letting off steam while waiting for the people to board.

"Whenever I hear that sound today, it takes me back to the camps."

During 1942-45, a total of 107,000 people passed through Westerbork camp on a total of 93 outgoing trains. Only 5200 of them survived, most of them in Theresienstadt or Bergen-Belsen, or liberated in Westerbork by the Canadians.

Nederland Spoorwegen took the trains to the border, after which they would be handed over to German crews.

None of the Dutch railwaymen appeared to know where the trains were going, said Steven. "They knew that they were being transported eastwards, and following orders."

FRIENDLY FIRE

While he was in the camp, Steven like many other inmates suffered from an infestation of parasitic worms. After the war, it would take 18 months of treatment in London's Great Ormond Street Hospital to be rid of it.

The Franks became friendly with an elderly couple in their Sixties who reminisced with their mother about holidays

in England. "They became surrogate grandparents to us," recalled Steven.

However, in May 1944, a British fighter aircraft mistook Westerbork for a German army training camp. Steven saw holes suddenly appearing in the roof of their hut, and bullets ricocheting off the bedsteads.

Instinctively, he ran through a hail of bullets to get away. But he found his 'grandfather' lying dead, riddled with bullets.

"It was the first time that I had come face-to-face with death," he said.

The camp was never a pleasant place, and there were health hazards at every turn. Yet it was infinitely better than many other Nazi camps. It was intended as a transit camp rather than an extermination camp.

Indeed, Westerbork camp developed many of the features of a small town.

It had an 1800 bed hospital with a maternity ward, laboratories, pharmacies, dental clinics and around 120 doctors and 1000 staff. There was an old people's home, a school for children aged six to 14, an orphanage and religious services.

The camp had workshops for tailoring, furniture manufacturing and even bookbinding. Tradesmen such as locksmiths, decorators, bricklayers, carpenters, opticians and gardeners found work.

It even had a garage and a telephone exchange as well as its own sewage works. By 1943, more than 6000 people were employed there. Sporting activities were encouraged, along with entertainment such as a choir and cabaret. There were football

tournaments, but the member of the teams changed as the weeks went by, as more and more players were shipped to the East by train, never to return.

Indeed, while Westerbork may have seemed by comparison a comfortable place in which to be incarcerated, many of the inmates would have made use of the amenities for only a few days, and a few days after that, would die in Auschwitz.

All the amenities came at a price, but not to the Germans. Again, the commandant funded it all out of stolen Jewish property which the Nazis had plundered.

THEIR NAME ON THE LIST

One Monday in September 1944, the feared list was posted as usual – but this time with the Franks' names on it.

They were to be taken to Theresienstadt.

His mother got their clothes ready and filled a rucksack with a few personal belongings.

They and other passengers were led to a ramp where he saw cattle trucks with 'Theresienstadt' written on the sides.

The people were packed into the freight wagons so tightly that many of them found it difficult to breathe. The rucksacks were placed in the corners to create more space. "There was a great bang as the door was shut," Steven recalled.

Eyewitness Philip Mechanicus, a journalist who kept a camp diary, described the typical departure scene: "The train, a long scabby snake that cuts the camp in two.

"The Boulevard des Misères (the main

The SS mess hall in Westerbork camp at Christmas. Peace on earth and goodwill to all men had by then clearly gone out of the window.

Westerbork Commandant Albert Gemmeker with his secretary and his dog.

A monument at Westerbork showing a length of track with the rails turned up, showing that no trains will ever run from the site again.

ANNE FRANK

Diarist Anne Frank and her family were deported on the last train ever to run from Westerbork concentration camp to Auschwitz, on September 3, 1944, arriving there three days later. Aged 15, on arrival at the death camp, she was stripped naked and disinfected, had her head shaved, and was given a tattooed number on her skin, but was not selected for the gas chamber. She was later transferred to Bergen-Belsen where she died from typhus.

street in Camp Westerbork) where it stands, blocked by men from OD (Joodsche Ordedienst, the camp's Jewish police force) to keep out everyone who is not needed there, and then the people, packed with a bread-bag hanging from their shoulder, a rolled blanket bound to the other side with a piece of rope swinging on their back. Shabby vagabonds who own nothing but the clothes they wear and what's hanging from them. Men with silent, stiff faces, women often in tears. Older people, stumbling over the bad road, through pools of mud. Patients on stretchers, carried by OD men.

"At the platform the big chief (Commandant Albert) Gemmeker himself, usually with his little dog, the green police, a number of prominent inmates among whom is Schlesinger, in riding-breeches and boots, with straw coloured hair and wearing a flat cap."

Philip wrote about a particular transport which departed on February 8, 1944, describing it as perhaps "the most fiendish".

More than 1000 Jews boarded the train to Auschwitz-Birkenau. They included 268 of the camp's hospital patients, including children with scarlet fever and diphtheria. Many of them were so ill that they were carried to the platform on stretchers.

At Auschwitz-Birkenau, 142 of the men and 73 women on board were allocated work at the camp. The other 800 passengers, including all the children, were gassed.

Steven's memories of the trip he and his family endured from Westerbork would never fade.

"We were in that cattle truck 39 hours," he said. "We had no food or water. We had no sleep. I will never forget the stench. It was a mixture of human sweat, vomit, poo and pee."

All the

passengers could do was stand and suffer, as if they were being deliberately stifled to death.

But suddenly the train stopped.

"I remember a great wrrmmm noise as the door was opened," said Steven. "An enormous waft of ice-cold air came in.

"Suddenly we were able to breathe again."

Knowing a little about rail freight in my capacity as editor of *Heritage Railway* magazine, I am familiar with the historical methods of transhipment of whole herds of livestock by rail across Britain, when a farmer decided to uproot and move lock, stock and barrel across the country.

Even when sending cattle to faraway markets, steps would be taken by the railway company for them to be fed and watered en route, and even in the days when animal welfare laws were far less stringent, no cattle would be expected to travel without sustenance for 39 hours.

Here, however, was sheer brutality and deliberate and callous neglect in the worst extreme, and when railway officials and staff claimed that they did not know what was happening, my initial reaction is one of disbelief.

On a local level I concede that they might not have known about the exact purpose of Auschwitz, but what level of IQ did you need to realise that treating people or animals like this is tantamount to a death sentence in many cases (as happened regularly).

In my view no attempt to show basic value for human life was shown by those who organised these trains, so how much would they care about what happened to the passengers at the other end?

For a railwayman of even modest experience, something would have been clearly amiss with these transports.

Maybe those who suspected knew better than to ask. Maybe they were scared for their own families. Or perhaps, maybe they knew and they just did not care.

As it was, for three years, railway staff went along with the Westerbork transports, obeying orders to the letter.

THERESINSTADT – THE MODEL CAMP

The Austrian Emperor Joseph II ordered the building of the fortress of Terezin in north-west Bohemia and named it after his mother, Maria Theresa of Austria. It comprised a small fortress for military purposes, and a large fortress adjoining it, in the form of the walled town of Theresienstadt.

Redundant as a fort by 1800, afterwards it was used to hold military and political prisoners. From 1914-18 it housed Gavrilo Princip, whose actions started the First World War when he shot dead Archduke Franz Ferdinand of Austria and his wife on June 28, 1914. Princip died in cell number one from tuberculosis on April 28, 1918.

In the summer of 1940, the Gestapo turned the small fortress into a prison using Jewish slave labour and the town of Theresienstadt into a ghetto.

Infamously, it was from time to time dressed up as a 'model' concentration camp as a propaganda effort by the Nazis, to show the world – and possibly the German public – that they meant no harm to those who they deported on the trains, and all would be well. The Nazis originally intended it to house educated, middle-class Jews from Germany, Czechoslovakia, and Austria.

The Nazis made much out of the rich cultural life in the walled town, providing musical instruments for orchestras, chamber groups and jazz ensembles. Several stage performances were produced and attended by camp inmates including scholars, writers, artists, scientists, diplomats, musicians, and lawyers – much of the surviving Jewish intelligentsia of Europe.

As with other ghettos, it was run by a Jewish council, which did its best to see that

Monument at Westerbork: Each single stone represents a single person that passed through Westerbork and died in a concentration camp.

the children who passed through the camp continued to be educated, even though much of it was under the nose of the Nazis.

In 1943, 456 Jews from Denmark, a country which for pragmatic reasons had not resisted the German invasion and had generally co-operated rather than sought open confrontation, were sent to Theresienstadt. The Danes insisted on the Red Cross being allowed to visit the ghetto, and the Danish King, Christian X, managed to win the freedom of all Danes held there on April 15, 1945. A total of 413 survived.

But the underlying truth was that it was a brutal concentration camp in miniature, where sadism ruled supreme alongside hunger and sickness, all of which claimed around 33,000 lives. Once the outside world was no longer looking, once the international visitors had gone home, inhumanity returned to normal.

Czech Gendarmerie guards worked alongside the Nazis in the enslavement, deportation and murder of Jews, more than 50,000 of whom were crammed into space intended nearly two centuries before for just 7000. Indeed, in 1942, the Nazis turned out the 7000 non-Jewish Czechs living there to make way for Jews.

It was also a main transit camp for Jews being ferried in from other parts of occupied Europe for onward transport to Auschwitz or Treblinka, for Sonderbehandlung or 'special treatment'. Many of the 80,000 Czech Jews who fell victim to the Holocaust perished in Theresienstadt.

CAMP LIFE

Slave workers housed in Theresienstadt worked splitting locally-quarried mica, making boxes – and coffins – and spraying military uniforms with white dye to camouflage them for use on the Russian front.

Former prisoners told how shipments of clothing stolen from Germans Jews were sent to Theresienstadt to be sorted and repackaged before being sent back out as emergency aid for German people whose homes had been bombed in Allied air raids.

In Theresienstadt, Steven's mother volunteered to work in the camp hospital laundry. At the time, a typhus epidemic raged through the camp.

She and her children had to live on one or two slices of bread a day. However, because of the heavy work she had to do, she was given

The inner gateway at Theresienstadt. FELIX TRILLER*

Destination boards were clear and open about where each train was going, but how many passengers knew what awaited them at the journey's end?

Railway Siding left in situ at Theresienstadt.

A partially-restored camp hut at Westerbork today.

What appears to be an opening train pulls into Theresienstadt station behind an ancient 0-8-0 on June 1, 1943.

There were no gas chambers at Theresienstadt, but there was a crematorium. MARTIJN MUNNEKE

Jewish deportees at Theresienstadt in 1943.

extra food, and saved it for her children.

Still, that did little to curb their prolonged hunger.

Steven recalled: "There was a real pain inside your stomach like toothache.

"I sucked buttons of my clothes to pretend they were sweets in a bid to relieve their pain.

"But we were so really lucky that we were being fed at all."

Steven became fascinated by a special section of the camp in the small fortress, which had a slogan painted above it: 'Arbeit Macht Frei'.

His mother told him in no uncertain terms not to go there, because "people inside had lost their minds".

From 1940, the Gestapo used the small fortress – which remained separate from the Jewish ghetto in the main fortress on the river's right side – as a prison. Around 32,000 people passed through its gates, many on the way to concentration camps, while an estimated 2600 people were executed, starved, or succumbed to disease there.

In 2001, prison guard Anton Malloth was sentenced to life imprisonment after being convicted of beating at least 100 prisoners to death, after escaping justice for 55 years.

Stephen recalled the June 23, 1944, visit of the Danish Red Cross and the International Red Cross to the "model camp", and how some of the emaciated elder Jews had been shipped out beforehand to improve the general appearance.

The Nazis tried to make everything look less overcrowded by the only way they knew

how – send more Jews on a one-way train to Auschwitz.

Fake shops and cafes were built to show the comfortable lifestyle that the deportees enjoyed, and the visited Danes were seen in freshly-painted rooms not shared by more than three people.

The party included E Juel-Henningsen, the head physician at the Danish Ministry of Health, and Franz Hvass, the top civil servant at the Danish Foreign Ministry. Dr Paul Eppstein was instructed by the SS to appear in the role of the mayor of Theresienstadt

The VIP guests were treated to a performance of a children's opera written by an inmate, and helpful German escorts asked questions of the inmates on a predetermined route around the camp, and of course received favourable replies.

RED CROSS FOOLED

The Red Cross visitors appeared to have been well and truly fooled by the whole show laid on for them, and afterwards the Nazis went one better by making a propaganda film about the camp, with the intention of dispelling all those vile lies about murder camps once and for all.

Production of the film began on February 26, 1944. Directed by Jewish prisoner Kurt Gerron, a director and actor who had appeared with Marlene Dietrich on screen, the aim was to show how the Third Reich really cared for the Jews under its protection. Shooting of the film, its title translated into English being Terezin: A Documentary Film of the Jewish

Resettlement began in February 1944. After it was finished, most of the cast along with Gerron himself were deported to Auschwitz by train. He was murdered in the gas chamber on October 18, 1944.

At periodic intervals, German officials would visit the camp's children's home to select those for onward transport to Auschwitz, and most likely death within days.

Steven remembers the screams of siblings who were being deliberately parted from each other.

"When children had lost their homes and their parents, the only thing that they might have left to hold onto was a brother or a sister," said Steven. "The last thing they had left was that last sibling. I will never forget the crying, sobbing and screaming."

Most of these youngsters would last little more than a few hours after their train reached the ultimate terminus, Auschwitz, from which for them there would be no return journey. The architects of the Holocaust were getting exactly what they wanted – extermination. So why exacerbate the misery of defenceless children who were already scheduled for oblivion?

At this point it becomes clear that the Holocaust had long since stopped being a mass pogrom of Jews. Those children were no longer being punished for their ancestry or culture. It was nothing less than a final attack on their basic humanity.

The 'master race', whose armies had fought their way to the gates of Moscow and into Stalingrad, was now reduced to taunting innocent harmless little children whose days

Steven Frank and fellow prisoners watched the glow in the sky as Dresden burned.

they had numbered.

The advancing Red Army was the first to reach one of the big concentration camps, arriving at Majdanek near Lublin, Poland, in July 1944.

Taken aback by the speed of the Soviet advance, the Germans demolished the camp in a vain attempt to hide their atrocities.

The large crematorium was set on fire, but staff did not have time to demolish the gas chambers which were left standing.

Soon after, the dismantled sites of the Belzec, Sobibor and Treblinka murder camps were in Soviet hands, and more and more evidence was being presented to a shocked world.

On January 27, 1945, the Red Army liberated Auschwitz, only to find only a few thousand emaciated prisoners alive. The rest had been forced to march in icy conditions and with inadequate clothing westwards, on pain of death, or shipped out by train, again to remove evidence and witnesses.

In the warehouses that had not been destroyed by the retreating Germans, the Soviets found personal belongings of the victims: hundreds of thousands of men's suits, more than 800,000 women's outfits, and more than 14,000lb of human hair.

Steven remembered a different form of train coming into Thereseinstadt. These were arriving from Auschwitz, filled with prisoners, as opposed to going out in the opposite direction.

Some Auschwitz prisoners dressed in their distinctive striped camp uniforms came in the box wagons that they and so many others described as cattle trucks. Some were so ill that they were taken straight to the Thereseinstadt hospital – at least, for the moment, receiving better treatment than would have been the case had they arrived at Auschwitz in that condition.

Others, however, were corpses that had frozen solid during the journey.

KEEPING THE PIECE

One day, while playing inside one of the parts of Thereseinstadt fortress, Steven noticed a trapdoor in the ceiling. Mischievously he climbed inside, and gingerly made his way through the loft space until he came to another trapdoor.

He opened it, and to his astonishment found an Aladdin's cave in the room below, unguarded and unoccupied.

It was full of clothing and possessions presumably stolen from previous occupants of the camp before they were sent on their way by train to their deaths.

By now, the Nazi recycling process had ceased to function.

Excitedly, Steven retraced his steps and told his mother.

The discovery meant that in the harsh winter, warm clothing would be available.

Steven was particularly delighted at finding a chess set in the room. It would give him and his brothers hours of relief from the cold, boredom and hunger.

He still has a piece from that set today, and forever wonders what happened to its

Memorial honouring the families and children who died at Theresienstadt. LEANDRO KIBISZ CC

rightful owner.

On the night of February 14/15, the Franks were awoken up by the sound of a tremendous bombardment.

The whole sky was glowing crimson in colour.

What they did not realise at the time was that they were witnessing the carpet bombing of Dresden, Germany's seventh largest city, by the Allies.

Dresden, a major communications centre with a sizeable railway marshalling yard which could handle east to west military traffic for the Reich, had already been targeted. However, when the air raid sirens sounded at 9.51pm, few might have imagined the sheer scale of the destruction that followed.

In the first attack, Bomber Command sent in a group of Lancaster bombers carrying 500 tons of high explosives and 375 tons of fire bombs, some of which had the capacity to destroy a city block.

The first bombs fell at 10.14pm, and virtually all had been dropped within eight minutes, all within an area between 1.25 miles and 1.75 miles wide.

By the time a second wave of bombers flew in, the thousands of fires from the burning city could be seen more than 60 miles away on the ground, and 500 miles

away in the air, with smoke rising to 15,000ft.

The attack continued in daylight the next day, when 316 USAAF B-17 Flying Fortresses dropped 771 tons of bombs.

Then at 12.17pm, the USAAF 379th bombardment group started to bomb marshalling yards in the Friedrichstadt district west of the city centre as the area was not obscured by smoke and cloud. Further groups followed in rapid succession but had finished by 12.30pm.

On February 15, the 1st Bombardment Division bombed the suburbs and nearby towns after finding their primary target, the Böhlen synthetic oil plant near Leipzig, obscured by clouds.

HELL ON EARTH

The city became engulfed by a raging firestorm, with around 25,000 people being killed.

Those casualties that were not burned to death died through lack of oxygen, while others threw themselves into the river to escape the flames.

Churchill, who had authorised the attack, later tried to distance himself from it. Historians have ever since debated as to whether the bombing of Dresden was disproportionate, whether it served any practical purpose and whether it might itself

Memorial cemetery in front of the Little Fort in Terezín.

Brass plaque recalling the fate of some of those for who Theresienstadt was not the final end of their train journeys. LAVENDER DREAMER

be considered to be a war crime.

US Army Chief of Staff General George C Marshall conducted an inquiry into the raid. The inquiry declared the elimination of the German ability to reinforce a counter-attack against the Red Army or to retreat and regroup using Dresden as a base of operations, were important military objectives, and that the Soviets had requested the bombing for this very reason.

A secondary objective was to disrupt the industrial use of Dresden for munitions manufacture, which American intelligence believed to be the case.

LEGITIMATE TACTICS?

The attack came less than three weeks after the horrors of Auschwitz were exposed to the world. At the time, there were no initiatives by the Nazi government to sue for peace or call a ceasefire, and V2 rockets had been poured on to London regardless of the casualties.

Also, who knew what further atrocities awaited discovery in the remaining German concentration camps?

If area bombing could shorten the war by even a day, how many innocent lives in them might be saved?

Those who had seen the newly-liberated Auschwitz, or heard the stories about children being thrown alive into its crematoria, might not have wasted too much time deliberating on the merits or otherwise of the 'overkill' of what seems to have been a legitimate target. Perhaps they had by then reached the point where they could no longer care less.

That again was the multi-faceted dehumanising aspect of the Holocaust.

On February 5, 1945, Himmler allowed a transport of 1210 Jews from Theresienstadt, most of them originating from the Netherlands, to be taken to Switzerland. He had reached an agreement with Jean-Marie Musy, a pro-Nazi former Swiss president, to free the group released after $1.25 million was placed in Swiss banks by Jewish organisations in that country.

Steven recalls that someone in Theresienstadt had an illicit radio, and inmates were able to listen to Churchill broadcasting on the BBC Overseas Service.

It was clear that the war was approaching a conclusion, but the prisoners were still fearful about Nazi reprisals.

Rumours spread that the Germans had built improved gas chambers at Auschwitz, the camp's true purpose as a killing field by now being common knowledge thanks to the tales being told by returning survivors.

On May 1, 1945, the Nazis transferred control of the camp to the Red Cross. The mortality rate was high due to disease and malnutrition. A week later, on May 8, 1945, Terezín was liberated by Soviet troops. It was the last of the camps to be freed.

The tables were turned, and two days later Theresienstadt became used by Czech partisans and former inmates to hold German SS personnel and civilians suspected of war crimes. Among the interned Germans were former Nazis such as Heinrich Jöckel, the former commander of Terezín and other SS members. The last German prisoners were freed on February 29, 1948.

Because of a typhus epidemic, nobody was able to leave Thereseinstadt for nearly a month.

NEW LIFE IN ENGLAND

In early June 1945, Dutch prisoners were sent by train back to the Netherlands. Steven's mother did not want to go, fearing there would be no survivors there who knew her family, and asked instead to go to England.

The crew of an RAF plane took pity on the Franks and agreed to fly them to England. Taking off from Pilzen in southern Czechoslovakia, they flew to Paris and on to Croydon Airport south of London.

In a matter-of-fact way, they were unceremoniously dumped on the runway. Another aeroplane arrived shortly afterwards and the family joined this group. Next day, Steven's mother was reunited with her father.

Out of around 144,000 Jews sent to Theresienstadt, there were 17,247 remaining at the end of the war. They included 5000 from the Netherlands.

Around 88,000 were deported to Auschwitz and other murder camps including Treblinka.

Steven and his family settled down to life

in England. For many years afterwards, he would never mention to anyone that he had been in a concentration camp.

Back in Theresienstadt, the Nazis had predictably banned religious instruction. However classes were held in secret, in the hope that some of the children might survive and would then have knowledge of where their roots lay.

On January 21, 1943, a group of children secretly gathered in a courtyard near their barracks to celebrate Tu B'Shevat, 15th of Shevat 5703 in the Jewish calendar, the festival of the new year of trees. Teacher Frau Lauscher organised a tree-planting ceremony to celebrate the occasions and persuaded one of the men who worked in the fields to smuggle a seedling into the camp. He brought it in hidden in his boot.

TREE OF LIFE

This little tree became a symbol of hope, and successive groups of children took great care of it. After they were herded into trains bound for Auschwitz and elsewhere, other children took their place at Thereseinstadt and continued to nurture the tree.

The tree survived the war, along with Frau Lauscher, her husband and daughter. She returned to Theresienstadt and found the tree again. It was later transplanted in the cemetery just outside the camp.

Over the decades, it grew into a 60ft sycamore tree, as a memorial to the murdered children and mark of defiance against oppressors.

Steven made an emotional return visit to Theresienstadt in 1993, visiting the room where his family first arrived by train from Westerbork. "I just could not eat in the place," he said, recalling those extreme pangs of hunger.

He and others began the gathering of seeds from the original tree to grow saplings to be planted as a symbol of hope and survival.

Saplings have been planted by Steven at several sites in England, including Britain's first dedicated Holocaust Memorial and Education Centre, Beth Shalom, the House of Peace, which opened in September 1995 in the two acre grounds of a former farmhouse in the village of Laxton, near Newark, on the edge of Sherwood Forest in

Nottinghamshire.

In 1981, brothers Stephen and James Smith and their parents took a family holiday to Israel, and realised just how far Christianity has moved from its Jewish origins. They saw that contemporary anti-Semitism was as Christian as it was evil.

Ten years later, the brothers, by now in their 20s, spent a day at Yad Vashem, the memorial centre in Jerusalem, and realised that the Holocaust is not a Jewish problem, but has implications for everyone.

They returned, determined to bring the issues and challenges set by the Holocaust to Britain, which, Channel Islands apart, had not been occupied by the Nazis. Stephen and James therefore felt that the vast majority of British people had managed to avoid confronting the reality of the Holocaust, and decided to create an exhibition.

Around 20,000 people visit Beth Shalom each year, some lucky enough to hear talks given by none other than Steven Frank, now 77, who is committed to letting today's youngsters hear his story of survival against the odds and learn from it.

HISTORY LESSON

The extensive museum and exhibition tells the whole story of the Nazi persecution from start to finish, and as an educational resource in Britain is unsurpassed. In short, every child of school age should visit.

In the garden stands a fully grown sapling from the Terezin Tree. The memorial gardens contain a beautiful rose garden, where more than 800 visitors, including survivors and their families, have planted roses in memory of Holocaust victims. A tag by each rose bears their names.

The Nazis committed millions of innocent people to oblivion, erasing every trace of them from the face of the earth.

So every name that reappears in the rose garden at Beth Shalom is an act of defiance. They may have destroyed the person, but their identity cannot be wiped out, and will outlive their oppressors.

Each rose is testimony to the fact that mankind is capable of much better things, and while beauty and truth may be stamped on by the jackboot, they can never be vanquished.

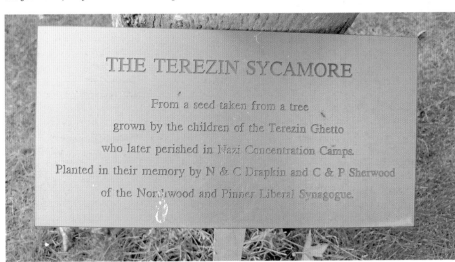

THE TEREZIN SYCAMORE

From a seed taken from a tree
grown by the children of the Terezin Ghetto
who later perished in Nazi Concentration Camps.
Planted in their memory by N & C Drapkin and C & P Sherwood
of the Northwood and Pinner Liberal Synagogue.

The Terezin Sycamore at Beth Shalom near Newark today. ROBIN JONES

The rose garden at Beth Shalom keeps the names alive of those who the Nazis murdered.

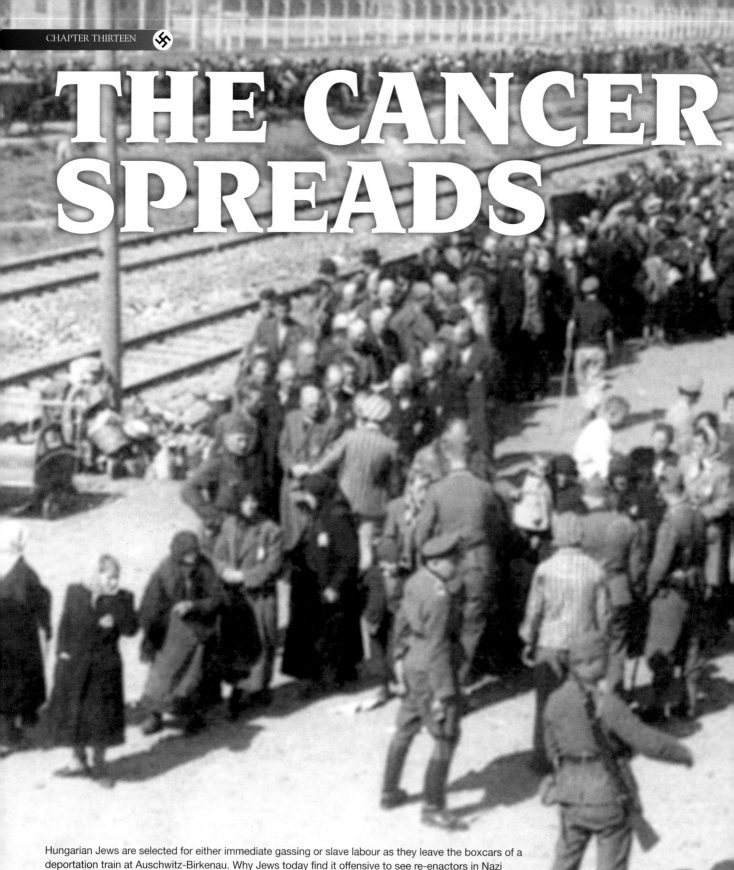

THE CANCER SPREADS

Hungarian Jews are selected for either immediate gassing or slave labour as they leave the boxcars of a deportation train at Auschwitz-Birkenau. Why Jews today find it offensive to see re-enactors in Nazi uniforms standing alongside trains at heritage railways in the UK might just about be understandable.

Shipping Jews and other unwanted people to their deaths was big business for the Deutsche Reichsbahn. Not only was it paid an estimated 240 Reichsmark to ship eight million people, but took its cut from the one-way tickets that the Jews themselves were forced to buy, after already being charged for accommodation in the ghetto. It was a win-win situation: the Nazi ideologists could humiliate the Jews even further, while there

were big bucks for those who took them to their deaths.

The Reichsbahn transported people from all over Germany to a central point of no return, travelling beyond the landmass of Axis-occupied Europe, Norway and North Africa. One day, had it not been stopped in its tracks, it could have been used on a sizeable portion of the British population, Jewish or not.

Belgium became the first country in Nazi-

occupied Western Europe to transport Jews to Auschwitz, sending them aboard so-called 'phantom trains' to France in the first instance.

Hitler placed General Alexander von Falkenhausen in military control of Belgium and Northern France, with SS Gruppenführer Eggert Reeder as his administrative deputy. Von Falkenhausen disagreed with the Nazi ideologists over Jews, and Reeder negotiated an agreement

Buchenwald and Auschwitz instead of Prisoner of War camps as per the Geneva convention.

The carriages and boxcars were packed as tightly as possible in order to maximise revenue. Railway staff forced all passengers, including young children and the elderly, to stand throughout trips which lasted several days, with no food, no drink, and no toilet facilities, and fewer than 3% of all those deported survived. SNCF staff even complained when Red Cross workers tried to provide food and water to the victims because it slowed down the deportation schedules. Senior rail officials accompanied the trains to the French border.

One SNCF train left the holding camp at Compiegne on July 2, 1944, with 2166 passengers. When it arrived at Dachau three days later, 536 people were already dead. SNCF employees cleaned the cars and disposed of the bodies of the deceased.

The internment camp at Drancy, built as subsidised housing in the form of tower blocks and run until August 1944 by Alois Brunner, a Nazi who ended up spending his latter years holed up in Damascus and might still be there alive today, was the deportation train transport hub for the Paris area. By February 3, 1944, 67 trains had departed for Birkenau.

Under the direction of Heinz Röthke, between August 1942 to June 1943, nearly two-thirds of those deported in SNCF boxcars requisitioned by the Nazis from Drancy were sent to Auschwitz.

It was also from Drancy that Klaus Barbie, the 'Butcher of Lyon', transported 44 Jewish children that he seized in a raid on a children's home at Izieu on April 6, 1944, to Auschwitz. There were 42 children and five adults, while two of the oldest children and the home's superintendent were killed by a firing squad in Estonia.

The last train from France left Drancy on July 31, 1944 with more than 300 children on board.

Independent studies have, over the ensuing decades, concluded that SNCF collaborated with the Nazis. In the first meeting with the Nazis concerning the deportations, it was agreed that SNCF would retain control and responsibility for the trains, including the technical arrangements. It has been said that while SNCF protested at any German order which could reduce profitability, not one voice was raised in anger over the death camp trains.

It was discovered that even after the Allies had liberated Paris following the D-Day landings in 1944, SNCF still submitted invoices for the deportations. The postwar French government declined to pay.

SNCF later publicly argued that its staff would have faced execution had they refused to operate the trains. Yet while it has been shown that some railway workers showed solidarity with deportees, only one footplateman refused to drive a deportation train. A man named Léon Bronchart refused on October 31, 1942, to work on such a train, and was given only a brief suspension for his

to allow native Belgian Jews to remain in Belgium, in a bid to encourage less resistance by local population to the German' rule.

A total of 2250 of unemployed Belgian Jews were sent to forced labour camps in Northern France to build the Atlantic Wall, while in 1942, 10,000 non-Belgian Jews were sent to Auschwitz, which received its first Belgian Jews on August 5 that year.

Between then and July 1944, 28 trains transported more than 25,000 Jewish deportees to Auschwitz.

THE WILLING FRENCH

The track record of France with regards to deportation trains could be judged appalling.

Between March 1942 and August 1944, SNCF shipped 76,000 Jews and other unwanted people to Nazi concentration camps – including US and Canadian pilots shot down over France who ended up in

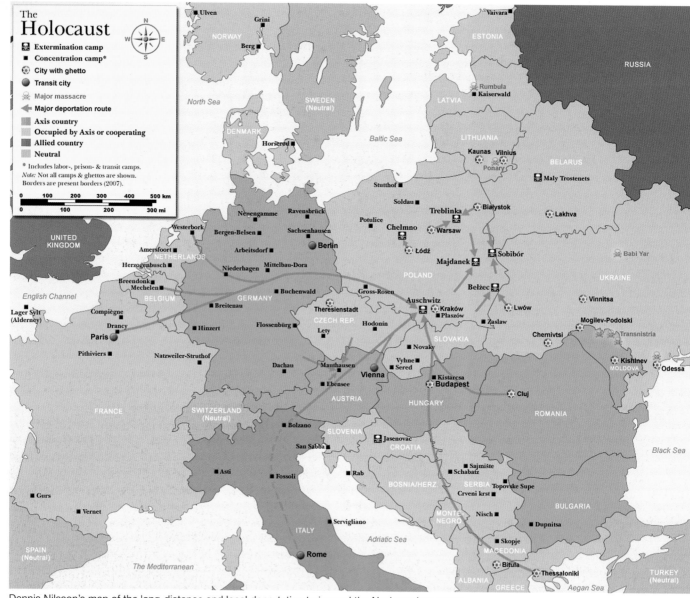

Dennis Nilsson's map of the long-distance and local deportation trains and the Nazi murder camps.

action. He was not even sacked, and was later honoured by Yad Vashem in Jerusalem as a "righteous gentile", giving lie again to the 'only obeying orders' myth.

No SNCF deportation train was ever sabotaged. Indeed, the transports continued into August 1944, two months after the Normandy invasion and a week before Paris was liberated.

Only on November 4, 2010 did Guillaume Pepy, the then chairman of SNCF, issue a statement saying that, "the Nazis and their French Vichy collaborators directed these terrible actions". The statement conveyed "profound sorrow and regret for the consequences" of the actions of SNCF.

Not only were Jews deported by SNCF from German-occupied France, but also from the 'free' Vichy area to the south. It was essential to the Germans that the Jews should appear to have been arrested and deported by Frenchmen.

The Vichy Government readily produced the Statut des Juifs (Statutes on Jews) of October 4, 1940, by which refugee Jews who had been deprived of their German nationality forfeited all civil rights.

When the deportations began in 1942, the Vichy authorities, however, still made determined efforts to protect French Jews while leaving the Nazis a free hand with nationals of other countries and stateless refugees. The Nazis in turn persuaded some of their allies, such as Romania, to agree to the deportation of their Jewish nationals living in France. By contrast, Italy and Spain agreed to take back their Jewish nationals and would not allow them to be deported.

Following years of lawsuits brought against SNCF by former deportees and their families – and successfully defended by the company – in March 2011 the US Congress introduced the Holocaust Rail Victims Justice Act to allow US citizens and others to make claims and to take action against railroad companies that had deported them or their relatives to Nazi concentration camps on trains owned or operated by those companies. At the time of writing, the bill is still waiting to be passed.

THE HUNGARIAN GENOCIDE

At first, Hungary resisted the deportation of Hungarian Jews to its ally Germany, but did deport 100,000 Jews in the former Romanian territory of Transylvania, and others from occupied Yugoslavia to be taken out.

However, learning about secret talks between Hungary and the British and Americans about surrender, Hitler launched Operation Margarethe and ordered Nazi troops to occupy the country.

Almost immediately, mass deportations of Jews to the murder camps began, under the auspices of Eichmann. Between May 15 and July 9, Hungarian authorities deported 437,402 Jews, with all but 15,000 going to Auschwitz-Birkenau, with 90% of them gassed on arrival. Indeed, one in three Jews killed at Auschwitz were Hungarian.

In April 1944, Eichmann's officials offered to sell exit visas for 600 Hungarian Jews in exchange for $1,600,000 in gold, diamonds, and cash. A special train was organised with the aid of Hungarian journalist and lawyer Rudolph Kastner, who acted on behalf of the Budapest Aid and Rescue Committee and who included 388 people from his home town of Cluj on the passenger list as well as his own family, later claiming that was done to assure the other travellers the train was safe, and was not bound for Auschwitz.

The train containing around 1700 Jews packed into 35 boxcars departed from

Budapest on June 30, 1944, around the same time of the mass deportations of Hungarian Jews to the murder camps.

On the passenger list were around 273 children, many of them orphaned, and 150 of the wealthier passengers paid $1000 each, so others could travel free.

It was by no means plain sailing. The train was stopped at the Hungarian-Austrian border, from where it could have gone west as promised, or east to Auschwitz. The passengers started panicking, but Eichmann decided, for reasons unknown, to send the train to Bergen-Belsen.

It stopped at Linz in Austria, where passengers were sent to a military delousing station for medical inspection, strip searches showers. They also had their heads shaved.

OPEN SECRET

Several fearful passengers wrongly believed that the showers would be gas chambers, again highlighting the fact that the true purpose of Auschwitz was by this stage at least an open secret despite later claims otherwise.

The train reached Bergen-Belsen on Sunday, July 9, and the passengers were held for weeks and in some cases months in a special camp on a meagre diet.

Yet the passengers were allowed to continue their journey as promised, and reached Switzerland in two batches, the first in August, the second in December 1944, with 1684 saved. In the meantime, several had died, while babies had been born. Around 17 were kept behind in Bergen-Belsen.

Kastner was later publicly lambasted for knowing about the true nature of Auschwitz and failing to alert the wider community in Hungary while saving his own friends and family.

His defenders argued that the existence of the Nazi murder camps was known, and Kastner was powerless to do anything more to stop the deportations.

The Israeli government sued the publisher of a newsletter which accused him of being a Nazi collaborator, in a trial running from January 1954 to June 1955.

The judge found against the government, ruling that Kastner had "sold his soul to the devil" by negotiating with Eichmann. After being the subject of several death threats, Kastner was assassinated in Tel Aviv in March 1957. Nine months later the Supreme Court of Israel overturned most of the lower court's ruling, saying the judge had "erred seriously".

THE GREATEST WAR HERO?

By now, the world was watching the deportations, and tried to act.

The Pope, the King of Sweden and the Red Cross all brought pressure to bear.

On July 8, 1944, the deportations stopped.

However, a coup that October saw the Arrow Cross pro-Nazi party take control of Hungary, and 50,000 of the remaining Jews were forced on a death march to Germany, digging anti-tank ditches on the roads

A Hungarian Jewish woman and young children selected for gassing unknowingly walk to their deaths alongside the railway lines at Birkenau.

Journey's end: Hungarian Jews, mainly women and children, stand alongside the boxcars that brought them to Birkenau and imminent death.

The French internment camp at Drancy.

Not all Hungarian Jews made it to Auschwitz. Pro-Nazi Arrow Cross militiamen would herd them to the edge of the river Danube in the capital Budapest, force them to take off their shoes and shoot them so they fell into the water and were carried away. The Shoes on the Danube Promenade memorial created by Gyula Pauer and Can Togay remembers those Jews and comprises pairs of period-appropriate shoes out of iron and attached to the stone embankment.

This Holocaust memorial in Warsaw features tracks leading up to a train car filled with crosses and the names of families murdered by the Nazis. SCOTT ROZIC*

And a jolly good time was had by all: laughing Nazi officers and female auxiliaries serving at Auschwitz pose on a wooden bridge at Solahuette while celebrating Christmas. Karl Hoecker, who compiled an album of pictures of his time serving as an adjutant to several concentration camp commanders, is in the centre. At his trial in Frankfurt, he denied having participated in the selection of victims at Birkenau or having any knowledge of the fate of the approximately 400,000 Hungarian Jews who were murdered at Auschwitz during his time there. In August 1965 Höcker was sentenced to seven years imprisonment for aiding and abetting more than 1000 murders at Auschwitz, and on May 3, 1989, a district court in Bielefeld sentenced Höcker to four years imprisonment for his involvement in gassing to death prisoners, mainly Polish Jews, at Majdanek. Camp records showed that between May 1943 and May 1944 Höcker had acquired at least 3610 kilograms of Zyklon B gas for use in Majdanek.

westwards. Around 15,000 Jews died during the brief reign of Arrow Cross.

In the meantime, in stepped a true hero of humanity.

Swedish diplomat Raoul Wallenberg was sent on a mission of mercy to save as many Hungarian Jews as possible. Along with fellow Swedish diplomat Per Anger, he issued 'protective passports' which identified the bearers as Swedish subjects awaiting repatriation. They were not legally binding, but looked the part, and when German and Hungarian officials were not convinced, bribes played their part.

The Swedish legation in Budapest also succeeded in negotiating with the German authorities so that the bearers of the protective passes would be treated as Swedish citizens and be exempt from having to wear the yellow Star of David.

Wallenberg rented 32 buildings in Budapest and declared them to be protected by diplomatic immunity. In then, around 10,000 Jews found a safe haven from the Hungarian authorities on 'Swedish' soil.

Bravest of all, he shamed the Germans into stopping the deportation trains.

In one instance, he climbed up on the roof of the train and began handing in protective passes through the doors which had not yet been sealed.

The Germans shouted at him to get down, but Wallenberg ignored them.

The Arrow Cross soldiers at the station began shooting at him, but… aimed over his head, because they too were in aware of his sheer nerve and bravery.

Wallenberg then ordered everyone with a 'Swedish passport' to get off the train and head for a row of cars to take them away. The soldiers were dumbstruck, and allowed him to get away with it.

PLOT FOILED

Wallenberg also stalled a plan to blow up the Budapest ghetto and kill an estimated 70,000 Jews, by threatening to have the perpetrators prosecuted for war crimes.

Swiss diplomat Carl Lutz also issued protective passports from the Swiss embassy in the spring of 1944, and Italian businessman Giorgio Perlasca posed as a Spanish diplomat and issued forged visas.

Raoul Wallenberg disappeared after the Soviet invasion in January 1945, being summonsed to General Malinovsky's headquarters in Debrecen to answer allegations that he was engaged in espionage.

He was taken by train from Debrecen via Romania to Moscow, where he was transferred to Lubyanka prison. On March 8 1945, Hungarian radio announced that Wallenberg and his driver had been murdered on their way to Debrecen, possibly by the Arrow Cross or the Gestapo.

On February 6, 1957, the Soviet government released a document claimed that Wallenberg had died suddenly in his cell on July 17, 1947, "probably as a result of a heart attack or heart failure". His personal belongings were returned to his family in

1989, including his passport and cigarette case. In 1991, a Russian investigation concluded that Wallenberg had been executed in prison in 1947, although no explanation has ever been given, and there were reports that he had been seen years later in the Soviet penal system.

MUSSOLINI'S 'HAVEN'

Italy had become a staunch Hitler ally under the fascist leader Benito Mussolini. Yet while he had been preaching anti-Semitism as early as 1936, and two years later his government passed the Racial Laws which made Jews second-class citizens, he resisted the deportation of Italian Jews to Germany.

That all changed after the Allied invasion of Italy and the first overthrow of Mussolini. Following the September 8, 1943 Armistice with Italy, the Germans occupied northern Italy, where Mussolini was re-established in a Nazi puppet state, and deported 8000 Jews to Birkenau.

They were followed by around 10,000 Italian partisans, while between September 1943 and April 1944, at least 23,000 Italian soldiers were deported to work as forced labourers in German industry.

In October 1942, 770 Norwegian Jews were deported by boat to Hamburg and sent onwards by train to Auschwitz.

GREECE, BULGARIA AND ROMANIA

On February 22, 1943, the Bulgarian government agreed to allow the Germans to deport 11,000 Jews from today's territories of the Republic of Macedonia and Greece.

These trains took four days to reach Auschwitz and were so packed that they had to stop each day to dump the bodies of the newly deceased.

More than 40,000 Jews were deported from Greece to Auschwitz-Birkenau between March and August 1943 after, following the Nazi invasion, an internment camp was set up in Athens. From there, Jews were shipped to another internment camp at Thessaloniki, to which Jews from the Greek islands were sent.

Romanian Railways (Căile Ferate Române) carried Jews and gypsies to concentration camps in Romanian Old Kingdom, Bessarabia, northern Bukovina, and Transnistria. In some cases, the conditions on the trains were so bad that only a fifth of the passengers survived. The national railway company has still to issue an apology for what it did.

THE COUNTRY THAT PAID

While the Czechs suffered harshly under Nazi occupation, the eastern half of Czechoslovakia became a puppet state supportive of Hitler.

Uniquely among Axis-occupied territory, the normally-independent Slovakia actually asked the Germans if they could pay them to get rid of their Jews.

On September 9, 1941, the fascist parliament passed the Jewish Codex, a series of laws and regulations that stripped the little country's 80,000 Jews of their civil rights.

The Slovakian government then paid the Nazis 500 Reichmarks for taking each Jew on condition they would never come back. Altogether, the SS earned 40 million Reichmarks from this.

THE LAST TRAINS OF SHAME

Some even believe that deportation trains passed through neutral Switzerland en route from Italy to Austria and Germany, but there is no concrete evidence. Under previous treaties, Switzerland was forced to allow Germany to ship certain goods excluding soldiers and armaments through the St Gotthard Tunnel.

With the Red Army advancing, and the closure of the Birkenau death factory, Nazi deportation trains dwindled. Instead, the SS sent thousands of prisoners on death marches westwards, making use of the labour to build anti-tank ditches.

The last recorded deportation train shipped women from the Flossenbürg concentration camp who had been forced to take part in a death march.

On April 20, 1945, the SS began the forced evacuation of 22,000 prisoners including 1700 Jews, to Dachau concentration camp, shooting anyone too weak to keep up. By the time they reached Dachau, more than 7000 marchers were dead.

The remaining survivors were crammed into boxcars to be sent to Bergen-Belsen, and only 200 out of 1000 women survived the entire trip.

Had Operation Sealion succeeded, where would the Jews of Britain have gone? Transported by the Southern Railway to Dover and across the Channel to the great abyss beyond, probably followed by every able-bodied Englishman to reduce the risk of rebellion? Or perhaps there might have been a Belzec or Chelmno on Salisbury Plain, or in the Scottish Highlands. Had Hitler won the war, it's argued this certainly would have happened.

SS photograph of two Jewish women resistance fighters captured during the Warsaw ghetto uprising of April/May 1943. Somewhat miraculously, Malka Zdrojewicz (right), survived Majdanek extermination camp.

Raoul Wallenberg, the Swedish diplomat who defied gun-toting German and Hungarian guards to hand out hundreds of fake passports on the roof of a deportation train to save the Jews inside from certain death.

French railway operator SNCF is today facing lawsuits from survivors of deportation trains that it was pro Nazi. It was issuing invoices for payment of services rendered in organising, staffing and running the death camp trains even after France was liberated by the Allies. SNCF

ONLY DISOBEYING ORDERS

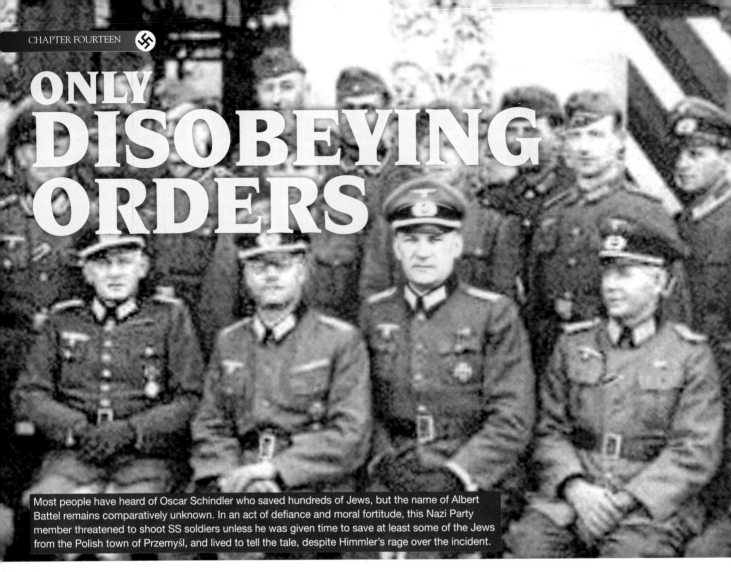

Most people have heard of Oscar Schindler who saved hundreds of Jews, but the name of Albert Battel remains comparatively unknown. In an act of defiance and moral fortitude, this Nazi Party member threatened to shoot SS soldiers unless he was given time to save at least some of the Jews from the Polish town of Przemyśl, and lived to tell the tale, despite Himmler's rage over the incident.

There is no doubting the fact that in Nazi Germany, thought could be considered a capital crime.

As the war progressed, it became increasingly clear that if the Gestapo chose to do so, anyone could be arrested on the most spurious of excuses and whisked off to a concentration camp or worse.

Take the case of armaments factory worker Marianne Elise Kürchner, a full-blooded Aryan German woman from Berlin, who told a silly joke to a fellow staff member: "Hitler and Goering are standing atop the Berlin radio tower. Hitler says he wants to do something to put a smile on Berliners' faces. So Goering says: 'Why don't you jump?'"

Don't all laugh at once for it isn't really that funny. Marianne's co-worker also clearly did not see the humorous side of it because she denounced her to the authorities.

Telling tales to the Gestapo usually led to an arrest and the offender was normally given a warning by a court, or at worse sent off to Dachau for a few months of hard labour re-education.

However, Marianne was called up before the People's Court, a body which did not adhere to any book of statutes and could dish out punishments as it saw fit. She appeared before its president, Roland Freisler, aka Raving Roland, who acted as prosecutor, judge and jury, and was infamous for his howling belligerent speeches and humiliation of defendants,

calling them names like "dirty dog" or "you lousy bastard".

Incidentally, if anyone reading this still thinks there is another side to the story and the Third Reich was not all as black or insane as has been painted by the victors, who of course write history, try a Google/You Tube search for Roland Freisler and watch the short film clips of him in action from the court bench. His crazed rants struck fear into the hearts of even hardened Nazis who could hear him shouting and screaming almost uncontrollably at defendants way down the corridors outside the courtroom, and in most cases he handed out pre-determined death sentences which were often carried out the same day.

Even some members of the Nazi hierarchy asked Hitler to rein Freisler in because they considered him to be an embarrassment, but the Fuhrer would have none of it.

Marianne admitted in court that she had made the joke but said she had not been herself at the time and had been feeling bitter about the recent loss of her husband at the front.

Freisler was unmoved. Individual suffering was no defence in his court.

He delivered his verdict on June 26, 1943: "As the widow of a fallen German soldier, Marianne Kürchner tried to undermine our will to manly defence and dedicated labour in the armaments sector toward victory by

making malicious remarks about the Führer and the German people and by uttering the wish that we should lose the war. She has excluded herself from the racial community. Her honour has been permanently destroyed and therefore she shall be punished with death."

Marianne was guillotined shortly afterwards.

Incidentally, Freisler (who had been a delegate at the Wannsee Conference) was conducting a Saturday session of the People's Court on February 3, 1945, and was in the process of trying Fabian von Schlabrendorff, a member of the July 20 bomb plot to kill Hitler, and who had resigned himself to certain death that day.

As Freisler adjourned for lunch, US bombers attacked Berlin and there was a direct hit on the People's Court. Was there a god somewhere guiding that bomb? Many indeed wondered, for a beam fell on Freisler, killing him outright, a cleaner death than those he meted out to those he found guilty, many of whom were slowly hanged with piano wire from meathooks a few hours later. When his body was brought into Luetzow Hospital shortly afterwards, someone commented that his death had been "God's will" and nobody there raised a voice in dissent.

Von Schlabrendorff not only survived but also became a judge of the Constitutional Court of the Federal Republic of Germany.

On October 15, 1941, Hans Frank,

Governor General of Nazi-occupied Poland, issued an order which clearly stated: "All persons hiding Jews outside (any) ghetto will be punished by death."

Poles, Germans and Jews alike knew he meant every word, for if you were found helping a jew, you could be shot or hanged in public.

On October 1, 1942, SS Commander Hans Rauter, military commander of Amsterdam, messaged Himmler: "Every Jew anywhere in Holland and non-Jews who help Jews will be rounded up and shipped to (Auschwitz)." Himmler replied: "Very good."

Yet the other side of the coin is that despite this widespread climate of terror, there were people who were ready to defy Nazi ideology, and not only lived to tell the tale, but went unpunished altogether. Earlier, we saw how public protests forced Hitler to stop the Aktion T4 programme in 1941.

In Minsk, the Nazi Generalkommissar of White Russia, Wilhelm Kube, declined repeatedly to allow mass murders of Jews who had been deported from Germany to the city, though he still allowed the killing of their Russian counterparts. However, he nonetheless objected to any sadistic and inhumane treatment of any Jews while they were alive. SS officials challenged his stance, but he went unpunished.

In Auschwitz itself, a number of doctors refused to carry out the medical experiments on prisoners and were merely reassigned to other duties, again without reprisals.

There are several documented cases of Nazis who refused to murder or take part in massacres, or even participate in anti-Semitic activities. They were simply switched to another job.

There was, however, a big difference between those who refused to murder Jews and those who were found to be helping or hiding them, for whom the repercussions were merciless.

Denmark was in many instances heralded by the Nazis as a perfect example of an occupied state: If you played ball with the German forces, you would come to no harm. The Channel Islands was highlighted by the propaganda machine in a similar manner.

The Germans invaded Denmark in 1940, but Danish officials from King Christian X down to police officers – and including railway workers – refused to help the Gestapo to find Jews or to introduce anti-Semitic measures. Not only were there no reprisals, but even the German Army declined to help the Gestapo round up Danish Jews.

There were around 7800 Jews in Denmark and more than 7200 were saved through a massive all-out effort to take them by boat to sanctuary in neutral Sweden. It is said that local German officials turned a blind eye to the transports.

It is clear that those at the head of Deutsche Reichsbahn knew about the purpose of the deportation trains.

Yet there are documented examples of senior officials who knew, and who refused to co-operate. And nothing happened to them.

In his book Hitler's Trains, Alfred C Mierzejewski cites several such cases.

Richard Neuser, a conductor based at Bialystok in Poland, where on June 27, 1941, up to 700 Jews were burned alive in the Great Synagogue, had been told by workmates about the appalling conditions on the Jewish deportation trains and the fate that lay in store at the end of the journey.

Neuser told the head of operations that he would rather have nothing to do with Operation Reinhard trains.

His wish was granted, and he was never asked to handle any of the deportation trains. Furthermore, nothing whatsoever happened to him in reprisal.

Then there was Alfons Glas, who worked in Office 33 at the headquarters of the Ostbahn, the Eastern Railway in occupied Poland.

His job included helping to schedule the deportation trains.

He surely cannot have been unique in wondering what happened to the huge numbers of passengers on board the trains, and what the camps were really like.

Glas worked out that many of the passengers were going to their deaths, and requested a transfer.

His superiors readily agreed to his request, and that was the end of the matter.

Historians have stated over the decades that ordinary railwaymen took the trains to the entrance to the camps. There, SS locomotive crews took over and drove the trains inside, closing the gates behind them.

Did none of the footplate crews ever ask why? Did they never wonder why men, women and children were packed inside boxcars and taken on lengthy journeys in appalling conditions for days at a time without food, water or even a toilet stop? Was it never asked why trains of apparently harmless and often malnourished people had to be accompanied by armed guards?

Of course, the Germans did take extraordinary steps to hide the true purpose of the deportation trains; on one hand to avoid another public opinion backlash in the Fatherland, and on the other to continue with the elaborate web of deceit that had persuaded many of the passengers to turn up in the first place.

It was even said by Auschwitz survivors that it was forbidden on pain of death even to talk about gas chambers in the camp.

Yet did these SS locomotive crews remain silent to a man throughout Operation Reinhard? Was Germany immune from the friendly banter which was part and parcel in every locomotive depot on every railway system (certainly those in Britain) throughout the world.

Even those who knew better than to ask questions – how did they live with their own silent suspicions?

Clearly, aware of the prevailing climate, many ordinary railwaymen would have been more concerned about the well-being of their own families than those of total strangers, whom others in far higher positions had given the authority to dispose of.

How many more railwaymen asked for

transfers rather than become tiny but crucial cogs in this steel-wheeled killing machine? There is no record of any such request from the railway sections themselves, nor of any other protest.

For me, it is too simple to say they did not know anything.

Mierzejewski highlights the case of Rolf Ruckel, who was employed in Office 23, which was responsible for the freight train schedules. He recalled that the real purpose of the deportation trains was general knowledge within the department.

Again, you have to look at the life and times before passing judgment. Berlin was at the heart of Nazi ideology and German patriotism. At best, a lone voice would

Wehrmacht commander Major Max Liedtke, another unsung hero of the Second World War, who said no to killing Jews.

Wilhelm Kube, the Nazi Generalkommissar of White Russia, who stopped the SS from killing German Jews sent to Minsk. He was assassinated in his Minsk apartment on September 1943 after a maid, Yelena Mazanik, hid a hot water bottle containing a bomb in his bed. The SS killed more than 1000 male citizens of Minsk in reprisals, although Himmler was pleased by the assassination as Kube did not support some of the harsh measures of the SS. The maid lived to joined the partisans and afterwards became a hero of the Soviet Union.

have been swimming against a tidal wave of negativity.

Deutsche Reichsbahn as an entity had, just like Britain's London & North Eastern or Great Western Railway, pride in performing its role to the best of its ability.

It was there to serve the government and the people, regardless of the demands placed on it. Many railwaymen saw it as a mark of honour to obey orders from their employer, just as it was their patriotic duty to serve the government.

Look at the French national railway operator SNCF, which like the rest of the country fell under German and collaborationist Vichy control in 1940. Recent figures suggest that 80,000 political prisoners and 76,000 Jews were deported from France between 1940 and 1944 on 475 trains. Yet records show that only one driver refused to take part. Again, ignorance of the nature of the deportation trains and the purpose of their ultimate destinations have been cited as reasons why French railwaymen contributed to the Holocaust.

In his 1992 book Ordinary Men: Reserve Police Battalion 101 and the Final Solution in Poland, the historian Christopher Browning looks at the role of German Ordnungspolizei (Order Police) Reserve Unit 101, used to massacre and round up Jews for deportation by railway to the murder camps in Poland in 1942.

He argued that the men who carried out such atrocities were by no means hardcore Nazi ideologists, but middle-aged working-class men from Hamburg who were otherwise unfit for military duty.

In some instances, these men were ordered to round up Jews and shoot them if there was insufficient space for them on the deportation trains.

Browning's case, which has its critics, was that Unit 101 members murdered out of basic obedience to authority and peer pressure rather than sadism or ancestral hatred of Jews. In a coherent group setting, he argued, most people will follow given commands, even if they believe them to be morally questionable.

Furthermore, Browning claimed people will more than likely follow orders, even those they might personally question, when they see them as coming from a higher authority.

The commander of Unit 101 gave his men the choice of opting out of massacring Jews if they found the job too unpleasant, yet the vast majority elected to carry on regardless. Less than 15 out of 500 men chose not to take part.

For me, two dissenting Nazi voices still sound loud and clear from those black days.

Wehrmacht commander Major Max Liedtke, the military governor of the city, and his lieutenant Albert Battel were stationed in the city of Przemyśl in southern Poland when the SS arrived to 'resettle' the substantial Jewish population, which had been persecuted since the Germans invaded on September 15, 1939, the first mass executions of approximately 600 Jews taking place over the next four days.

Oberleutnan Battel, then 51, had already been in hot water with the Nazi party, which he had joined in 1933, for friendly behaviour toward the Jews.

As the SS approached the town on July 26, 1942, Battel asked the Gestapo if he could keep the Jews who worked for the army, but the request was refused.

He gained the support of Liedke and in broad daylight ordered the bridge over the River San, the sole access to the Jewish ghetto, to be blocked.

The citizens of Przemyśl were amazed at what happened next.

As the SS troops prepared to cross the bridge, Battel's sergeant-major threatened to fire on them unless they pulled back.

After calling Julian Scherner, their commander in Krakow, the Gestapo gave in to Battel.

A few hours later, Battel sent an army detachment into the cordoned-off area of the town where the Jews lived.

He ordered trucks to evacuate around 80-100 Jews, who worked for the army, and their families.

These Jews were taken to the Wehrmacht barracks and placed under military protection. Sadly, Battel and Liedtke could do nothing to prevent the removal of the bulk of the Jewish population in the town in the coming days.

The SS entered Przemyśl, and 'evacuated' the Jews, including the head of the Judenrat, Dr Duldig, loading them on to trains which took them straight to Belzec.

During one mass deportation, an SS man was seen to catch a Jewish woman who was holding a baby in her arms. She began asking for mercy, pleading that she alone be shot, leaving the baby alive. Behind the fence stood a group of Poles ready to catch the baby, but the SS man snatched him from her arms and shot her twice, before, it was witnessed, he took the infant "and tore him as one would tear a rag".

Battel's Jews, however, survived.

The SS launched a secret investigation

SS Commander Hans Rauter, military commander of Amsterdam, threatened to send any non-Jew found helping Jews to hide straight to Auschwitz. Among his responsbilities was Kamp Westerbork from which 100,000 Dutch Jews were sent by train to the east and the death camps. After the Second World War, he was convicted in the Netherlands of crimes against humanity and executed by firing squad on March 24, 1949.

Hans Frank, Governor General of Nazi-occupied Poland, threatened anyone hiding Jews outside a ghetto with death. He once told his senior officers: "I must ask you to rid yourself of all feelings of pity. We must annihilate the Jews wherever we find them and whenever it is possible." He later claimed that he was unaware of the extermination camps in his territory until early in 1944, but was hanged for war crimes on October 19, 1946.

A typical Nazi poster designed to spread hatred of Jews. Despite Goebbels' propaganda machine, not even all Nazis were convinced.

into the embarrassing conduct of Battel, and Himmler soon heard about his escapade. Needless to say, he was livid. However, he chose not to risk a confrontation with Wehrmacht officers, but swore to take his revenge on Battel and have him arrested after the war ended, stating so in a letter to Martin Bormann, Hitler's right-hand man. Battel was unaware of the attention he was receiving in the highest echelons of hatred.

Sceptics might say that Battel and his superior chose to save Jews only because they were of practical use to his army detachment.

However, Battel had already been indicted before a party tribunal for having extended a loan to a Jewish colleague.

While based at Przemyśl, he was officially reprimanded for cordially shaking the hand of Dr Duldig.

Battel also received a reprimand for defying the SS at the bridge, but was later promoted. He was discharged from military service in 1944 because of heart disease. Back in his native Breslau, he was drafted into the Volkssturm, a latter-day German Home Guard. While serving in it, he was taken prisoner by the Red Army.

After his release, he settled in West Germany, but despite his heroic actions, which remained largely unknown, he was barred from practising as a lawyer, his profession before the war, because he had been a Nazi.

Battel died in 1952, outliving Himmler by seven years, but his stand against the SS became known only through the research of the Israeli lawyer Dr Zeev Goshen.

On January 22, 1981, the Israeli Holocaust Centre Yad Vashem named Albert Battel as one of the Righteous Among The Nations.

The same honour was bestowed on Max Liedtke, who was dismissed as military commander of Przemyśl on September 30, 1942, probably because of the Battel incident. He was redeployed in the 1st Panzer Army and at the war's end was sentenced by the USSR for war crimes allegedly committed in Russia. Three years younger than Battel, he died in 1955, still a Soviet prisoner.

The pair had, nonetheless, as in the case of Oskar Schindler, showed that even in members of a fascist party, human decency could still cast a blinding light.

Maybe Battel's genuinely heroic stand might come to be far wider applauded by future generations.

Research over the ensuing decades has brought to light at least 100 cases of German soldiers, policemen, or even members of the SS, disobeying orders to kill Jews, POWS or other unarmed civilians.

In some of these documented cases, the men concerned flatly refused to commit murder. In other cases, especially where police or army units not under the immediate control of the SS were asked to help out, they protested to their superior officers, citing their own mental torture, religion or conscience.

Some, like the above-mentioned

The Great Synagogue in Bialystok where, on June 27, 1941, up to 700 Jews were burned alive by the Germans. One train conductor said he wanted nothing to do with the deportation trains and was granted the request without reprisals.

Jews being forced over the railway bridge crossing the San River in Przemyśl.

railway official, obtained transfers, while others even feigned madness. One army officer in Poland told Jewish prisoners to run away while the security guard overseeing their round-up was not there. The subordinate guards assumed permission had been given and permitted the Jews to leave.

In other cases, dissenters deliberately lost their weapons, turned a blind eye to women and children hiding during searches, and even deliberately missed their aim while shooting prisoners.

In these cases, not one was shot for disobedience, and few were severely punished – bringing into question the excuse of 'only obeying orders'. Many historians have automatically considered in the circumstances of a terror state like the Third Reich that excuse to be watertight, but these cases show that in places at least, it was leaking like a sieve.

Despite widespread popular belief and the rantings of the likes of Roland Freisler, it has been demonstrated that there was not an effective automatic system of 'terror-justice' inflicted on those who refused to commit

atrocities such as the murder of harmless men, women and children.

Reprisals in two cases were that men were given a court martial and packed off to concentration camps, while others were punished by digging execution pits.

Most were merely given a warning or transferred, maybe with demotion to a lower rank, or given a slower promotion.

It has also been suggested that in many military cases, if a court martial had been held, the accused would have had the right to summon the person who gave the original order to kill, to give evidence to that effect. In theory, that would have gone right up the tree to Hitler himself. It is not known exactly when Hitler gave the order to murder the Jews, as no such document now exists, although there is no doubting the physical reality of the Holocaust. It may well have been that this order was never written down, so it could not be traced back to him or his close associates, and the last thing they would have wanted was for the burden of responsibility to have been revealed in court.

What would have happened if more Germans had said 'no'?

KINDERTRANSPORT
Nicholas Winton and other angels of mercy

Kindertransport children alighting in Britain, having gained the safe haven their families in Europe were to be denied by the Nazi killing machine. Millions of their counterparts would not be as fortunate.

New-build Peppercorn A1 Pacific No. 60163 *Tornado* storms through Chelmsford with the final leg of the 2009 'Winton Train' en route to Liverpool Street station. DAVID HAMILTON/A1SLT

Even the British began to sit up and take notice of the deterioration in attitudes towards Jews in Germany after Kristallnacht.

The British Government had refused to allow 10,000 Jewish children to enter Palestine, but in the wake of the visible nationwide outrage against the Jews on November 9, 1938, the British Jewish Refugee Committee appealed to the better nature of those in authority, including a direct approach to Prime Minister Neville Chamberlain, and accordingly a debate was held in the House of Commons.

As a result, the UK decided to allow an unspecified number of children under the age of 17 to enter the country from Germany and German-annexed territories on temporary travel documents, on the understanding that the children would rejoin their parents when everything returned to normal back home.

History was to record that it never did.

Most of the children who were evacuated from the darkening tyranny would never see any of their families alive again.

Appealing to Parliament, British Foreign Minister Samuel Hoare said: "Here is a chance of taking the young generation of a great people, here is a chance of mitigating to some extent the terrible suffering of their parents and their friends."

On November 25, the BBC Home Service broadcast an appeal by Viscount Samuel for foster homes.

An organisation for refugee relief had been established by Lola Hahn-Warburg several years earlier, with Lord Baldwin, Rebecca Sieff, Sir Wyndham Deeds, Viscount Samuel, and Rabbi Solomon Schonfeld, who

was to save about 1000 Jewish children. The Nazis agreed to a limited number of evacuation trains, but they had to be sealed. Furthermore, they demanded that the transports must not block German ports, so most of the trains went to the Netherlands, from where a cross-channel ferry from the Hook of Holland took them to Harwich in Essex. The Movement for the Care of Children from Germany co-ordinated many of the rescue efforts.

The first such train transport left Germany on December 1, 1938, with 200 orphan children on board, all of whom had left Germany with just 24 hours' notice and just two bags of clothing each. They came from a Jewish orphanage in Berlin which had been destroyed in Kristallnacht.

In Harwich the next day, the children who had been sponsored were whisked off to London by train to meet their new foster families. The rest were housed in the Dovercourt Bay holiday camp until foster families could be found.

Most of these trains departed from Berlin, Vienna, Prague, and other major cities in Central Europe. Children from smaller towns and villages travelled from their homes to these collection points to board the trains.

Jewish organisations inside the Greater German Reich – mainly the Reich Representation of German Jews, in Berlin, and the Jewish Community Organisation, in Vienna – drew up plans for the trains.

COMETH THE HOUR, COMETH THE MAN

At this time Nicholas Winton, a 29-year-old British Christian stockbroker, whose

parents were of German-Jewish descent, cut short a Swiss holiday and travelled to Prague after hearing of a growing refugee crisis resulting from the Nazi invasion of Czechoslovakia.

Martin Blake, a friend working in the British Embassy for the British Committee for Refugees from Czechoslovakia, and a master at Westminster School, was already helping adults flee the country, and after hearing that refugee children could not leave unattended, Nicholas decided to help.

He arranged for their evacuation from the Nazi-appointed Protectorate of Bohemia and Moravia to Britain by train, in what became known as Kindertransport.

He set up a team to identify those youngsters most at risk from persecution. Rescuers from his and other organisations and associations gave preference to children whose parents had been sent to concentration camps or who could no longer support them.

For each child to be accepted, British officials required a confirmed foster home and a £50 guarantee, and Nicholas went back to England to make arrangements for the children's arrival.

Starting in March 1939, he managed to organise eight trains, and saved a total of 669 mainly Jewish children, moving them from Czechoslovakia to Britain. A ninth train was due to depart the day the war broke out – it never left, and the children who were intended to ride on it suffered the fate of other Czech Jews.

The original trains left from Prague Wilson station, and while some children were placed with Essex families after getting off the boat, most travelled on to London's

Liverpool Street station. Organisations which helped the children start a new life included the Refugee Children's Movement, the B'nai B'rith, the Chief Rabbi's Religious Emergency Council, the YMCA and the Society of Friends. Some went to private homes across the whole of the British Isles and others to boarding schools.

Many who were over the age of 14 went into employment, often in agriculture.

As talk of the 'Englishman of Wenceslas Square' spread among the Czech Jews, more and more parents made contact and asked him to include their children on the list which would save their lives.

However, he was by no means alone. Among other remarkable angels of mercy was Gertruida Wijsmuller-Meijer, a Dutch Christian who badgered none other than Adolf Eichmann in Vienna until he suddenly agreed to release 600 children, thinking she would never manage to transport them. She defied him and succeeded, masterminding the first refugee train out of Vienna on December 10, 1938.

She also organised a transport from Riga to Sweden and helped smuggle a group of children onto the illegal ship *Dora* bound from Marseille to Palestine. She was also responsible for guiding the last transport through Nazi-bombed Amsterdam to the freighter Bodegraven in May 1940.

Lisa Midwinter, originally Lisa Dasch, who was born in Teplice in Czechoslovakia, was three when she boarded the train to England with her brother.

She recalled: "I remember this great big black object as high as you could see. I remember figures in blue, which must have been the train driver, singing and handkerchiefs, and terrific noise.

"I remember handkerchiefs being waved and crying, and seeing grown-ups crying."

She was later told that she had come from a middle-class Jewish family – a priority target for the Nazis who had occupied her homeland.

Evacuee Otto Deutsch, who fled by train from Vienna, said: "I never saw my parents again or my sister. My parents were shot and what they did with my sister I really don't want to know."

British author Vera Gissing, a passenger on a Winton train, wrote her biography and later turned it into a script for the film Power of Humanity.

She said: "He rescued most of the Jewish children of my generation in Czechoslovakia. Not many of us could reunite with our parents; they perished in the concentration camps. If we had not been separated from them, we would have died too."

The children saved by the Kindertransport programme also included British filmmaker Karel Reisz, who directed The French Lieutenant's Woman; British lawmaker and peer Alfred Dubs, who sat in the Blair cabinet; American physicists and Nobel laureates, Walter Kohn and Arno Penzias; Joe Schlesinger, one of Canada's most prominent TV journalists; costume designer Ruth Morley; Australian and German author Walter Kaufmann; Olympic and international footballer Rolf Decker; and Dr Ruth Westheimer, the American therapist and sex expert.

Refugee Eric Lucas later recalled his childhood journey on a Kindertransport, recounted on the Holocaust Research Project website at www.holocaust researchproject.org as follows:

"The town where we lived was the border-control point, as beyond it stretched the still free towns of Belgium and Holland. In just over an hour the train would speed through the fertile lowlands of Belgium, and would take me right to the Channel port of Ostend. I was the only passenger who boarded the train at that station. To travel abroad, to leave the country was only granted to emigrants and those who had a special reason connected with the interest of the State.

"The travellers were few, but the Customs officials and the guarding soldiers were many. The men on whose whim hung one's final leaving were the sinister tall figures in new black uniforms.

"When I was at last allowed to board the train I rushed to the window to look for my parents whom I could not see until I had left the customs shed. They stood there, in the distance, but they did not come to the train.

"I began to wave timidly and yet full of fear, after the control I had just passed, but even that was too much for the guards. A man in a black uniform rushed towards me: 'You Jewish swine – one more sign or word from you and we shall keep you here. You have passed the Customs.'

"And so I stood at the window of the train. In the distance stood a silent and ageing couple, to whom I dared neither speak nor wave a last farewell, but I could see their faces very distinctly in the light of the oncoming morning."

He added: "A few hours previously, first my father and then my mother had laid their hands gently on my bowed head to bless me, asking God to let me be like Ephraim and Menashe. 'Let it be well with you. Do your work and duty, and if God wills it, we shall see you again. Never forget that you are a Jew, do not forget your people, and do not forget us.'

"Thus my father had said and his eyes had grown soft and dim 'my boy – it may be that we can come after you, but you will never be away from me – or from your mother.'

"Tears streamed down her infinitely kind and sad face. With a last effort she continued in the old, so familiar Hebrew words: 'Go now, in life and peace.'

"Standing at the window of the train, I was suddenly overcome with a maiming certainty that I would never see my father and mother again.

"There they stood in the distance, lonely and with the sadness of death. Cruel hands kept us apart in that last intimate moment. A passionate rebellious cry stuck in my throat against all that senseless brutality and inhuman cruelty 'why, O God had it all to be like that'?"

Artist Frank Meisler's Kindertransport memorial stands outside Liverpool Street station. PAUL DEAN*

The headboard carried by the 2009 'Winton Train' during its British leg. SP SMILER*

Sir Nicholas Winton in the cab of A1 Pacific No. 60163 *Tornado*. KEN LORD/A1SLT

Kindertransport children in the holiday camp at Dovercourt Bay, near Harwich, at Christmas 1938.

A party of Kindertransport children crossing the tracks at Harwich station after disembarking from the ferry which brought them to safety from the Netherlands.

On display in a special Kindertransport exhibition in the Beth Shalom Holocaust Centre in Nottinghamshire is this bear, the symbol of Berlin, owned by Margaret Treharne. One of the Kindertransport children, she brought the bear on her trip to England and, in the decades that followed, took him as a mascot on every long-distance trip she made. ROBIN JONES

This statue of Sir Nicholas Winton was unveiled in Prague Main station on September 1, 2009. The girl is modelled on the granddaughter of a girl saved by one of Winton's original trains in 1939. Produced by sculptor Flor Kent, her other sculpture, Für Das Kind Kindertransport Memorial, was installed in Liverpool Street station, the other end of the transports. LUDEK KOVÁR

He continued: "There stood my father and my mother, an old man leaning heavily on his stick and holding his wife's hand. It was the first and last time in my life that I had seen them both weep. Now and then my mother would stretch her hand out, as if to grasp mine – but the hand fell back, knowing it could never reach.

"Can the world ever justify the pain that burned in my father's eyes? My father's eyes were gentle and soft, but filled with tears of loneliness and fear. They were the eyes of a child that seeks the kindness of its mother's face, and the protection of its father.

"As the train pulled out of the station to wheel me to safety, I leant my face against the cold glass of the window, and wept bitterly. Those who have crossed the Channel, escaping from fear of death to safety, can understand what it means to wait for those who are still beyond it, longing to cross it, but who will never reach those white cliffs, towering over the water."

Young Eric tried his best to get a visa for his parents Isaac and Sophie to follow him to England, but in vain, and four years later they died, probably in one of the murder camps, but precisely which one has never been established.

THE ONES THEY KEPT BEHIND

Tragically, a ninth and last Winton train with 250 children on board was stopped at the last minute, after war broke out. It had been due to leave Prague on September 1, 1939, but the Germans refused to allow it to depart. The children and their families were never heard of again.

The rescue operation saw between 9000-10,000 children, including 7500 who were Jewish, taken by train from Germany, Austria, Czechoslovakia, and Poland to Britain.

Bizarrely, British authorities interned as enemy aliens about 1000 children from the transport programme on the Isle of Man and in other internment camps in Canada and Australia. Nonetheless, several of the boys went on to enlist in the British Army and fight against Hitler.

The plight of the refugee children clearly did not elicit the same sympathy in the US as it did in Britain. In 1939, Senator Robert F Wagner and Representative Edith Rogers placed a bill before Congress to admit 20,000 Jewish unaccompanied children aged under 14 from Nazi Germany, but in February that year it failed to get Congressional approval.

Despite that setback, between November 1934 and May 1945, about 1400 unaccompanied, mostly Jewish children, between the ages of 14 months and 16 years, had been allowed entry into the US. However, while the UK government had waived immigration visa requirements, these children did not receive the same assistance, and there are stories that applications for entry were made notoriously difficult and took up to nine months to process. It was even harder for their parents to get a visa, and they were left behind in Europe as a result.

THE RELUCTANT HERO

Before the war broke out, Nicholas Winton sought registration as a conscientious objector and joined the Red Cross, but the following year changed his mind and joined the RAF, starting as an airman and rising to the rank of war substantive Pilot Officer and Flight Lieutenant.

However, his exploits in the face of Nazi terror came to light only after his late wife Greta found papers in their loft.

His work became public knowledge during the screening of a 1988 episode of the BBC TV series That's Life, when an unsuspecting Winton was invited to be an audience member.

However, during the programme, his scrapbook was shown. Hostess Esther Rantzen then asked if anyone in the audience owed their lives to him, and around 25 people stood up and applauded him.

In the 1983 Queen's Birthday Honours, Nicholas had been awarded an MBE for his work in establishing the Abbeyfield homes for the elderly in Britain, but in the 2002 New Year Honours he was knighted in recognition of his work in organising the Czech Kindertransport trains.

He received the Pride of Britain Award for Lifetime Achievement in 2003, and has also been honoured by the Czech government, and has been given the freedom of Prague. Prime Minister Tony Blair called him the 'British Schindler'.

A STEAMING TRIBUTE

In 2009 a special train was laid on to mark the 70th anniversary of the Kindertransport.

The train, carrying 22 of the original children on its three-day journey, departed from Prague on September 1 and ran through Germany and the Netherlands, tracing the route of its eight predecessors.

It was hauled by steam locomotives which would have been in use in the mid-20th century and comprised period coaching stock. Before it left, a statue of Sir Nicholas was unveiled at Prague station.

After crossing the North Sea to Harwich, the passengers were taken to Liverpool Street behind Britain's newest main line steam locomotive – Peppercorn A1 Pacific No. 60163 *Tornado* – which has been built by The A1 Steam Locomotive Trust (an organisation comprised of volunteers), at a cost of £3 million, and which had been officially launched into traffic by the Prince of Wales at York station that February.

Sir Nicholas, then 100, and largely confined to a wheelchair, was reunited with more than 20 of the children he had saved. Several of them had relived the journey they had made 70 years before, while others who could not make the trip greeted him at Liverpool Street, where a band played and hundreds of well-wishers crowded the platforms to greet the train.

He was presented with flowers, and climbed on to the locomotive's footplate.

Marianne Wolfson, 85, who flew from Chicago to ride on that train, said of the reluctant hero: "He doesn't think that what he did was a big deal, but we got our life back."

Alexandra Greensted, 77, from Maidstone, said: "It's a very emotional day for me. I can't remember much about the actual train journey. All I can remember is being at the railway station crying my eyes out. I left my father and two older brothers behind."

Sir Nicholas told 'his children': "It's wonderful to see you all after 70 years. Don't leave it quite so long until we meet here again."

Stefan Fule, the Czech Republic's Minister for European Affairs, said: "What Sir Nicholas did for these people is an amazing story - and it's a story that needs to be retold. Seventy years on, it's still taking our hearts and making people very emotional."

It is estimated there are about 5,000 people who today owe their lives to Sir Nicholas, comprising the 669 children he saved and their descendants.

Frank Meisler's Kindertransport memorial at Gdansk Główny station in Poland.

The Czech leg of the 2009 'Winton Train' was double-headed by preserved CSD Czechoslovak State Railway express 4-8-2s No. 486.007 and No. 498.022. Built by Skoda in the 1930s, No. 486.007 – known as Green Anton – was designed for heavy trains in hilly areas. Class members lasted in service until 1971. RAINER HAUFE

DRG Class 41 2-8-2 No. 41 018 hauled the 2009 'Winton Train' from Furth im Wald to Emmerich am Rhein in Germany. Built in 1939 under the Nazi regime, it is now based at the Augsburg Railway Park museum in Augsburg, Bavaria, and owned by DG München. From Linz am Rhein to Cologne, the train was double-headed with No. 41 360. RAINMOD SPEKKING*

CHAPTER SIXTEEN

Why wasn't Auschwitz bombed?

GAS CHAMBER

UNDRESSING ROOMS

CREMATORIUM II

ENGINE ROOMS

GAS CHAMBER

CREMATORIUM

CREMATORIUM III

AUCHWITZ-BIRKENAU EXTERMINATION CAMP
OSWIECIM, POLAND
25 AUGUST 1944

PRISONERS ON WAY TO GAS CHAMBERS

BOXCARS

PRISONERS

PRISONERS

WOMEN'S CAMPS

ENLARGED FROM THE ORIGINAL NEGATIVE AND CAPTIONED IN 1978 BY THE CIA

GUARD TOWERS

PRISONERS

MAIN GUARD HOUSE

US Air Force recognaissance aerial view of Auschwtiz-Birkenau clearly showing the killing apparatus.

The Allies has amassed a wealth of knowledge about the concentration camps long before they were liberated, despite the Nazis' exhaustive attempts to keep their true purpose a secret.

Jan Karski, a Polish resistance fighter and later professor at Georgetown University, reported to the Polish government in exile and the Allies on the Nazi ghettoes and camps, and spoke to anyone who'd listen, from the Pope to the Hollywood movie industry. Many didn't believe him, and it was said when he once spoke to President Franklin D Roosevelt he was suddenly asked about the state of horses in Poland.

However, aerial reconnaissance photographs taken in 1944 backed up intelligence reports from the ground and clearly showed the position of buildings including the chimneys of the crematoria, and even the cluster of dots between there and the railway line which comprised the latest consignment of victims to be shipped in.

The British Prime Minister Winston Churchill broadcast on November 14, 1941: "None has suffered more cruelly than the Jew the unspeakable evils wrought upon the bodies and spirits of men by Hitler and his vile regime. The Jew bore the brunt of the Nazis' first onslaught upon the citadels of freedom and human dignity. He has borne and continued to bear a burden that might have seen beyond endurance. He has not allowed it to break his spirit; he has never lost the will to resist. Assuredly in the day of victory the Jew's suffering and his part in the struggle will not be forgotten."

Reading in July 1944 the first detailed account of Auschwitz, Churchill wrote: "There is no doubt this is the most horrible crime ever committed in the whole history of the world, and it has been done by scientific machinery by nominally civilised men in the name of a great state and one of the leading races of Europe. It is quite clear that all concerned in this crime who may fall into our hands, including the people who only obeyed orders by carrying out the butcheries, should be put to death after their association with the murders has been proved."

At the time, it would be months before the US, British or Red Army got there, and how many countless numbers of innocent people would have to die before then? The gas chambers were capable of killing 10,000 people per day.

So... why not bomb Auschwitz-Birkenau?

True, there would have been a massive loss of life among the inmates, leading to Goebbels' propaganda ministry claiming that every single death that had ever taken place there had been due entirely to Allied bombing, just as several modern-day far-right groups try to convince the intellectually challenged that everyone who died in the camps was a plague victim.

Yet others say the risk would have been well worth it. The killing machine would have at least been temporarily disabled, and those killed in a bomb blast would die a 'quicker and cleaner' death than the Nazis had in store for them. The bonus would be that it could facilitate a mass-breakout, such as that engineered by the heroes of Sobibor on October 14, 1943. About 300 prisoners made it to the forest after killing some guards, and while many of them were subsequently rounded up or shot, up to 70 survived the war.

The question of why Auschwitz was not bombed has provoked debate for seven decades.

During his second visit to the Yad Vashem Holocaust memorial in Jerusalem in 2008, US President George W Bush said: "We should have bombed it."

Pragmatists, however, have pointed out that as with the case of Britain's rail network during the Second World War, it offered multiple routes to the same destination, so if one main line to Auschwitz had been damaged by an air strike, it would have posed little trouble to reroute the deportation trains while repairs were or were not carried out.

But what about the camp complex itself?

Until the Allies had gained a foothold in Europe following the Normandy landings, it would have proved difficult to bomb Auschwitz because of the limited range of aircraft. Historian David Wyman argues that the 15th US Army Air Force, which was based in Italy, had the range and capability to strike Auschwitz from early May 1944.

The bombing raid option appears to have been first mooted a month before D-Day, when allied forces were understandably busy 'softening up' the Atlantic defences prior to the invasion.

Slovak rabbi Michael Dov Ber Weissmandel suggested a bombing raid to the Jewish Agency on May 16, while two officials of the Jewish Agency in Palestine separately made similar requests around the same time.

Yitzhak Gruenbaum spoke to the US Consul-General in Jerusalem, Lowell C Pinkerton, and Moshe Shertok approached George Hall, the British under-secretary of state for foreign affairs. Yet the executive board of the Jewish Agency disagreed.

On June 11, 1944, the executive, with David Ben-Gurion in the chair, overwhelmingly rejected such proposals, because a raid would kill Jews.

On June 28, Aryeh Leon Kubowitzki, the head of the Rescue Department of the World Jewish Congress, voiced his outright opposition to the bombing calls made by Jewish leaders on the periphery, and wrote: "The destruction of the death installations cannot be done by bombing from the air, as the first victims would be the Jews who are gathered in these camps, and such a bombing would be a welcome pretext for the Germans to assert that their Jewish victims have been massacred not by their killers, but by the Allied bombers."

On July 7, soon after the US War Department refused requests from some Jewish authorities to bomb the railway lines leading to the camps, a force of 452 15th Air Force bombers flew along the five deportation railway lines en route to nearby oil refineries nearby. Indeed, one bomb fell into the grounds of Auschwitz.

Buna-Werke, the IG Farben industrial complex next to the Auschwitz III (Monowitz) slave labour camp just over three miles from Auschwitz I was the target of four bombing raids.

John Jay McCloy, the US Assistant Secretary of War during the Second World War, was asked outright on November 8, 1944, to bomb the camp. However, by that time, the camp was being wound down.

On December 26, 1944, the US 455th Bomb Group hit Monowitz and targets near Auschwitz-Birkenau, striking an SS military hospital.

During such raids, Auschwitz-Birkenau was photographed from the air several times (the first having been on April 4, 1944, in a mission to photograph the synthetic oil plant at Monowitz) but no serious attempt appeared to have been made to analyse the photographs and the layout of the buildings that were clearly visible.

On August 24, 1944, the US Army Air Corps bombed a factory adjacent to the Buchenwald concentration camp, killing 315 prisoners, seriously injuring 525 and wounding 900 others.

Some historians claim Churchill favoured bombing the camps. It was while writing to his foreign secretary on July 11, 1944 that he wrote the earlier quoted: "... all concerned in this crime who may fall into our hands, including the people who only obeyed orders by carrying out these butcheries, should be put to death..." However, the Air Ministry decided against the idea for "operational reasons".

There was also the strategic argument that the Allies were committed to bombing exclusively military targets in order to win the war as quickly as possible.

Furthermore, it was considered that airmen's lives would be at risk damaging railway lines which the Germans would have running again within days, and that disrupting rail supplies to the camps could lead to prisoners being deprived of food.

Laurence Rees, the writer and Bafta Award-winning producer of the BBC series which marked the 60th anniversary of the liberation of the camp in January 2005 Auschwitz: The Nazis & the 'Final Solution' said that the lack of proper consideration given to bombing the camp and a "dismissive tone" in some of the documents of the time give the sense that "no one was bothered enough to make bombing Auschwitz a priority". He remarked: "If they were exterminating British POWs do we seriously think that we wouldn't have done all we could to stop it?"

One Auschwitz survivor later recounted: "We were no longer afraid of death; at any rate not of that death. Every bomb that exploded filled us with joy and gave us new confidence in life."

Dr Alfred Gottwaldt of the Deutsches Technikmuseum in Berlin, a published expert on the deportation trains, believes that the explanation is much simpler.

"President Roosevelt would not want to be seen fighting for the Jews. Nationalist Americans would not want to die for Jews."

His words echo the anti-Semiticism that was rife in the US before the Second World War, and which clearly not only inspired the Nazis but gave them some sense of justification.

Churchill, said Dr Gottwaldt, was not anti-Semitic, but he was also aware of the mood of sections of the British public of the day. In a country which had seen marches by Oswald Mosley's Union of British Fascists, would Churchill have wanted to tell the electorate that he had "let our boys die for the Jews?"

THE TRANS-SAHARAN RAILWAY:
the persecution the world forgot

The use of railways by the Nazis to persecute the Jews and other minorities they found undesirable is automatically associated with Europe.

However, slave labour concentration camps were also established in North Africa after the fall of France and the founding of the Vichy government.

Thousands of Jews were deported across the Mediterranean to work on Hitler's grandiose scheme to build a railway that crossed French West Africa – one which would have provided no less than a springboard for world domination.

Had it been completed, it would have provided the Axis powers with a quick and efficient means to reach the tropics – and place South America within a 1600 mile bombing range.

On March 22, 1941, the collaborationist Vichy leader Marshal Philippe Pétain authorised the construction of a Trans-Saharan Railway, more correctly known as the Mediterranean-Niger Railway, using Jews, Czechs, Poles, and Spanish Republican soldiers as slave labour.

At the same time, Pétain's administration enacted legislation that stripped Algerian Jews of their French citizenship and extended the racial laws enacted in the French non-occupied territory to Tunisia, Algeria, and Morocco.

More than 1500 Jews who had fought in the French Foreign Legion against Germany in 1940 were deported to the Saharan slave labour camps.

A total of 17 slave labour concentration camps were located in North Africa: three in Morocco, three in Algeria, seven in Tunisia and four in Libya. Overall, there were said to be around 30 'detention' camps, Djelfa being the largest, holding 700 to 1000 prisoners.

The camps were administered by former officers of the Foreign Legion, who often made no effort to hide their sympathy for Nazi Germany.

At the camp at Hadjerat-M'Guil, for instance, many were sent to work on the railway project, while around 170 prisoners were tortured and murdered.

It was estimated that on the eve of the American invasion of North Africa, on November 8, 1942, around 4000 Jews were being held in camps in the south of Morocco and in Algeria.

Overall, it is estimated that there were 500,000 Jews living in French North Africa during the war. Thanks to the Vichy attitude towards the victorious Germans, they, like their European counterparts, also suffered the build-up to the Final Solution, with anti-Jewish laws, deportations, and slave labour camps, but not the gas chambers.

The Germans wanted the Mediterranean and the South Atlantic linked by a land route across Africa, but since time immemorial the Sahara Desert had provided a far more formidable barrier than the sea lanes of the Atlantic.

Hitler quickly recognised the enormous economic and military importance of Africa, and the potential that a Trans-Saharan railway could unlock.

Firstly, Germany would gain access to Central Africa's vast resources of cotton, rice, rubber, zinc copper, tungsten, peanuts (a source of oil), bananas, cocoa, coffee and many other overseas products, supplies of which had been cut off by the British blockade. With a railway to export them, Germany could become self-sufficient.

Once the 2200 mile railway from Algiers reached its intended destination of Dakar in Senegal, the Nazis would be able to attack British shipping routes around the Cape of Good Hope to India and South America.

Furthermore, a naval base at Dakar might give Germany a perfect launch pad for a future attack on South America. Bombers could reach Brazil from there in six hours.

As it was, the southern portions of the French West Africa empire were practically isolated, the vast interior regions presenting an almost insurmountable barrier between them

Slave labourers working on the Trans-Saharan Railway near the notorious work camp of Bouarfa.

and Algiers. The war with a strong naval power like Britain placed the southernmost French territories at great risk, but if a railway offered speedy transport from Algeria, it might well be a very different matter.

There had been a confrontation between the British and the Vichy navies at Dakar early in the war. The Battle of Dakar, also known as Operation Menace, was an unsuccessful attempt in September 1940 by the Allies to capture the port and install Free French Forces under General Charles de Gaulle there.

The Vichy forces did not back down, and while the battle was in progress, Vichy bombers based in North Africa attacked the British base at Gibraltar. Eventually, after a few days, the Allies withdrew, leaving Dakar and French West Africa in Vichy hands, and a ripe destination for Hitler's railroad to be built by his new French puppets.

A Trans-Saharan railway was first proposed in 1873, when Paul Solleilet presented a project to the Ministre des Communications et Colonies. Six years later, Armand Duponchel published Le Chemin de Fer Transsaharien, proposing a trans-Saharan railway scheme at a cost of 1.6 million francs per kilometre. For various reasons, these came to nothing, but like Britain's Channel Tunnel project, they were reconsidered every two decades or so. It received serious consideration in the 1900s, and in 1928, the French parliament commissioned a study, only for the Great Depression to sink the scheme again.

Small sections of the route had been built before the Second World War. In 1931 a standard gauge line had been completed by the Mediterranean Niger Railway Company between the coal mining region near Bouarfa in the east and the Algerian rail system at Oujda. In 1940 construction was begun on the Algerian segment of the proposed railway, linking to the Moroccan segment, completed in 1931, at Bouarfa and continuing into Algeria to connect with the 1055mm narrow gauge line at Colomb-Bechar.

The section of line which ran south to Colomb-Bechar, deep in the interior of Algeria, and another running north from Dakar to Bamako, in what is now Mali, are still in use today.

In the Thirties, while Britain and Germany were breaking speed records on existing lines, the French government again looked seriously at the project to build the whole route. After the fall of France, the scheme was seen by Hitler as a perk of the conquest, and for him it opened up new horizons.

The idea was the link up existing short stretches of line, one running south through Algeria to the city of Colomb-Bechar, on the southern slope of the Atlas Mountains, and the other running from Dakar through tropical West Africa to Segou.

The line would not be built on sandy desert, as that would be incapable of holding the tracks, but on nearby hard ground comprising rock and pebbles.

Slave labourers were moved into place in late 1940. On February 8, 1941, the construction of the first 100 miles of the section between Bouarfa and Kenadsa began. Jean Berthelot, the Secretary of State for Communications, visited Africa to open the first section of this railway amid much pomp. The Vichy regime pledged up to 5000 million francs.

Indeed, the construction of the railway became a pet project for Vichy France. On March 22, 1941, a law was passed formally authorising its construction from Bouarfa and continuing through Béchar, Kenadsa, Beni Abbès, and Adrar. In Tassit in Niger, the route would split and then reach its final destinations, Segou and Niamey.

"France builds road of imperial conquest for Hitler," ran the headline in the New York Times of August 5, 1941, with the sub heading "French and Nazi engineers speed construction of railway vital to attack on western hemisphere."

The scheme looked brilliant on paper, but the practicalities were very different. The scarcity and poor quality of the water obtainable in the desert areas of the Sahara precluded the use of steam locomotives, and there would be insufficient time to carry out geological surveys and exploratory drilling for underground reserves.

So diesel and electric locomotives would have to be used. The Vichy scheme proposed the use of hydro-electric power from a dam on the Niger River built in 1929 to power electric locomotives, while the use of diesels would permit the 1200 kilometres of the Sahara to be crossed from north to south without stopping.

The war had by then made it impossible to import powerful locomotives from the United States. After the French defeat, locomotives that had been ordered remained in the possession of the Allies.

Under the plans, a journey from the Mediterranean to Niger would take two days at 40mph. What was a French/German equivalent of the Trans-Siberian Railway would be built in three years, but to aid the war effort, a temporary field railway might

be built in six months. The French press made much of the grandiose scheme. However, on the ground, the reality was very different, if only in human terms.

The construction workers lived in barracks, hovels made from wood and clay, with sub-basic toilet facilities. SNCF staff who had been delegated to the project slept in their offices.

In daily conditions of blistering heat, the work was carried out by bare hand.

Many of the workers quickly succumbed to diseases such as typhus and perished on the construction sites.

One story of acute hardship was told by Morice Tondowskia, a Jewish tailor's apprentice who left Poland at the age of 26 in 1937 for France to escape what many by then saw as an inevitable war.

When war broke out in 1939, all male refugees in France were ordered to register for military service and Morice joined the Foreign Legion, which posted him to Meknes in Morocco.

One day after the Vichy regime came to power, Morice was stripped of his rifle by his French commanding officers without any warning or explanation, and sent to the edge of the Sahara.

From the hot springs oasis of Berguent, he and other Jews, either regular soldiers or illegal refugees, were marched at gunpoint to an empty expanse of desert five miles away.

His party was told to dig holes in the earth to sleep in, covered with a thin canvas to protect them from the desert night frost.

He and the rest had unknowingly become slave labourers, for no reason other than they were Jewish. Indeed, it was France's only all-Jewish labour camp in North Africa, and among its 7000 prisoners were around 2000 Jews.

The prisoners toiled from dawn to dusk with little food, water or rest, let alone medical care.

They were ordered to collect, break, load and move rocks to pave the way for the Trans-Sahara Railway.

A 1940s poster advertising the Trans-Saharan Railway.

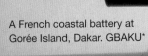

A French coastal battery at Gorée Island, Dakar. GBAKU*

A contemporary artist's impression of a diesel train running on the Trans-Saharan Railway.

If the weather or work did not get to them, the brutal camp guards, mostly Legionnaires, would. Torture was rife. Misdemeanours such as escape attempts were punished by throwing the offender into an open pit where he would be ordered to lie still, boiling in the day and freezing by night, without food or water, until he died.

Another Jewish Legionnaire, Conrad Singer, was discharged in 1940 after the fall of France and interned by the French at a camp near Boubouda on the fringe of the Sahara, completing the last part of a horrendous journey in freight wagons.

Conrad spent two years there extending the Trans-Saharan Railway line over the Atlas mountains.

The camps for the railway workers were short of water, while dysentery, jaundice and typhus raged. He and two other fellow Jewish prisoners then spent nine months working down a mine.

Even that was better than the fate meted out to Jews in Tunis after the Germans took over control in November 1942.

The Nazis established a local Jewish Council, took hostages, seized Jewish property and imposed heavy fines, while turning the synagogue in Tunis into a storeroom. Jews were forced to wear the yellow badge of the star of David and 4000 were packed off to concentration camps in Tunisia. Others were shot in their own homes and a few ended up being exported to the extermination camps.

SS-Obersturmbannführer Walter Rauff arrived in the country with an Einsatzgruppen commando unit to step up the murders of Jews.

He had previously been responsible for equipping the death squads in Eastern Europe with gassing vans to eliminate Jews, gypsies and Russians.

A top-secret letter sent to Rauff by SS-Untersturmfuhrer Dr August Becker, who had designed gas vans for use in Smolensk, read: "…if it has been raining for half an hour, the van cannot be used because it simply skids away. It can only be used in absolutely dry weather…

"I ordered the vans of group D to be camouflaged as house-trailers by putting one set of window shutters on each side of the small van and two on each side of the larger vans, such as one often sees on farm houses in the country… The vans became so well known not only the authorities, but also the civilian population allude to it as the 'death van' as soon as one of these vehicles appears. In my opinion even with camouflage the van cannot be kept secret for any length of time…

"The gassing usually is not undertaken correctly. In order to come to an end as fast as possible, the driver presses the accelerator to the fullest extent. By doing that the persons to be executed suffer death from suffocation and not death by dozing off as was planned.

"My instructions now have proved that by correct adjustment of the levers death comes faster and the prisoners fall asleep peacefully. Distorted faces and excretions, such as could be seen before, are no longer to be seen…"

After Tunisia, Rauff was reposted to Italy.

Rauff surrendered to the US Fourth Army on April 30, 1945, but escaped from a POW camp near Rimini in December 1946 and despite his war crimes, was given sanctuary in a monastery in Rome for 18 months.

He eventually fled to Chile where he faced several extradition attempts, but died of heart failure in 1984.

Dr Erwin Michel was president of the German radio industry until Hitler came to power.

His family took refuge in France, where his son Peter tried to enlist in the army the day before war with Germany broke out, but was refused as a foreign national. However, the French Foreign Legion was willing to accept him.

Peter Michel served for a year in French North Africa before being 'demobilised' on September 22, 1940, at Meknes, a Moroccan military post and railway centre west of Fez. He signed a set of demobilisation payments in exchange for a sum of money worth around $25, but later he and his comrades found to their horror that they had been tricked.

Instead of being free to leave, they found out four weeks later they had inadvertently signed up as members of a labour force to build the Trans-Saharan Railway.

They protested loudly, but were told that they had each signed a declaration of willingness to join up for voluntary labour service. The commander showed them the demobilisation forms which had been signed, and between sentences of the original text the authorities had stamped in the words "wishes to join Group A of foreign labourers". That made it all legal and above board.

Peter worked at various sites on the railway for a year, in appalling conditions. Eventually they were taken by rail – in cattle trucks – to Bouarfa, an inhospitable place where the climate was judged to be so hellish that until two years before, the French government had banned Europeans from going there. The ban was lifted so that the French could send Spanish refugees there as slave labourers too. Peter arrived there on Christmas Day 1940.

In the tent camp, all discussion of political or religious matters was supposedly barred, both for officers and men alike. One day, however, the whole labour regiment was assembled and the officer in charge began ranting: "You dirty Jews – it's because of you we lost the war!"

Peter stepped out of line to answer him. When forced to get back to get back into line, he tore off his corporal's stripes, provoking a great uproar. The camp

A rare picture of Spanish prisoners working to build the Trans-Saharan Railway. Pictures of the project of any quality are very rare.

commander sentenced him to eight days in military prison.

Truckloads of French soldiers from Oujdu arrived at their tent encampment. They pulled down all their tents, saying that they were army property and not for the use of men who had been demobilised.

"That night we slept in the open desert," he recalled. "The sand was freezing cold, the wind penetrating. The captain had a bed in his tent and a stove."

Peter described the typical working days as follows: 5am – reveillé; 5.30am breakfast of one sardine, three slices of bread and ersatz coffee; 6am-noon – work; noon – lunch of dishwatery soup, some meat bones, lentils or beans, usually with a little sand mixed in. On holidays there was a ridiculously small helping of potatoes added. After lunch, between 1pm and 4pm, they rested because of the heat; 4pm-8pm – work, often until after dark; 9pm – dinner, exactly like lunch, only a little less. Food was not only scarce but of the worst quality. It was always icy cold because the kitchens were in Bouarfa and the food was brought out along the line in trucks.

Each man was paid one franc and 25 centimes a day, around three US cents. If they saved up three francs and 50 centimes, they could buy a packet of cigarettes. A glass of lemonade would cost two francs. It would take 12 days of work to save up for a piece of shaving soap.

Their guards carried riding whips and were renowned for their brutality, as were the punishments. One was to remove the leather shoulder straps from the legionnaire's canvas covered wooden knapsack and replace them with wires to cut deep into a victim's shoulders. Stripped to the waist, the victim was forced to march miles through the desert, his knapsack filled with bricks, and often without wearing shoes.

As the months passed by, the workers' clothing fell to shreds, and they ended up labouring in blazing heat stripped to the waist without any protection from the sun.

Peter was one of the lucky ones, eventually, at the age of 23, managing to obtain papers to allow him to leave and reach the USA, where his ordeal was told in a series of newspaper articles in late 1941.

Some apologists claimed that the use of the slave labour in North Africa was a means whereby Jews could be hidden from Nazi

Dakar station, seen today, never received a single train from Algeria. JWH VAN DER WAAL*

An 0-6-0T shunts freight wagons at Dakar in 1910, as seen in an old postcard.

persecution. Those who had to toil in the inhospitable conditions, or who happened to be in Tunis in late 1943, might beg to differ.

After the British liberated North Africa in 1943, beginning with the capture of Tunis on May 19, Conrad was shipped to Glasgow and eventually joined the Pioneer Corps of the British Army.

The local Arab population responded in much the same way as the peoples of the occupied countries in Europe. Many actively co-operated with the Nazis, while some risked all to support persecuted Jews. Robert Satloff, author of Among the Righteous: Lost Stories from the Holocaust's Long Reach into Arab Lands, relates the story of Si Ali Sakkat, a former mayor of Tunis, who sheltered 60 Jewish workers when they showed up at his farm, and Si Kaddour Benghabrit, rector of the Great Mosque of Paris, who gave 100 Jews counterfeit Muslim identity papers.

Ultimately, only a tiny section of the railway as envisaged by the Nazis and their Vichy puppets was built, between Bouarfa and Oujda. Limited traffic ran on one small section from January 15, 1942.

It seemed every bit a French scheme to many in the outside world, but orders for the contracts to build the railway came from the German armistice

commission in Casablanca. The Nazis would never visit the labour camps personally, as they knew that the French censorship of letters was poor, and they did not want their involvement emblazoned across the world.

In 1941, supplies of steel for the railway dried up, as with the entrance of the USA into the war, no more would be coming across the Atlantic. Cement produced at factories in Casablanca also became difficult to obtain. Accordingly, the 10 hour shifts for slave labour gangs were reduced from six days to four and then just two, out of necessity rather than any spark of compassion.

It seemed that the senior officers wanted to keep their jobs going for as long as possible, and whether they believed in the viability of the project or otherwise, did their best to make the contract last as long as possible.

Construction finally stopped in 1944 due to lack of financial support. The Trans-Saharan Railway was never finished, and in 1945 the project was finally abandoned by France. Hitler's Third Reich was meant to last 1000 years, and managed 12; the Trans-Saharan Railway did not even manage five minutes.

However, it did achieve something: testimony that the Holocaust was never an exclusively European phenomenon. Thankfully, it never became a worldwide one.

This tent city at Bouarfa was home to forced labourers working on the grandiose railway scheme.

CHAPTER EIGHTEEN

WHEN HITLER MET BRUNEL

Remember those days when video recorders were new and we had that battle between the big, bulky VHS tapes and the smaller, sleeker but supposedly better quality Betamax? After several years of slogging it out, VHS became the undisputed market leader and consigned Betamax to the car boot sale.

Much the same happened with Britain's early railways. George Stephenson and his 4ft 8½in gauge got in first, but Isambard kingdom Brunel did not let him have it all his own way.

When Brunel was appointed engineer of the Great Western Railway, he astonished everyone by choosing a whopping 7ft 0¼in gauge for his trains.

Indeed, in many respects they were superior to those running on the Stephenson gauge, offering faster locomotives – at one stage, those on his Bristol & Exeter Railway were the fastest in the world, and his carriages and freight wagons could carry much bigger loads.

The problem was the break of gauge.

When a Brunel route met a Stephenson gauge, passengers had to change trains and the freight had to be moved across too. Until a third rail was laid between the Broad gauge tracks, there was no interchangeability. Eventually, in 1845, the British Government said that no more broad gauge should be built, but it took until 1892 before the last of them, Paddington to Penzance, was converted to 'Stephenson' or 'standard' gauge.

Hitler faced a similar problem when invading Russia. In the century before, the Russians had deliberately chosen 5ft gauge, as opposed to the Stephenson gauge of Western Europe, to make it difficult for an invading force to run military trains. Indeed, it may be the only reason why the Nazis failed to take Moscow in 1941.

During the Second World War, the bulk of long distance transport by the Wehrmacht was by train. When Operation Barbarossa began in 1941, the Germans were forced to change the gauge of all the tracks as they steamrollered through Russian territory so the gauge could accommodate German trains. Accordingly, the invasion was slowed down, as the panzer tank units pushing ahead needed regular supplies of oil and ammunition, which had to be brought by rail. If the German army had reached Moscow a week sooner, and it probably would have done if not for the break of gauge, the war may well have had a very different outcome.

Hitler, however, was not dreaming of a standardised gauge, but a new railway to serve the postwar Third Reich which would dwarf even Brunel's broad gauge lines.

While the world was in flames around him, Hitler began planning a great transcontinental rail network which would be built to 3m gauge, 9ft 10⅛in. His project was known as the Breitspur Fernbahn, or Broad Gauge Long Distance Railway.

Steam, diesel and electric locomotives as big as two-storey houses would pull multi-deck carriages 2ft high out of gargantuan monumental stations and over the length and breadth of conquered or collaborationist

Two gargantuan electric multiple units are seen departing Munich. This is another of artist Robin Barnes' paintings from his book Broader Than Broad.

The final Brunel broad gauge train departs from Paddington to Penzance on May 20, 1892.

Isambard Kingdom Brunel, whose GWR was built to broad gauge.

Europe and Asia. Big locomotive builders of the day were taken on as consultants and designers – including Krauss-Maffei, Henschel and Borsig among others.

Hitler dreamed of building the network from Brittany and Spain to Rome, Moscow, Vladivostok and even India. Ukraine and the Volga Basin were seen as key destinations because of their huge prairie-like wheat fields, not to mention Romania and the USSR's oil wells.

The gigantic trains would offer every luxury to their 2000-4000 passengers, each around 1640ft, nearly a third of a mile long, fitted with a restaurant, cinema, swimming pool, barber shop and sauna, and would travel at up to 200mph. Freight tracks would have been capable of carrying ships on low-loader wagons.

The massive scale of the new railway was planned to match the monumental architecture that Hitler planned for Berlin, which was to become the world capital of Germania.

The idea was not Hitler's – it came from Fritz Todt, who had been appointed inspector general for German Roadways after the Nazis came to power, and who in 1938 founded the Organisation Todt, joining together government firms, private companies and the Reich Labour Service to build the Siegfried Line. On March 17, 1940, he was appointed Reich minister for armaments and munitions. However, for Hitler it became a pet project.

Railway experts argued that having a different gauge would, as in the days of

Brunel, create difficulties, and especially with the advent of motor transport, could not see where the huge loads for the Breitspur would originate.

Hitler would not listen and ordered work on the first lines – between Hamburg, Berlin, Nuremberg, Munich and Linz – to begin, with 100 officials and 80 engineers working on the initial survey and blueprint.

There would be a ballastless track, pre-empting the German high speed lines of four decades later, with two parallel pre-stressed concrete 'walls' sunk into the ground, joined at the top by a flat tranverse slab. The rails were fixed on top of the 'walls', with an elastic material between rail and concrete. Lacking sleepers, the track could have doubled up as a road for military purposes.

Ten types each of diesel and electric locomotive, 16 steam turbine locomotives and 10 traditional steam locomotive types – some of them behemoths with 10 cylinders – were drawn up.

However, no actual construction work was begun, and the broad gauge dream died with Hitler in his bunker in 1945.

Experts believe that while a basic demonstration line might well have been built, war-torn Germany would never have had the resource to take the project much further, and indeed the cost of building monstrous locomotives that worked would probably have crippled the project.

Had Hitler won the war, his navy would have snatched command of the seas, rendering one of the primary aims of the broad gauge system, the conveyance of bulk

freight, largely redundant. Also, rapid advances in aircraft technology would have led to stiffening competition from this quarter.

If the Trans-Saharan Railway had been a goal too far, the Breitspur Fernbahn could have turned into Hitler's worst nightmare.

There again, we might choose to look at it as the misery we never had.

Finance for the Breitspur Fernbahn would likely have come from the millions of tons of booty seized during the Europe-wide persecutions, but even that probably would not have been enough to finance it.

Look at Werner von Braun's rapid strides in rocket technology and the V1 and V2 missiles that were raining down on London, which had been achieved on the back of an army of slave workers.

With every Jew in Europe, and probably gypsy too, scheduled for death by 1946, from where would the thousands of gangs of unpaid navvies for the Breitspur Fernbahn have come? First stop might have been every able-bodied British man, who following a Nazi victory would have been deported to Europe in order to neutralise the threat from the island fortress once and for all.

Worst hit however, would almost certainly have been the Slavonic peoples, for while the Poles and Czechs were most likely the target for the next Operation Reinhard, after the last Soviet POW had been worked to death, those Hungarians and Ukrainians who had so willingly done the Third Reich's dirty works as guards in the murder camps might have found their names on the bullets too.

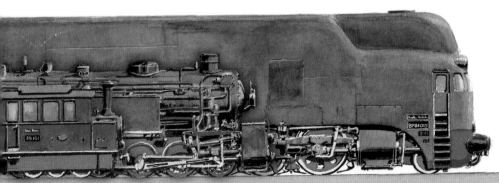

Imagine an N gauge model railway locomotive stood against an OO gauge counterpart, and you would have a rough comparison between the sizes of traditional railways and Hitler's impossible broad gauge dream. The painting is from Robin Barnes' definitive text on the subject, Broader Than Broad, published by Camden Miniature Steam Services in 2012, £16.95, ISBN 978 0 9564073 6 8.

DAYS OF RECKONING

US 7th Army soldiers force suspected members of the Hitler Youth to examine boxcars containing bodies of prisoners starved to death by the SS. The Dachau death train consisted of nearly 40 trucks, containing the bodies of up to 3000 prisoners.

In each and every concentration camp, the liberating Allied forces were met with scenes of horror and disgust beyond any normal person's worst nightmares. Piles of bodies lying unburied, the living reduced to skeletons by starvation regimes and many often just hours from death, and disease rife everywhere. The jubilation of the inmates was also indescribable, but often short-lived, as they met a new deadly enemy: kindness. Their bodies had deteriorated to the point where they could no longer digest solid food, and many died after eating normal food, despite the best efforts of armies of medics to save them. Inmates kept dying for months afterwards from typhus, dysentery and exhaustion.

There are many reports of brutalised prisoners rising up at the moment of liberation and meting out their own revenge on their persecutors. In one instance, it was said that a camp commandant was thrown alive by inmates into a crematorium.

The Nazi atrocities continued right up to the moment of surrender. The US Army entered Leipzig to find the bodies of murdered prisoners burned to death by flame throwers still smouldering. Loyalist Nazi groups hanged people for showing a white sheet from their windows for the crime of 'defeatism', even though it was clear to anyone with the lowest IQ that there was then no Fuhrer and no Germany left to fight for.

The trains of shame also rolled on to the bitter end.

In the article A Child in Auschwitz, written by survivor David Kaye and published in the Summer 2012 edition of Everyone's War, he described his family's horrific journey from the Lodz ghetto in a goods van to Auschwitz on August 8, 1944, before he was parted forever from his mother and younger sister on the selection ramp.

After being sent to work in horse stables, on January 18, 1945, with the Red Army approaching, David, then 17, was sent on a nonstop two day death march to the west, with anyone who dropped out being shot by the SS. After 75 miles the survivors were loaded on to open wagons at a railway station. The train took them to Weimar, from where they walked 10 miles to Buchenwald concentration camp and its by them familiar brand of hell on earth.

On April 8, 1945, with the Allied guns reverberating in the west, the SS rounded up David, along with around 5000 other inmates, and forced them to march back to Weimar to catch another train of open trucks, with 150 people crammed like sardines into each wagon, with, of course, no food or water. An SS guard sat on the top of every wagon and one wagon held a contingent of them.

The train set off towards the Czechoslovak border. It did stop at times, and the guards allowed the prisoners to get out and cook any food they could find: some ate wood to stop their hunger pangs. Every morning, the guards would approach each wagon and tell the prisoners to bring out the fresh corpses, which would then be loaded on to wagons.

The train rolled on aimlessly for weeks, as more and more 'passengers' died, and even the SS guards began to look ill. One day, David awoke to find that he had been lying on dead bodies all night. He witnessed a starving Russian prisoner cutting flesh from a dead body to eat, and when he was spotted by an SS guard, he was machine-gunned.

Finally, the train reached Terezin in Czechoslovakia on May 8 and stopped in a siding. After a few hours, it became clear that the SS guards had all run away, as the Red Army had liberated the town. By then, the survivors were in such a bad way that they could not eat properly.

Like Stephen Frank, David was lucky enough to be flown to England three months later, and started a new life.

LAST MASSACRE AT DACHAU

Young David was indeed among the fortunate ones. On the evening on April 27, 1945, days before the war ended, a train rolled into Dachau concentration camp from Buchenwald.

When it had set out, there had been as many as 4800 prisoners on board. When it arrived, there were just 800 survivors. More than 2300 bodies were left both inside the train and lying on the ground around it.

The next day, Dachau Camp Commandant Martin Gottfried Weiss, along with most of his guards and administrators, had run away, with the Americans advancing. A Red Cross official persuaded his adjutant, Untersturmführer Johannes Otto, to leave guards posted so as to keep the 32,000 starving and sick prisoners inside until the Americans arrived, because it was feared that they would spread typhus in the locality. Otto also ran away, but some of the guards remained behind in the watchtowers, while hoisting a white flag the following day.

It was then that Untersturmführer Heinrich Wicker, an officer in the SS Totenkopfverbände, and an aide formally surrendered the camp at the main gate, in the company of the Swiss Red Cross representative. The SS-Totenkopfverbände, or Death's Head Units, was the SS branch that was responsible for administering the camps, including Auschwitz-Birkenau, Treblinka, Bełżec extermination camp and Sobibor, and they were universally feared for their fanatical and murderous brutality, mostly towards harmless and helpless people.

The two SS officers explained that they had arrived at Dachau only the night before, in order to hand over the camp to the Americans, and that the 100 remaining guards had mostly put down their arms.

The Americans found 1600 people crammed into each of 20 barracks, which had been designed to house just 250 people.

The liberating troops were so sickened by the sight that met them inside the gates of Dachau that several of them killed some of the SS guards even though they had surrendered. Brigadier General Felix L Sparks, who was in command of the liberating battalion, said that between 30 and 50 guards had been shot, but researchers in later years put the figure at between 122 and 520. Other guards were killed by the prisoners, blurring the responsibility.

Preparations for Sparks and his officers to be court-martialled over the massacre were drawn up, but the charges were dismissed by the US General George Patton, who by then had become the military governor of Bavaria.

At a sub-camp of Dachau near Landsberg, US troops arrived to find around 400 bodies burning on a fire. They rounded up male civilians in the town and marched them to the camp, where the commandant was forced to lie down between the corpses. The locals were then ordered to walk past and spit in the face of the commandant, who was then handed over to a group of freed inmates.

At Dachau and many other liberated camps, local people were forced to view piles or corpses or bury them, Many claimed that they were shocked and had no knowledge of what thad been going on at the camp just down the road.

THE SAVIOUR OF NAZI WAR CRIMINALS

The Roman Catholic Church and Pope Pius XVII have, ever since the end of the Second World War, been the subject of great debate among Holocaust scholars. On one hand there is a widespread belief by that, by and large, the Pope did not speak out sufficiently against the murder of Jews, and that had he done so, more of the German population, especially its Catholics, might have opened their eyes and wavered, just as public opinion uniquely forced Hitler to climb down over the Aktion T4 Euthanasia programme.

On the other hand, other scholars argue that the Pope may have saved hundreds of thousands of Jews. In 1940, Pius asked members of the clergy, on Vatican letterhead, to do whatever they could on behalf of interned Jews.

However, on July 26, 1942, bishops in The Netherlands, including Archbishop Johannes de Jong, issued a decree which openly condemned the Nazi deportations of Dutch workers and Jews. The SS responded by arresting more than 40,000 Catholics of Jewish descent for the deportation trains, and they were never heard from again. Pius XII often repeated what he told the Italian ambassador to the Vatican in 1940: "We would like to utter words of fire against such actions and the only thing restraining us from speaking is the fear of making the plight of the victims even worse."

In September 1942 Myron Taylor, the US representative to the Vatican, warned the Pope that the Vatican's 'moral prestige' was being injured by its silence over the atrocities. Representatives from Great Britain, Brazil, Uruguay, Belgium and Poland reiterated the warning, but the Cardinal Secretary of State's reply was that the rumours about genocide could not be verified. That year, British representative wrote that "a policy of silence in regard to such offences against the conscience of the world must necessarily involve a renunciation of moral leadership and a consequent atrophy of the influence of the Vatican".

In spring 1943 Italian priest Pirro Scavizzi told Pius that the murder of the Jews was "now total" and even infants and the elderly were being destroyed "without mercy". The Pope reportedly broken down and wept uncontrollably and allegedly told the priest: "I have often considered excommunication, to castigate in the eyes of the entire world the fearful crime of genocide. But after much praying and many tears, I realize that my condemnation would not only fail to help the Jews, it might even worsen their situation."

In 2010, 19 Catholic scholars wrote a letter to Pope Benedict XVI asking that the process of according sainthood for Pius XII be slowed down, saying that "Pope Pius XII did not issue a clearly-worded statement, unconditionally condemning the wholesale slaughter and murder of European Jews".

At Bergen-Belsen, British liberators made SS women bury their victims with their bare hands, irrespective of whether they would catch diseases from the rotting bodies.

The first Nuremberg Trial involving the major surviving Nazi leaders: Hermann Goering (far left) instructed Adolf Eichmann to begin the deportation of Jews.

The three judges at the trial of Adolf Eichmann, who ordered the deportation trains as part of Operation Reinhard.

The finger of blame: a Russian prisoner of war at Mittelbau-Dora concentration camp, a sub-camp of Buchenwald, demands answers from one of his persecutors after it was liberated by the US 3rd Armoured Division. About a third of the 60,000 prisoners who passed through Mittelbau-Dora died. Many were used as slave labour to build the V1 and V2 rocket installations nearby. Many were burned to death just hours before the liberation.

April 30, 1945: Railway truck loaded with the bodies of prisoners who died during a seemingly-purposeless transport to Dachau from other concentration camps, when the war was already clearly lost.

However, while that debate continues to rage, the stance of one of Pius XII's bishops, the Austrian Alois Hudal, is unequivocal. It was Hudal, history records, who helped some of the worst Nazi monsters to flee justice in Europe and escape to the safe havens of South America.

Hudal made his sympathies clear in his 1937 book On the Basic Foundations of National Socialism, which distanced himself somewhat from Rome. He proposed an alliance between the Catholic Church and the Nazis to create a "truly Christian National Socialism" and supported discriminatory segregation legislation against Jews. Pope Pius XII eventually broke off all contact with Hudal, after trying to change him, but during the Second World War he continued as pastoral head of the Anima Church and College in Rome.

His isolation from the mainstream Vatican hierarchy continued after 1945, when Hudal began his activities in the so-called 'Ratlines' which helped the most-wanted criminals to escape.

Hudal viewed this work as "a charity to people in dire need, for persons without any guilt who are to be made scapegoats for the failures of an evil system".

Read those words again and think about their literal meaning. Then look closely at the list of some of the Nazi fugitives who were helped by his 'Ratline':

Franz Stangl, commandant of Sobibor and Treblinka.

Alois Brunner, who organised all deportation trains from France and Slovakia and who, thanks to Hudal's assistance, was last heard of in a bolthole in Syria.

SS Captain Eduard Roschmann, known as the 'Butcher of Riga' because of his numerous atrocities in Latvia.

Gustav Wagner, the commanding officer of the Sobibor murder camp.

The abomination that was Josef Mengele.

And last but not least, Adolf Eichmann, who masterminded the Operation Reinhard deportations and trains, and also sought to profit big-time from genocide. It was Hungarian Franciscan Father Edoardo Dömöter who forged the identity on Eichmann's passport, issued by the Red Cross in the name of Riccardo Klement.

In 1945 Hudal gave refuge in Rome to Otto Wächter, a leading proponent of mass murder of Jews in German-occupied Poland. He was allowed to live in a Rome monastery as a monk under Hudal's protection.

Monsignor Karl Bayer, the Rome-based director of Caritas International after the war, admitted in the Seventies that he and Hudal had helped Nazis flee to South America with the Vatican's support, and claimed that some finance had even been provided by the Pope.

In memoirs published after his death in 1963, Hudal wrote that he never gave up in trying to obtain an amnesty for Nazis and maintained to the end that his actions were "those of a true Christian". He wrote: "We do not believe in the eye for an eye of the Jew" and said "I thank God that He opened my eyes and allowed me to visit and comfort many victims in their prisons and concentration camps and (to help) them escape with false identity papers".

These 'victims', as he saw them were in reality Nazi Prisoners of War who were being held in Allied detention camps.

Maybe he was thinking of the Christian act of forgiveness. The drawback to this argument was that these monsters had done him personally no harm: surely those who logically and exclusively have the ability to forgive are the victims, most of whom by then were piles of ashes in the grounds of murder camps and whose opinions on the matter could not be sought. Plus – it is not known that any of these men ever actually admitted their guilt and asked for forgiveness.

A wandering Jewish preacher, who lived in Palestine with a band of male and female camp followers about two millennia before, might have been able to offer Hudal some clear guidance in this matter. A book containing many of this man's teachings and adventures was freely available in Nazi-occupied Europe, although the ideologists did not always approve of its contents. Maximilian Kolbe certainly had a copy.

JUSTICE FOR THE DEATH TRAINS

As we have seen, hundreds of thousands of railwaymen throughout Nazi-occupied Europe became small cogs in the greatest organised act of mass murder that the world had ever seen. It has been shown that key figures in the Deutsche Reichsbahn were happy for the death trains to run; countless others knew what was going on, and looked after Number One, despite evidence that, had they refused, they may well have come to no physical or financial harm.

For them, there were no Nuremberg Trials or other courts where they were brought to answer for their crimes, and given the opportunity to state their side of the story, a luxury never afforded to the millions of boxcar passengers.

There was, however, justice seen to be done in the case of Adolf Eichmann.

As we have seen, Eichmann masterminded the mass deportations to the ghettos and murder camps. When Germany invaded Hungary in 1944 amid fears that the Red Army was to invade and occupy that country, the ever-enterprising Eichmann made an offer through Joel Brand, a member of the Hungarian Aid and Rescue Committee which had brought Jewish refugees to Hungary, to effectively sell Jews to the West.

Eichmann asked Brand to act as an intermediary in a deal between the SS and the Allies, whereby the Nazis would free up to one million Jews in exchange for 10,000 trucks for the Eastern Front, and large quantities of soap, tea and coffee.

Brand went to Turkey to inform the British about Eichmann's offer, and was promptly arrested by them. The BBC broadcast details of the offer on July 19, 1944.

Clearly such a deal could never be brokered, as it would split the Allies, with

In a scene repeated at many liberated concentration camps, on May 11, 1945, US Army Signal Corps soldiers force German civilians to walk past bodies of 30 Jewish women who had been starved to death by the SS.

The scene moments after disgusted American soldiers shot SS troops in the coal yard at Dachau, after viewing what had been going on inside the camp.

American and British hardware used to fight the Soviets. The Jewish Agency for Israel was also strongly opposed.

This matter had been the subject of a bitter debate ever since, with Hungarian Jews and Brand claiming that they were betrayed. When Eichmann received no answer, he started sending 430,000 Hungarian Jews by train to Auschwitz-Birkenau.

Himmler, thinking about saving his own skin, as if that would ever have been possible, told Eichmann in 1945 to stop gassing Jews and remove all evidence of the Final Solution. Eichmann ignored this order and carried on with his work in Hungary, fleeing only when the Red Army crossed the border.

He was captured by the US Army, which fell for his fake identity of Otto Eckmann, in early 1946. Later that year he escaped from US custody and hid for several years in the Lüneburg Heath area, the scene of the unconditional surrender of German forces in northern Germany, Denmark and The Netherlands to the Allies, under Field Marshal Bernard Montgomery on May 4, 1945.

On July 14, 1950, Eichmann fled to Argentina, where for the next decade he worked in several odd jobs in the Buenos Aires area, even becoming a professional rabbit farmer, later being joined by his family. Documents released in 2006 indicated that Eichmann had lived under the name Clemens there since 1952, but the CIA took no action because Eichmann's arrest could embarrass both the USA and Western Germany by bringing attention to the fact that both had recruited former Nazis after the war.

They were shamed by Israel's secret service Mossad which, to cut a long and complicated story short, tracked down Eichmann and kidnapped him on May 11, 1960. He was smuggled out of Argentina on an El-Al plane, heavily sedated and dressed in air crew uniform, and arrived in Israel on May 21, 1960.

The kidnap led to right-wing anti-Semitic riots in Argentina, but when Eichmann's capture was announced to Israel's parliament, the Knesset, two days after he landed, Prime Minister David Ben-Gurion received a standing ovation.

There are those who think that Eichmann did not even deserve the decency of a fair trial, and a bullet in the head in Buenos Aires would have given him a cleaner death than he meted out to the millions forced on to his transport trains. Yet Israel wanted the world to see that justice was done and Eichmann's crimes laid bare for all to see.

He was indicted on 15 criminal charges, including crimes against humanity, war crimes, crimes against the Jewish people, and membership in an outlawed organisation.

At his trial in Jerusalem, which began on April 11, 1961, Eichmann sat inside a bulletproof glass booth to protect him from victims' families.

One key witness for the prosecution was an American judge named Michael A Musmanno, who had questioned the Nuremberg defendants in 1945, and who testified that Goering "made it very clear that Eichmann

was the man to determine, in what order, in what countries, the Jews were to die".

Eichmann claimed he was, yes you guessed, "only following orders" and said: "I never did anything, great or small, without obtaining in advance express instructions from Adolf Hitler or any of my superiors." Yet even depositions from fellow high-ranking Nazi survivors, who refused to travel to Israel to speak on Eichmann's behalf despite being granted immunity from prosecution, did not support these explanations. A former SS brigadier-general said that Eichmann was an absolute believer in National Socialism and would act to the most extreme end of the party doctrine, and that Eichmann had greater power than other department chiefs.

The 14 week trial included testimony from 90 concentration camp survivors and ended on August 11. The three judges deliberated in secret and on December 11 announced that Eichmann was guilty on all charges. Four days later, the inevitable death sentence was imposed.

On May 29, 1962, Israel's Supreme Court, sitting as a Court of Criminal Appeal, rejected Eichmann's appeal, which again leaned on having "only obeyed orders".

The court then delivered its own verbal verdict on the overlord of the trains that had shamed all of humanity: "Eichmann received no superior orders at all. He was his own superior and he gave all orders in matters that concerned Jewish affairs... the so-called Final Solution would never have assumed the infernal forms of the flayed skin and tortured flesh of millions of Jews without the fanatical zeal and the unquenchable blood-thirst of the appellant and his associates."

Eichmann was hanged shortly before midnight on May 31, 1962, at a prison in Ramla. For him, there would be one final journey on rails – a set of tracks carrying his body into a specially-designed furnace, ironically similar to the fate suffered by millions of his victims, of many nationalities, not just Jews and gypsies. We must never forget that: despite the specific groups whom it set out to eradicate from the face of the earth, the Holocaust ended up as an all-out assault on all of humanity.

Nazi supporter Bishop Alois Hudal.

Master race beauty contest: SS women guards at Belsen-Bergen captured by the British.

American troops guarding the main entrance to Dachau just after the camp was liberated.

Inmates of Dachau celebrate liberation.

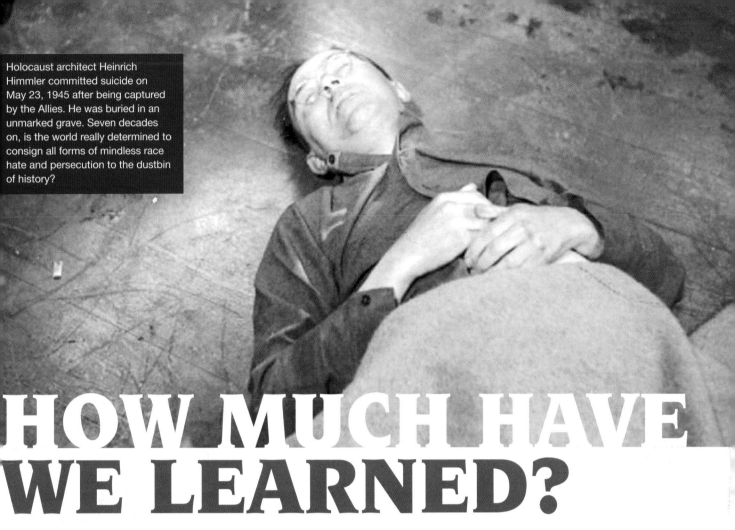

HOW MUCH HAVE WE LEARNED?

Per Anger was another Swedish diplomat in Budapest – second secretary from 1943-45 in the Swedish Legation.

He once rushed to a station where a large group of Jews was being loaded for deportation. Protesting loudly, Anger pushed forward and said that a dreadful mistake had been made, for in this group were persons with Swedish papers and they could be being deported by error!

He then demanded to be allowed to climb into the train, to check the papers of the deportees and threatened to send a diplomatic protest if this were denied him.

In the train there were actually only two people with Swedish papers. When, however, Anger realised that none of the German guards could read Hungarian, he tricked them and freed from the train more than 100 people who had any form of documents about them – a driving licence, inoculation pass or even tax forms!

Romanian-born Jewish-American professor and Holocaust survivor Eliezer 'Elie' Wiesel, whose mother was murdered in Auschwitz and father in Buchenwald, and who won the Nobel Peace Prize in 1986, wrote in a foreword to Anger's memoirs: "When one reads what a handful of men and women were able to achieve, then one attempts to imagine what could have been achieved had only more people shown the same initiative and sympathy."

According to some modern estimates, between five and six million Jews, more than three million Soviet prisoners of war, more than two million Soviet civilians, more than

one million Polish civilians, more than one million Yugoslav civilians, more than 200,000 gypsies, around 70,000 men, women and children with mental and physical handicaps and an unknown numbers of political prisoners, resistance fighters, homosexuals and deportees died in the Holocaust.

To place these numbers in context, the total figure compares with nearly a quarter of the prewar population in Germany of 69,623,000.

Two thirds of the total European Jewish population, and two-fifths of the Jews in the entire world, perished. Altogether, an estimated 60 million people were killed in the Second World War, more than 2.5% of the world population.

On April 29, 1945, the day before he committed suicide, Hitler remained unshaken. He ordered "the government and the people to uphold the race laws... and to resist mercilessly the poisoner of all nations, international Jewry".

Compare that figure for the German population (of which up to 10% were killed in the war), with the 510 Germans who Yad Vashem has listed as among the "Righteous Amongst the Nations". As well as the better-known names such as Oscar Schindler, there were decent people in the Third Reich who risked their lives to shelter Jews, from Army officers to ordinary families. Captain Albert Battel was not unique: there were the likes of Major Karl Plagge, a Wehrmacht officer, engineer and Nazi Party member who used his position to employ and protect about 1240 Jews so they would escape the annihilation of their race in Lithuania. Yet

the figure of 510 is miniscule compared with the size of the German population.

To me, at times it seemed that after Germany's defeat in 1945, the number of people who did not know about the murder camps was greater than the total population of the country. Always someone else gave the orders.

Deutsche Reichsbahn, which made the Holocaust possible, had more than a million employees.

If, for argument's sake, we accept the 'explanation' that they did not know about the gas chambers or life in the camps, because SS train crews took over at the entrances and closed the gates behind them guarding their dreadful secrets, then what about the appalling conditions in which prisoners were transported for days without even a cup of water? No railwaymen in any country would treat livestock like that, for they would know only too well there would be dead cattle long before the journey's end.

Then there are countries such as France, on our own doorstep, some of whose railway officials seemed on occasion even more eager than the SS in transporting deportees to the east en masse in sub-barbaric conditions, and even after tens of thousands of Allied servicemen gave their lives to liberate their country, were still trying to exact payment for arranging and running the death trains.

British historian Ian Kershaw wrote: "The road to Auschwitz was built by hate, and paved by indifference."

Since the days of Trevithick and the Stephensons, the railway concept changed the world forever, reaching a zenith in the world speed record runs of the Thirties as described in Chapter 1. Railways had untold power to do enormous good, and for the most part they did, but placing them in the hands of an empire of sheep dominated by a neanderthal leadership was akin to giving a nuclear bomb to a Stone Age tribe engaged in petty squabbles with their neighbours.

Back in February 2002, I walked around Berlin while on a trip to photograph steam trains at the Wolsztyn Experience in Poland. Although such material was not readily available to the visitor, I managed to get a map showing where the Third Reich government buildings had been, and saw the site of Hitler's bunker, unmarked and buried beneath a children's playground outside a block of social housing.

I came to the site of the transport ministry in Wilhelmstrasse. The building was no longer there and the vacant site had also been grassed over. In the middle of the green space, where the compliant DB hierarchy once plotted to transport millions of innocent people to their deaths, some had planted a wooden sign to display a poster. It advertised a concert by the American singer-songwriter Brian Wilson. I had tickets for his London show the following week. His final encore at every show concludes with a ballad containing the lines "*love and mercy, that's what we need tonight*".

If only those precious eight words would forever stand above the irrational yet consuming ancestral hatred that lay buried in the ground directly below!

But let us never delude ourselves. We the human race invented the computer age internet. We can fly faster than the speed of sound. We can send spaceships to moons of distant planets. We have made enormous strides in medicine and increased life expectancy.

Yet we cannot draw a line under ancient prejudices and hatreds, and wherever we see persecution, we are still so often powerless or unwilling to intervene.

Nobody has ever conquered Russia so we don't know exactly how the worst of the Soviet gulags matched up to their Nazi counterparts. Reports from North Korea about secret concentration camps filter out, but we don't know how accurate they are, and even if they were true, what would we do about it? The political spectrum has, at the time of writing, left us powerless to act against any atrocities committed by Syria's President Bashar Assad against his own people, and what about the human rights record of the economic powerhouse that is China on who we now so heavily depend?

Back in the 1940s, the formal bastions of the moral high ground, including areas of the Christian church, were found to be sadly wanting.

Nearly a century ago, it was proven beyond any shadow of a doubt that the Protocols of the Elders of Zion, a significant plank of 20th century anti-Semitism, was an outright fake. Yet even today, there are still regimes, especially in the Middle East, which have endorsed the book as an authentic portrayal of the true plans of Zionists. The late Colonel Muammar Gaddafi was such a leader, following in the footsteps of Presidents Gamal Nasser and Anwar Sadat of Egypt, while the 1988 charter of the Palestinian Islamist group Hamas proclaimed the book as genuine.

The Holocaust, however, remains as scientific proof that racism cannot win.

Hitler's Germany persecuted the very people who might well have helped him win the war, from the slave labourers who were gassed leaving munitions orders for the eastern front unfulfilled, to the top scientists who fled in the wake of the Nazi rise to power.

Among them was none other than Albert Einstein, a professor at the Berlin Academy of Sciences, who renounced his German citizenship before emigrating to the United States and whose works were among those targeted by Nazi book burnings in April 1933, when Goebbels announced: "Jewish intellectualism is dead."

I don't think so. At the start of the war, Einstein alerted President Franklin Roosevelt that Hitler might be developing an atomic weapon, and recommended that the US start similar research, leading to the Manhattan Project and the bombs on Hiroshima and Nagasaki. If Germany had not fallen by the time they were ready, Berlin might well have been a target for the first one.

I remember a science fiction TV show about a brilliant scientist who created a race of mutants whose sole purpose in life was to destroy any species that was different to theirs. Frustrated at the eventual lack of success, he then devised a bomb to destroy the entire universe apart from a handful of planets and an artificial sun reserved for his 'master race'. Had he succeeded, what would have been his creatures' purpose in

life, if there was no one left to hate? At what point would they have turned on themselves, and eradicated the last vestige of life in the cosmos?

Had it not been for diversity, there would never have been a human race. Evolution would have halted at the apes. Yet the likes of Hitler, Himmler and Heydrich were zealously determined to stamp out anything that disagreed with their would-be godlike view of the universe, regardless of its potential value. What began as a paranoia-fuelled war on a homeless nation ended up as an all-out assault on basic humanity itself.

Drawing on the alien analogy again, had a visitor from another planet been sent to earth to identify the master race after viewing our world in flames for six years, and had to decide between a nation which excelled in the systematic murder of millions of harmless people, and one which subsequently turned a thin slice of eastern Mediterranean pasture land, for defensive motives, into a micro superpower homeland within a few decades, I do not think he would be submitting a large bill for overtime in coming to his decision.

There will always be prejudice and hatred: it seems to be par for the course. Indeed, everyone has the human right to retain their own opinions within the confines of their head and maybe within their home, no matter how obnoxious they might seem. Nobody, however, has the right to lift a finger outside those limitations to harm the freedom of others.

We may become complacent of the lessons of history and repeat the same mistakes. On the other hand we cannot all be Wallenbergs, Battels and Angers. We just have to do what we can, each in our own small way.

The far right still very much has a presence, with representatives both at European Union level and in local towns across the continent. Those who are only too aware of the potential of public eagerness for a convenient scapegoat can be found everywhere.

Each of us has the obligation to look back in recent history, and say 'never again'.

Love and mercy. That's what we need tonight.

This monument in the grounds of Beth Shalom, the Holocaust resource centre in Nottinghamshire, is a depiction of the briefcase of Swedish diplomat Raoul Wallenberg, who could never produce enough false papers from it to save the lives of Hungarian Jews otherwise set for one-way train journeys to Auschwitz. ROBIN JONES